ADDITIONAL P

THE ONE Y

"An utterly unique memoir...a portrait, not only of the boy, but also of the man using a set of tools, including social theory and neuroscience, to disentangle the strands that make the self. Whether we are shocked by the conditions of his young life—addiction, abuse, mental illness, mosh-pit erections—is up to us. Tougaw's just trying to get to the bottom of it all."

—Vestal McIntyre, *Lake Overturn* and *You Are Not the One*

"Tougaw's book is about the ways we explain ourselves when our histories are complex, when they don't fit what most people understand as a story. This is a book for those of us who understand how complicated, torturous, joyful, painful, funny, and lonely family can be."

—Kaitlyn Greenidge, *We Love You, Charlie Freeman*

"A marvel of investigation and invention. This is a boy's life, down to the cellular level, peppered with rumination on everything from dream theory to neuroscience, punk rock and new wave lyrics. It is like nothing else in this world, pure body and soul, and I love it."

—Scott Cheshire, *High as the Horses' Bridles*

"Tougaw's intelligent, funny, and deeply moving memoir is that rare thing: the story of a family that is at once particular and universal. The variously wild, tender, deluded, suffering, incorrigible, and resilient people who are so vividly portrayed in this book are nothing if not idiosyncratic. At the same time, this story of a boy growing up in California during the years of a waning counterculture deftly incorporates sophisticated reflections on the brain science of human memory and development and the ongoing mystery of why some of us survive a chaotic and brutal childhood and others don't."

—Siri Hustvedt, *A Woman Looking at Men Looking at Women*

THE ONE YOU GET

PORTRAIT OF A FAMILY ORGANISM

JASON TOUGAW

5220 Dexter Ann Arbor Rd.
Ann Arbor, MI 48103
www.dzancbooks.org

Library of Congress Cataloging-in-Publication Data

Names: Tougaw, Jason Daniel, author.
Title: The one you get : portrait of a family organism / by Jason Tougaw.
Description: New York, NY : Dzanc Books, 2017.
Identifiers: LCCN 2017003746 | ISBN 9781945814327
Subjects: LCSH: Tougaw, Jason Daniel--Family. | Authors, American--21st century--Biography. | Gay college teachers--United States--Biography. | Families--Health. | Identity (Psychology)
Classification: LCC PS3620.O8877 Z85 2017 | DDC 813/.6 [B] --dc23
LC record available at https://lccn.loc.gov/2017003746

First US edition: September 2017
Interior design by Michelle Dotter
Cover design by Driverworks LLC
Jacket design by Steven Seighman

Printed in the United States of America

10 9 8 7 6 5 4 3 2 1

CONTENTS

For Nichole and Buffy, who lived it with me.

And for Summer, who lived it until she didn't.

1

THE SAN LUIS REY

"FUCK THE BABY," I shout from the toddler seat of the shopping cart. It's my first sentence, announced with glee at Jonathan's, San Diego's most expensive grocery store. Nanny is taking my mom shopping to celebrate our new life without Charlie, my father, who's probably in prison by now.

"Fuck the baby," I shout again. My mom and Nanny are quiet at first, but they give in and let their laughter splutter. Jonathan's is huge, a chaos of clean light. My sentence bounces off the jars and cans that line the polished aisles.

"Cathy, shut him up."

"Why me? Just find the Grey Poupon and let's get out of here."

"Because you're his mother, for Godssake."

A pair of women in their sixties round the corner. You can tell they belong from their penciled eyebrows, pearls, and pocketbooks. "Fuck the baby." My mom presses a hand over my mouth. The women have stopped their carts to observe. I yelp a muffled four syllables. If you've heard me already, they're unmistakable.

I don't remember this, but I knew what I was doing, they'll tell me later. I was conscious of their embarrassment, egged on by their blushing and laughing.

"Let's get out of here," Nanny says, and the laughter bursts through their ribs again. The women with pocketbooks push by, careful to avert their eyes.

"Okay, we just need bread and a can of salmon," my mom says, rolling the cart at top speed, one hand still clamped over my mouth.

"And a bottle of wine," Nanny says. "I think he wore himself out anyway. Didn't you, Unigagin?" (Unigagin is her nickname for everybody.) They collect the salmon, seven-grain, and Chianti and head for checkout.

"You finished, Boog?" my mom asks.

"Fuck the baby." All eyes are on us—women shopping, checkout clerks, the pharmacist thirty feet away. Nanny and my mom are beyond controlling themselves.

"Sssh. Jason, shush," my mom says.

"For Godssake, Jason."

My mom's hand is back on my mouth. Nanny has tightened her face and reached into her purse. She presses her lips together as she pays, but the cashier's stare lets her know her laughter is still visible.

The three of us are collaborators in this scene. We'll pass the blame around later. *I was just a baby. Who'd I learn the words from, anyway?* I'll say. *Certainly not me,* Nanny will say, not even convincing herself. *Yeah right,* my mom will chime in. *Who was the one laughing?* The truth is, we all want the blame. We love this idea of ourselves, a trio of rabblerousers enjoying the clean-lit luxury of Jonathan's while raising our middle fingers to its propriety.

If "fuck the baby" really was my first sentence—as my mom and Nanny will insist—it's almost too good to be true. How could I, at eighteen months, have found a sentence wry enough to bundle the terrifying, liberating, and hilarious chaos of being raised by Southern California hippies during the 1970s, in a family that had just fallen from wealth and celebrity, trying to figure out how to live as the counterculture revolution evaporated like a dream?

When I moved to New York in 1993, I found myself telling people about my California hippie childhood. Distance seemed to loosen my lips. I talked about the near abortion, living on a converted school bus, my heroin-addict father in prison. About growing up hippie and poor in the shadow of luxuries we no longer enjoyed, except by talking about them, constantly. About Ralph, my famous jockey grandpa who squandered his fortune; about Nanny (or Midge), his wife, whose best friend was Betty Grable. About the drugs my elders swallowed and the addicts they became. I listed mental illnesses and described our endless moving from house to house, my mom's many abusive boyfriends, her many marriages and divorces. "Why aren't you more fucked up?" people kept asking.

At first, I'd shrug. My family's lore had done its job. While the sensational details are largely true, they've also been refined, through decades of retelling, to provoke questions like this. Of course, what people really meant was, "How did you survive?" and "Why do you seem so different from the people who raised you?" The first question is the one the lore is designed to elicit. Its answer casts us as unlikely heroes, survivors. The second is less self-serving, a version of an undeniable philosophical question that haunts us all: "How did *I* become *me*?"

It's a hard question to answer. You might say it started with a fetus not flushed down a Tijuana river that's really an estuary in North County. You might say you have to understand California in the seventies, or the tenderness of both my mom and Nanny, or genetics and human physiology. You might have to shoot x-ray beams through my head at various ages and develop cross-sectional photos of the meat inside; slide me into a noisy fMRI and measure the oxygenation of cerebral blood flow; saw through my skull and insert tiny electrodes that measure localized energy exchanges; inject me with radioactive materials so the PET can measure their emissions as they decay; and poise a halo of helium-soaked coils over my head to measure the faint magnetism of the electricity buzzing around in there. Even if this were possible, the yield of information would likely be modest. You might learn some things, and some of them might be telling. But despite what some neuroscientists think, neural networks and selfhood are not the same thing. They are fundamentally related, and their relationship is fascinating. But neurons alone do not explain self, or if they do, we are not even close to knowing how.

In the meantime, here's my plan. I can tell the story, with the benefit of my unforgiving memory and the brain science that's beginning to offer new ways of understanding the development and experience of self. It begins with the fetus.

This story is family lore.

It's seventy-something degrees at 4 a.m. in Del Mar in November, even right on the beach. Doug closes and locks the door gently behind them. The air is visible as ocean fog. Cathy focuses for a second on the foam splattering in the darkness as it bounces off the shore, like staring at it might dissolve the moment. All three shuffle across the sandy driveway to Doug's Chevy station wagon, surfboard still strapped to the roof rack. Cathy protests, but Doug and Midge hold her snug and squeeze her into the backseat. Doug starts the car, turns on the wipers to slice a sheet of dew off the front windows.

Doug manages to make even the engine seem quiet and calm. As they turn out of the driveway, to begin the forty-minute drive to the border, Cathy feels the nauseating pull of morning sickness. It's 1968, and abortions are legal in Mexico.

It's been less than fifteen minutes since Doug nudged her awake. His hands are gentle and solid—as opposed to the tiny, manic hands of her father—and so at first they just made sleep more comfortable. "Cathy," he whispers, pulling strands of iron-straightened hair from her face. "Cathy, wake up, honey. Wake up. Get some clothes on. Your mother's waiting."

He is insistent enough to persuade her, so she throws on a filmy white embroidered blouse and some jeans, size one. Doug leads her down two stories of steep and winding stairs. Midge sits in the cavernous terracotta-tiled, tall-ceilinged foyer at the bottom, clenched from head to toe. Mother and daughter exchange a glance, and daughter knows. She turns back toward the stairs, but Doug is there, like a gentle roadblock. "Come on, Cathy."

"No. Let me go."

"For Godssake, Cathy." Midge can't find much to say.

"Let me go."

"Just come along, Cathy. I'll explain in the car." He is firm.

"You don't need to explain," she says.

Doug knows how to get things done. He's a blond, surfing, Qiana-clad car salesman, twenty-nine to Midge's forty-six. He calls her "my silver fox." He opened a surf shop with my uncle in the mid-sixties. It was Cathy who discovered their affair, when she came home one night and caught them making out in the driveway before the divorce from Ralph, her dad, was even final.

Doug calms Cathy as he drives. Renowned for her histrionics, her nickname has been Sarah Bernhardt since childhood. One famous story has her ranting to newscasters about how neighbor Desi Arnaz tried to shoot her with his rifle. Today she has a reason for hysterics.

"Just think about it. Just come to the clinic," Doug repeats. "If you still don't want to do it, we'll turn around and drive home." She can trust him. Midge is another story. Her silence is a sign of duplicity.

"This is the only thing you can do, Cathy. You're not ready to be a mother," Midge finally blurts out. Cathy is pissed, but Doug keeps driving. Her brothers were grown before the divorce. They got everything they needed: cars, college tuition they traded for drugs, their father's door-opening notoriety. She got a single parent panicking as her fortune dwindled, and now an abortion. Her body carries a fetus too tiny to show but real enough to retool her physiology and alter her already volatile moods.

The sun has not even begun to rise, but there is a small line of cars at the border. Somebody must be getting searched. "Cathy, don't worry," Midge tries to find something to say.

"Shut up, Mom. Don't worry?"

"Goddamn you listen to me Cathy. You—"

"Ssshh. Midge, calm down, hon. We're almost there." He wants to say, *Does the world really need another Neves? One more baby with the blood of the Portuguese Pepper Pot sloshing around in its veins? With a teenage junkie for a father?*

Doug pulls the car up to the booth, quiet and confident. The border guard, who looks like a San Diegan with his feathered hair and mustache, bends to peer into the car. He looks Cathy up and down with Tijuana suspicion. "What's the purpose of your visit?" he asks in perfect Southern California English.

"Shopping," Midge says.

"So early?"

"And surfing," Doug intervenes. "You ever ride a few while the sun rises?" he asks, glancing toward the roof, where his board is strapped.

"Can't blame you," the guard says, nodding. "We got better waves in Mexico."

They drive another thirty minutes of empty highway, parallel to the shore, before they reach the clinic. Doug and Midge stand on either side of Cathy. The sun, just beginning to rise out of the east, casts a butterscotch glow on the clinic's entrance, streaming in as they enter and disappearing when the door clicks closed.

Five feet tall, ninety pounds, pretty in a dark, Liz Taylor way, Cathy looks much younger than her eighteen years.

A nurse comes at her speaking gentle Spanish, nudges her sympathetically into a room. "Como está?" she asks, handing her a gown. "Que linda," she says. Cathy could almost be Mexican, with her straightened hair and tan skin. They could pass for mother and daughter.

Cathy shakes as the nurse guides her onto an examination table. Her feet are hopping in the rests, "like Mexican jumping beans," she'll recall later. "Cálmate, niña," the nurse says. "Cálmate." She must think Cathy is twelve or thirteen. "Cálmate."

For just a second, the nurse's brown eyes sink into Cathy's and swim there. It's all the encouragement she needs. Cathy rises from the chair. She storms back through the waiting room, collects Doug and Midge, and pushes her way into the blazing Mexican dawn.

"I guess you're gettin' another grandchild," Doug says to Midge. The trio drive back to Del Mar in silence.

"It's my fault," my cousin Bryan says. He's schizophrenic, so nobody pays him much attention, but he keeps saying it. "It's my fault Jason is the way he is."

I can't be sure which *way I am* he means, but he's making me self-conscious about my black cherry hair and matching lipstick. He might mean the way I'm in my own world, or contemptuous of my surroundings, or the way I've become a Newro (short for New Romantic, the most fey of new wave styles), but I'm pretty sure he means gay.

It's 1985, my sixteenth birthday party, and for some reason I'm letting it happen at Ralph's mobile home. *It's not a trailer*, I think to myself, *or I wouldn't be in it.* Ralph, divorced from Nanny almost twenty years, during which we hardly heard from him, returned a couple of months ago. This is a story about comings and goings.

"Shut up, Bryan." My cousin Nichole tries to make a joke out of it. She's my closest family ally. She's seven months younger than me, and her style is the lighter side of new wave: hair dyed auburn, bangs teased just a little, rhinestone broach cinching her collar. I can tell she and I are both wondering if Bryan's talking about the time he taught us to play "naked in the bag" when we were kids. But we also both know that his delusions don't require any shared reality.

"What the fuck is he talking about?" Ralph asks. He's four eleven, with tiny feet, a huge ego, and a filthy mouth. He's the living legend responsible for the destruction of the family—Ralph Neves, the famously reckless jockey who returned from the dead three times, who raised his kids among Hollywood royalty, who finally grew bored and left right around the time Bryan, his first grandchild, was born. The press called him the Portuguese Pepper Pot. Now he and his hair plugs live in a doublewide. He has returned—and this is the all-important detail—without his fortune. There was a time, I've heard all my life, when he and Nanny could have bought nearly all the beachfront property in Del Mar. Nanny pleaded with Ralph, but he said money was for spending. Hence the mobile home. Ralph's current interior is at odds with my personal aesthetic. The decor clashes with my hair, shaved up the back with long bangs I tease.

"Bryan," Nanny says. "Can we just enjoy the party?"

"It's my fault," Bryan repeats.

"What is he talking about, Jason?" my mom asks, sipping red wine, a terrifying bloodshot gleam in her eyes.

"What?" I say. My reply makes no sense, but it's all I can muster.

"Cathy, let's just enjoy the party?" Nanny says. That's enough to set my mom off. Nanny and I are in cahoots. I idolize her and resent my mom. She's sick of it.

"Why don't you tell him?" she asks, one brow raised a little higher than the other.

"Can we just have a nice party, Cathy? For once?" Most of our family parties involve a scene.

"Your Nanny wanted to flush you down the San Luis Rey." She's chosen my sixteenth birthday to tell me the story for the first time.

"Bullshit, Cathy," Nanny replies. But my mom tells the story of the clinic by the river anyway. "Bullshit," Nanny keeps repeating.

The rest of the evening is a blank. By this time, I've developed a technique for dealing with these situations. I become all brain, retreating to the land of mind, where the rest of my body, which has to live in the world and deal with its challenges, seems like an unpleasant prosthesis. The next day, and for the rest of our lives, Nichole and I will talk about what a bizarre and fucked up night this was. We'll laugh about it. We'll wonder how Bryan could remain such an effective instigator even though he lives in his personal psychotic world. But for the moment, all we do is exchange glances to affirm we'll debrief later. In the meantime, I focus on imagining what it would feel like to whirl down the San Luis Rey, tiny and translucent, bobbing with the current, banged up and bleeding from the rocks. I can see all my tiny organs, including the blobs of cells accumulating to form my brain and spinal cord. I wouldn't have felt anything. I'd have been recycled into universal matter and redistributed.

I do wonder whether those cells would have had the capacity, in their lingering moments of life, to send out a panic signal, like the ones I have spent years trying to understand, control, and dampen. Since childhood, an excruciatingly slow terror has been a trademark experience for me—measured in recurring nightmares, in the countless hours I spent as a kid examining my skin for signs of leprosy or in my twenties envisioning my blood, which I was sure was full of HIV. I try to trace the panic back to my fetus, when my cells might have mustered a last-minute attempt to communicate.

But if brain science has taught me anything, it's that no experience or personality trait can be traced to a single point of origin. Becoming somebody is a tangled process whose strands are well beyond our comprehension. There's no end point, no finished self. Even death is a moment in this process. But I imagine the waste of my underdeveloped brain matter anyway. I picture it disintegrating from exposure or devoured by river snakes, a lifetime of thoughts and feelings gobbled up and digested. I look for meaning in the fantasy. Looking without comprehending seems to be what we humans are built to do. That's why life can be so scary.

The San Luis Rey will become family lore—like Ralph's near-death encounters, Nanny's endless stream of pink T-Birds (a new one every year, in the fifties and early sixties), or the converted school bus we lived on when my mom was married to Stanley. After this night, the story will be refined and expanded at virtually all our gatherings. It will spawn bloodshot arguments.

After the birthday party, I drew the wishful and melodramatic conclusion that I was born at the wrong place and time, to the wrong family. *My mom had no business giving birth*, I decided there in Ralph's trailer, *and I had no business being born*. In fact, my birth was really no more or less an accident than anybody else's. In fact, the story turns an accident into a choice—my mom's choice. But it took me a long time to figure that out.

I was never sure if the San Luis Rey was real, so I did a little research. The only body of water I could find with that name was in North County, San Diego, and was an estuary used for drainage. The drainage part sounded right, but how did the San Luis Rey migrate in my family's imagination from North County to Tijuana?

The question is hard to answer, as hard as *Who am I? Who are these people who raised me? Why am I so unlike them? Why am I so like them?*

I spent a lot of my childhood asking these questions, and I spend a lot of my adulthood trying to read and write, think, and talk my way to some answers. I became fascinated with the fact of consciousness early on. We're aware of our own existence and at least a good chunk of our experience and our personal history. But where does this awareness come from? How does it work? I'm fascinated with these questions. I write about them. I teach college courses about them, leading students through fourteen weeks of literary, philosophical, and scientific attempts to find answers. None of these attempts settle the matter.

I love this effort to look for certainties that don't exist, and I think this must be related to the tall tales I was raised on. When I was younger, I thought science was the enemy. As a kid, I'd have told you

I'd become a writer, a pop star, or a music journalist, which seemed like an acceptable compromise between the first two. I didn't like my science teachers, with their formaldehyde frogs and multiple-choice exams. I was a child of psychedelic fog, not scientific facts.

But I was a kid who got fixated on things, and I always wanted to know how we come to be who we are. I was interested enough to try to understand something about neuroscience and physiology, because right now they seem closest to getting us some new answers. Still, the questions remain murky, the answers hard to come by, and I'm at least as fascinated with what neuroscientists don't know as what they've learned. The murk seems fitting, given my family lore.

I've learned from neuroscience that a fetus starts building its brain by the fourteenth day after egg and sperm commingle to make zygote. Fetal cells number in the mere hundreds, but a clique of them has already formed an embryonic nervous system, folding in upon itself and excluding cells concerned with vulgarities like fingernails or intestinal lining. The ball stretches until it becomes a tube, eventually developing into a spinal cord and brain.

The cells in the clique had to differentiate so my brain could develop. Which would have made for a lot of strife—cells abandoning cells and signing treaties with other cells who would in turn do their share of abandoning and signing. Neurons are social creatures, according to the neuroscientists. Those that don't form networks wither and die. Otherwise their extraneous presence would have cluttered my brain's delicate architecture, like empty boxes piled up in hallways.

Neuroscientists used to think cells in the fetal brain were coded for the roles they would play after birth. Now they believe the process is altogether bloodier. The function of a cell is determined by a game of musical chairs in which the losers are slaughtered. If a cell lands in a spot where it's needed—to help the organism hear or taste or feel pain, for example—then it assumes that role. If it migrates to a spot where other cells ignore it, busy doing their jobs, it is sacrificed. It ends up in the body's San Luis Rey.

There's a good reason for this. Too many cells making too many connections create brain chaos. Imagine yourself as an infant encountering the flood of information you face as you emerge from the womb, fight your way down the birth canal, and tear open your mother's vagina to greet the light of day. But you don't know the light of day from the cold, harsh fluorescence of an operating room. You don't know a nipple from a scalpel. Your brain contains too many cells making too many synapses, and it is only upon the elimination of nonfunctional synapses that the world comes into focus. *Massive cell death* is a prerequisite for development. The surviving networks shape the contours of a self.

Sometimes, when she was mad, my mom used to tell me she didn't have to keep me. She could have let Nanny's Tijuana doctors flush me down the San Luis Rey. Was there a reason for me to survive, I wondered. Now I wonder if there's analogy between my non-flushed fetus and the non-flushed cells. A cell survives because it's in the right place at the right time. The cell that survives molds the reality of the brain in question.

2

ACCIDENTS

It's been nineteen days since insemination. They don't know about the accident in her womb or the wedding. The sand in their toes and the sound of the Pacific Ocean might as well be in another dimension from the near future that is their fate.

The moon is a blazing chartreuse bopping around the night sky, a glowing pinball bouncing off planets and stars. The light tints their tan skin a nuclear yellow.

"Usually, you think the moon hangs in place," Charlie says. "But you're just *thinking* it."

"I know," Cathy replies. "What a drag."

"But that's the beauty of Johnny May's acid. I told you, didn't I? It's not a drug, it's a prayer. I wasn't shitting you, was I?"

"Nope."

"It's proof right there in front of our eyes that all that Galileo reality crap is bullshit."

"An illusion."

"Exactly."

They're in front of The Mausoleum, which is what Charlie and his friends call the house Midge and Ralph built on Nineteenth Street. It's a three-story latte-colored neo-Classical cake with dark brown shutters and a wall of windows that lead out onto the patio on the beach side. The lights are all off, but the moon shines bright enough that they can see the interior of the first floor, crystals in the chandeliers beaming yellow splinters onto terracotta tiles.

"I think someone's playing the piano," Cathy says. "Do you hear that?"

"Jim Morrison."

"The End" pumps out of The Mausoleum, the impatient blood in its pliable veins. Morrison's voice oozes right through the glass into the moist, salty air, singing about the end of elaborate plans and everything that stands.

"But they're all asleep," she says.

"Go with it. Just listen." When space and time disintegrate, reckless rock stars climb through black holes and play recitals in beachfront mausoleums. Out here in the beach air, the music isn't bloody anymore. Jittery atoms of Morrison's voice cling to the fog. They feel beads of it on their skin. Everything seems just right. The beach is a world without accidents.

"You know how when it's really hot you can see waves in the air?" Charlie asks.

"Heat waves," she says.

"Yeah, exactly. Well, I can see cool waves. I'm looking at them right now. They have to be there, you know. We just can't see them. But here they are, coming right toward us."

"Look," Cathy says, on her feet and running to the edge of the ocean, her feet sinking in wet sand. "Dolphins."

Charlie's at her side, looking out at the cavorting dolphins, squinting to keep sight of them as they leap over rising crests and disappear.

"They're mammals," he says. "Just like us," groping her hip and pulling their torsos together, finding her mouth and pressing his tongue into it until their faces dissolve into moon haze.

"Everybody smoked back then," people used to say, referring to the fact that pregnant women commonly smoked cigarettes in the sixties. "But your mom," my stepdad Stanley would joke, "your mom, she dropped acid."

It seems obvious that what biologists call the *internal milieu* or *chemical bath* of a pregnant woman's body would suffuse the embryo in her womb. It's a given that I soaked in my mom's chemical bath, absorbing substances her body needed to make the proteins that enabled mine to grow and develop. Her chemical bath was full of the food she ate, the air or smoke she breathed, and the acid she dropped.

I still don't know how true Stanley's story was. It probably depends on the exact date of conception. But either way, LSD is a big part of the early story, everywhere in the *external* milieu of my early life. Acid seemed preferable to the dull middle-American life my mom and her brothers were rejecting, even though they had never lived that life. Few have been raised with greater liberty than the children of the Portuguese Pepper Pot.

My parents and uncles didn't know the discovery of Lysergic Acid Diethylamide (LSD-25) was an accident, like my conception. I didn't know about it when I started dropping acid myself as a teenager.

We didn't know about 1938—the year chemist Albert Hoffman stumbled on LSD when he synthesized the twenty-fifth compound of an experimental drug derived from ergot, a fungus that grows on rye and has been used as both poison and medicine for centuries. Hoffman was experimenting with derivatives that might treat migraines. He spilled some of the compound on his hands, and it went to his head. The effects on his imagination piqued his curiosity, so he ingested 250 mg of the substance, two and a half times its hallucinogenic dose. Hoffman had a bad trip. He thought a demon had invaded his body; his furniture morphed into a tribe of monstrous enemies; his neighbor, he swore, was a hideous witch.

After Hoffman's discovery was made public, researchers began feeding LSD to humans and monkeys and rats, with two goals in mind: to figure out how it worked and to find some concrete applications for it, applications as diverse as neurological warfare and mapping the path to enlightenment. They'd dose the subjects and watch them trip, prodding them with swirling psychedelic patterns and colored lights.

A century of questing has yielded modest results. We now know that Hoffman's compound stirred itself into the chemical bath of his internal milieu. It traveled through nerves in his digestive track to his brain stem, which connects brain and spine. First stop, the *reticular activating system* (RAS), a very important collection of neurons. The RAS punctuates our days. When you wake up, you're putting it to work. When you go to sleep, the RAS again. The management of its trinity—sleep, dreams, arousal—is a grand responsibility.

When my parents dropped acid in 1968, their RAS sent neuronal axons far and wide, into the perceptual, cognitive, and emotional systems of their brains—just as mine did nearly twenty years later, when I put that first blot of paper with a picture of Snoopy on my tongue. According to some theories, the RAS is also a way station for basic emotion and helps regulate the body's homeostasis, or chemical balance. It traffics in feelings, and it monitors the body for imbalances. Antonio Damasio, probably the world's most famous neuroscientist, believes this monitoring may be a key to understanding consciousness itself.

Many of Damasio's colleagues disagree, but my parents could have told you a version of his theory, and so could I—or just about anybody you talk to after a first acid trip. Hoffman's compound has a way of convincing people they are privy to the secrets of consciousness. This has to be because RAS is involved in the basic processes that shape us.

When the alarm buzzes and you feel dread, that's the RAS strong-arming emotion networks of your brain. That's the everyday experience with RAS we all have. When hyper-stimulated by LSD, it snaps dormant networks into action, too much action. Otherwise routine sensory stimuli cross paths, trade details. Profound synesthesia ensues. Music becomes color, furniture marches, your own viscera transmutes into a demon, countertops melt, thoughts kill words and words fight back. Life is like a dream.

If infants are synesthetes anyway, is life an acid trip for them? Like a dream? I don't think anybody can tell you precisely how acid affects fetal development, but it's interesting to think that my teenage parents were replicating the sensory experience of the infant I was yet to become when they stood on the beach in front of my grandparents' mausoleum of a house.

Of course, acid trips wear off. Homeostasis does its work. You come down, buzzing and aching. The world gradually shakes itself still, squeezes itself ordinary. But the drug leaves traces, shifts perspectives, shapes worldviews. Whatever acid might do to the internal milieu of a person's body, the external milieu—which my teenage parents were about to face, with all its expectations and responsibilities—becomes subject to doubt. Sometimes I think my childhood was a nonstop, wobbling war between our species' default drift toward homeostasis and the determination of my family to throw our world off balance.

The way I imagine it, Cathy didn't expect the walkway to the front door to be lined with pansies and sweet peas. *Ding dong.* She didn't expect the house to be red. *Knock knock.*

"Coming." The call doesn't contain a hint of impatience. The door squeaks open, revealing Nancy: a spotless floral apron, wide hips, playful eyes.

"Oh my," she says. "Can I help you, dear?" The screen door is between them, softening the impression on either side. The tiny girl, belly exploding, looks familiar, and the familiarity accounts for her size. "You're Ralph Neves's girl," she says, knowing where the sentence leads. "Come in. Come right in, dear."

The house is carpeted in aquamarine and is full of blue antiques—ceramic bulldogs from China, decorative plates with pastoral scenes. *Madama Butterfly* glides from big speakers on the floor. "Would you like some toast and jam? It's all homemade. I have buttermilk bread or whole wheat. I have passion fruit, grape with the skins on, and orange marmalade."

"Thank you. I'm not hungry."

"It's like Charles not to mention this." Cathy's never heard him called that.

"It was an accident," she blurts, tears bursting out of her. "It was my first time."

"Phil's a big fan of your father's," Nancy says, finding a subject to erase the image of this girl's *first time*. "We love the races. Go every Sunday during the season. Phil likes to place a small bet every now and then."

"My dad is living in Arcadia now."

"Oh, yes, I read about the divorce. A shame. I suppose he's up there to be near the track at Santa Anita."

"Yeah, and Kay." Nancy is puzzled. "His new wife."

"Your father is quite a legend. The Portuguese Pepper Pot, the paper calls him."

"I'm not speaking to him."

"Charles didn't mention that."

"That figures," Cathy says.

"Charles's father will not take to this. He's a kind man but he's very stubborn, and he won't like it."

"He said you'd be mad. He said you'd never understand. We're in love."

"Now listen, Cathy. This was an accident." It's weird to hear this woman repeat her words. Women like Nancy rarely affirm the statements of girls like Cathy. "I'm going to help you and Charles," Nancy continues. "Phil won't like it, but the baby is our grandchild, and I'm going to help, if I can."

The evidence was in the slides, before they burned with most of my mom's possessions in the nineties.

Cathy, her white lace mini struggling to climb over her six-and-a-half-month belly, is giggling as Midge leads her down the aisle. "Stop it, Cathy," she mutters. "What the shit is so funny?" Cathy knows her mom knows exactly what the shit is so funny.

Cathy joins Charlie on the sacred stage. The setting is intimate: eight or nine people at the front of the church.

"Do you, Charles, take Cathy to be your lawfully wedded wife? To have and to hold? For better or for worse? In sickness and in health?" He does. Cathy's giggling has given way to genuine joy, plastered across her face. "Do you, Cathy?"

"I do."

A human life is a product of biology and culture, the internal and the external milieus collaborating. Two people unknown to the future human have sex; an embryo develops into a fetus and, if all goes well, a baby is born, composed of cells patched together from genetic blueprints laced through the viscera of the parents' bodies. These parents, themselves accidents of biology and culture, figure out what to do with their baby—how to raise it (or not raise it), where it will live, what and how it will learn. Before long, the rest of the world intervenes, steering the parents' influence in unexpected directions.

The many cumulative acts of others shape what it's possible to do, to know, and to be. *You have to take care of it*, they say. *You're not ready. For Godssake, then you have to get married. You have to grow up. You have to take care of yourself. You have to take care of this baby.*

Protect your internal milieu, they're saying. *Find homeostasis. Be sensible about your external milieu.* But the internal milieu has a way of interfering with reasonable decisions, with the will of the organism. My mother asserted herself, kept the baby. My parents did the sensible thing. They got married. They tried to turn an accident into a choice. But those Godforsaken milieus—as Nanny would have called them, in the language of her Scottish Catholic parents—have a way of turning choices back into accidents.

I'm lucky. I won't have to fight my way through my mother's birth canal. Her body is just too small to squirt out the six pounds, seven and a half ounces. Thirty-six hours of labor is more than her frame can handle, but she has no choice but to handle it.

When they finally cut me out, my body is fucked up. I'm not a fully functioning organism. I can't eat. In my mom's words, "Every time he ate, he threw up all over me." The condition is called *pyloric stenosis*. The pyloric valve separates the stomach from the small intestine. It's an accident of the genes. Due to a genetic disorder that affects every second generation of male children, mine is spasmodic.

At six weeks, they roll me into a bright, sterile operating room. A surgeon holds a scalpel to my belly, cuts it open, and scrapes out the excess tissue. There is no anesthesia. It's too dangerous, and besides, the doctors agree, infants don't feel pain.

When the blade slices skin, it's just another sensation, like the sound of sunlight on my face or the prick of my parents screaming their lungs out at each other. As the surgeon scrapes flesh from the valve, Charlie is somewhere guiding the point of a needle into his arm. Infants might not need anesthetic, but he does. My mom is in the waiting room, with Midge, Phil, and Nancy. The operation works, the genetic accident reversed with a knife and some very skilled hands.

The scar will grow with me, eventually, in adulthood, six inches long. It will never tan. I'll develop a strong affection for it. The scar is indelible, but it's not legible.

3

GUESTHOUSE

"What do you think, Jas? All packed up." Mother and child rock in a chair on the grass, next to a small pile of boxes and furniture.

"All packed up," she tells me, "but Daddy's not home from work. You ready for Cardiff?" she asks. "You ready for the Tougaws? Am I?"

We're moving into Charlie's parents' tiny guesthouse, to save money. We'll end up moving into and getting evicted from dozens of houses before I'm eighteen, sometimes more than one or two in a year.

"Hi, Cathy." She looks up, to see Mr. Diamond, our landlord. "Hot enough for you?"

"Great weather for moving," she says.

"I got the new tenants showing up in a couple of hours."

"Charlie's not home from work yet," she admits.

"I got my truck."

"I should wait for Charlie," she says.

"No time," he says, and kneels to pick up the nearest box.

Cathy spends the fifteen-minute drive talking to me. "Your grandmother's going to be so happy to have you so close. You can eat all the peaches you want. And onions and spinach. You like veggies. Your grandfather will teach you to be a little gardener."

"You're gonna live here?" Mr. Diamond asks as they pull into the driveway. "All three of you?"

"We don't need much. We're not materialistic."

In just a few minutes, our belongings are stuffed into one rectangular room twenty feet from the Tougaws' back door. Cathy slides the screen door shut as Mr. Diamond backs out of the driveway.

Cathy sits down in the rocker, feeds me, rocks me to sleep, and puts me in the crib. Feeling brave—Phil and Nancy are out of town—she ventures into the garden, through the orchard of plums, apricots, and passion fruit and into the vegetable beds, careful to step between rows. She snatches a head of red leaf lettuce, two tomatoes, a cucumber, and a green pepper.

She makes the salad, eats the salad, watches the baby, wonders what to do. The sun sets, but the heat lingers. No Charlie. She finally starts to cry. She rocks the tears for who knows how long, until she hears an engine, the squeak of a break, the click of a door, and a slam of steel. She runs out to greet him. "Charlie, there you are. Where—?"

"Why are you crying?" is all he says.

"Are you drunk?" she asks.

"Yep?" He grins at her. "You cryin' in front of the kid?" he asks, stepping past her. "Where's my kid?"

"Don't go in there. Don't. Why are you acting like this?"

"Just let me see my kid," he says, holding a palm up like he might push her over.

"Don't, Charlie. Just stop it, please. What's wrong with you? Stop! Who were you with? What are you on?"

When she gets inside, Charlie is standing over the crib, a finger in the baby's belly button. "Charlie," she whispers. "Let him sleep."

"What the fuck do you know?" he roars.

"He just finally got to sleep."

"What the fuck do you know?" he repeats. Now he's in motion, storming at her.

"Stop, Charlie," she says. "Please."

He lifts her off the ground. With her body in his arms, he storms toward the back wall of the guesthouse and pounds her head against it. The shock cancels her out, turns her into an inanimate object. When he stops, her hair is matted and wet and shiny with blood.

"*You're killing me!*" she screams, in genuine anguish. He drops her to the floor and goes back to the crib. When she walks out the door, he doesn't even look. She runs straight into the orchard, thankful for the dark, looking for the spot where the night is most concentrated, finally falling against a trunk.

Charlie walks outside, crunching leaves underfoot. He looks for her, but not very hard. "Fuck this," she hears him say.

If the lore is accurate, this is the first brutal scene I witnessed. This pattern will play out with Charlie several times before the two of them give up their brief experiment in domestic living. It will be replayed with other husbands, other boyfriends. My mom will acknowledge the brutality after it happens and apologize for making me a party to it. But she'll replay the pattern like it's pre-programmed. I'll learn to watch as bruises and hurt feelings fade, as things get patched up. I'll learn to expect the next scene, to clench and get through it.

For me, the clenching and watching became skills, waiting for childhood to end.

It's midnight. Charlie and Cathy are parked at Cardiff Beach in his faded metallic brown truck. I'm between them on the front seat, face up, wriggling on flaking gold vinyl. Cathy is red-faced from crying. "Jennifer told me where you were. I know what you were doing." The experiment failed. Those few months living like a family stretched and strained them.

"Fuck Jennifer," Charlie says. "What the hell does she know?"

"Heroin, Charlie? Heroin?"

Charlie shrugs and squints. "You don't get it."

"You're right, Charlie, I don't. I don't get the fact that you have a baby, an infant who's been sick practically his whole life, who still has a raw scar across half his stomach. And you're out shooting heroin. I don't get it. Maybe I'm just not smart enough."

"Shut the hell up. Be silent."

"Take a look at that baby. Take a hard look."

"You care so much about the baby you're gonna use him as a shield."

"Heroin," she yowls. Her voice cracks in its higher register. The word sounds obscene, slowed down and drawn out like a malfunctioning eight-track tape: "Haaaiiiirrooohhhiiiiinnnnn." She doesn't say *smack* or *horse* or *junk*, despite all the friends she has who live and die on it.

"Jason," he says. "Cathy, wait. Wait."

"Are you high now?"

"Just wait. Just listen."

"Are you?"

Can a person be enraged on heroin? She doesn't wait to find out. She runs through the night with me in her arms. When she reaches the payphone outside the Fish House West, she collapses into it and shuts the door. "Doug, it's Cathy. Can you pick me up?"

She holds me under her macramé sweater while we wait, closing its spearhead wooden fasteners to tuck me in against her breast. *At least he's too young to know what's going on*, she tells herself.

The front seat of the brown metallic car is my first memory. I must have fabricated it later, since I was still an infant, too young to remember. I'm sure that car never existed. But if I made it up, I did it by the time I was six or seven, because it's a memory I carried all through childhood: a car, a big man, good-looking, slow-moving—my mom, with long, straightened hair, screaming *heroin*.

I've never tried heroin. I heard a lot about it as a kid. "I hate heroin," my mom would always say, but she kept choosing men who loved it. "It killed so many of my friends." I knew this was an indirect reference to my father. We always called him *Charlie*, never *father* or *dad*. The word *heroin* conjured Charlie's image: hazy, floating, just out of reach.

The ghost of heroin—which is also the ghost of Charlie—adds another hazy layer of unreality to my childhood. When I was a teenager, I became obsessed with Jean Cocteau and his opium. I even tattooed Cocteau's Orpheus on my arm. I didn't make the connection between the French artist and my imprisoned father. But an opiate is an opiate. As far as I can tell, it evaporates pain and manufactures peace.

Charlie's brain, like all brains, contained built-in receptors for heroin, because our bodies traffic in their own natural opiates. Neuroscientists call them *opioids*. These receptors—they're called *kappa*, *mu*, and *delta*—attach to a cell's oily surface and dig roots. The calculated prick of an acupuncture needle can incite the circulation of opioids. So can a sugar pill, or a severe accident or trauma. Charlie preferred the reliability of a syringe.

Charlie already knew his brain was an illusionist. LSD had taught him that. But an opiate illusion is less work than an acid trip. Opiates target an area of the brain called the *nucleus accumbens*—the pleasure center, a small glob of cells housed in the forebrain and networked directly to the amygdala, an almond-shaped cluster responsible for basic emotions like fear, anger, and pleasure. The nucleus accumbens traffics in dopamine, and so the theory goes that it can tip the amygdala's balance toward pleasure and away from fear and anger. Roughly speaking, this is how Charlie found peace in the prick of a needle.

The natural opiates live in the nervous system. When things get really bad, they have to be able to manufacture well-being from scratch. They replace external horror or pain with relative internal ease, restoring homeostasis. They don't have to wait for an injection or a decision or even a craving. But the manufactured cousins have a secret weapon: addiction. Their doses can be manipulated. They seduce bodies for whom the ordinary rhythms of daily life are unbearable. When they gain entry to the nervous system, they disarm their endogenous cousins. The body enters into a symbiotic relationship with its opiate of choice, achieving a new, drugged-out homeostasis.

Opiates short-circuit the nervous system and wash the outside world in a shadowy haze. The shadows subsume sharp corners and hard facts. Obstacles give way to open road. Opioid realism is thoroughly convincing.

I've mostly given up blaming him, but I wonder what it was in Charlie that made the hard corners too hard. Why did he need heroin to create an illusion of homeostasis? Was it something in his cells, something I might have inherited? Was it something that happened to him, and if it was, did I inherit that, in the form of the hazy heroin ghost that trails me?

4

DNA

Great-Grandpa Neves is directing traffic on the Golden Gate Bridge, naked. By 1930, he's been in California long enough to perform the signals on instinct: palm out front for "stop," a backward wave for "move along." He mumbles the Portuguese to himself, "Pare. Siga em frente." He hasn't been here so long to forget how the world sounds in words with soft edges.

"What's the matter with you, mister? Get out of the way. Jesus Christ, he's cracked."

From a distance, the Golden Gate Bridge shines red like giant candy, but now that he's here, it's hard to see that. The wind whoops so hard he has to fight just to stay in one place. With each foot braced on a plank, he envisions a moving snapshot of his naked body floating, buoyed by the wind, threatening with every dip to zoom straight down and gulp the Bay until it floods his lungs and strangles him for a gasping seven minutes before he finally deflates.

He came to get the cars off, and he's going to do it. They're an eyesore. They make the bridge look like it's crawling with black ants. When he looks at the bridge, which he does hundreds of times a day, he feels the ants under his skin. These red steel beams, so majestic from afar, turn out to be the limbs of a giant scorpion surveying its ant prey.

"Run the sonofabitch over." The wind carries the driver's shouts. *Stop*, he commands. *Move along*. If he can just let the wind take him, if he can just let himself float, the world will fade white and disappear. *Stop. Move along. Pare. Siga em frente.*

The Golden Gate Bridge story is the centerpiece of my family's lore. Our blood flows from Ralph's schizophrenic dad right through each and every one of us. We're obsessed with this blood, and by *blood*, we mean *genes*. It could be any one of us up there on that bridge. Don't forget it.

Port-a-ghee blood. There's a problem with our blood, and it affects our brains. This is our family mantra. My mom and her brothers are only half Portuguese, but the Port-a-ghee blood cancels out other strains.

This blood is the reason Ralph ended up in an orphanage, with nuns. Hell, it's probably why he ended up riding. Even the press got the point: the *Portuguese* was the blood, and the *pepper* was the problem. Ralph's little body is the Pepper Pot. The rest of us are the Petri dishes into which the stew was served, in variable portions.

We told his story so many times it's hard to choose an example. But you have to make choices when you tell a story, what to tell, what to leave out. I'll choose Thanksgiving 1991.

Here we are, descendents of schizophrenia and recklessness. We cousins are in our twenties. My mom and her brothers are in their forties. Nanny is sixty-nine; Ralph, who's been back with us seven years now, is seventy-three. We're all here, significant others in tow.

Nanny is pouring Grand Marnier into the whipping cream when someone brings up Mrs. Bowman. "She tried to drown me," my mom says.

"Oh Cathy, she did not," her brother Gary says. His son Trever laughs. Nichole, my closest cousin, gives me a look to say *here we go*. Nichole's my uncle Craig's daughter, but I see her more than he does.

"She was going to watch me drown, if Uncle Angus didn't happen to walk around the back of the house and see me."

"Cathy, you and I both know it didn't happen that way," Nanny says.

"Who the hell knows," Ralph interjects. "It probably did. That crazy German bitch."

"See?" my mom says. "He even admits it. You guys were always gone and you left us with crazy, mean Mrs. Bowman."

"Cathy, she wasn't crazy," Gary says. Which is when my mom digs her hand into the cream and smears a handful over his head. The cream is beading in his kinks and dripping over his left eye. He's got a handful now too and is backing my mom slowly into the corner by the sink. He smears it all over her cheek, and it drips onto her black rayon blouse.

"That's it," she says, squeezing past him for the stainless-steel bowl.

"Jesus, Mary, and Joseph," Nanny says. "You're wasting all my Goddamn whipped cream."

"Whip some Goddamn more," Ralph says.

"Is the moon full?" my mom asks. "It's the Port-a-ghee blood." She says this every Thanksgiving, between bites of cranberry relish and gravy-soaked mashed potatoes. "It's especially bad when the moon is full."

"The moon is not full," I say, as though logic might matter here.

"I think it might be the red wine," my mom's husband Ryan says, smiling.

"That'll do it," Ralph says.

"This is what my family's like," Nichole explains to her rockabilly boyfriend Josh. "It's always like this."

"It's the Port-a-ghee blood," my mom repeats.

"Yeah, right," Ryan says. "It's the wine."

"The wine is for the Port-a-ghee blood," she says. "It keeps it healthy."

"See," Trever says to the onlookers, "it all started with our great-grandpa directing traffic on the Golden Gate Bridge."

"In the nude," my mom interrupts.

"Right," Trever says. "In the nude. And this is why my adorable Auntie Cathy acts the way she does." Gary and Trever both like to tease my mom about her penchant for hysteria, even though they know they risk pushing her into a bout.

"Very funny, Trever," she says. "Very funny. If anything, it's because of Mrs. Bowman. And Gary and Craig. And the fact that you two," she says, pointing to Nanny and Ralph, "were never home. You were always traveling around, or out partying."

"Okay, Cat," Ryan says, "let's clean up."

Great-Grandpa Neves might offer a partial explanation for Bryan's schizophrenia. But the rest? We've got diagnoses: bipolar disorder, depression, alcoholism, brain tumors. We've got behaviors: suicide attempts, drug overdoses, near-fatal accidents. We've got consequences: the metal plate in Ralph's head, Charlie in prison, the faded scars on my mom's wrist. There's a problem with our blood, and it affects our brains.

The math doesn't stretch far enough to explain our family disorders. Sequences of DNA, delivered from one generation to another, tell you only so much. Bryan's schizophrenia may be the only traceable legacy of our Port-a-ghee blood. You might be able to argue recklessness is a genetic trait that led to Ralph's many accidents or the metal plate in his head. You might even make a case that the blood in Cathy's veins metabolizes into a craving to fall in love with assholes and dropouts. But nobody can tell you how blood from Portugal caused Charlie's heroin addiction, or Nichole's ex-husband Geoff to crash his motorcycle, or the tumor that grew in Nanny's brain for years before anybody knew it was there. Intimate contact with the Port-a-ghee blood we're so proud of seems to place people at risk. We tell the stories because they stretch farther than the math.

When I was a kid, I thought I was from a different gene pool. But the evidence suggested otherwise. I had my disorders too. Dyslexia and hypochondria, when combined in the same brain, have an unexpected side effect. They produce a fixation with making illegible signs legible. Black marks on the page float until one word becomes another; sensations under the skin irritate until they are identified as symptoms of leprosy or AIDS. The need to crawl inside an obviously mythologized story and fuck with it until it makes sense may be a variation of the genetic sequence that enables schizophrenia.

I have a plan. If I can master genetics and quantum physics—and then map the quantum leap of genes from Ralph's bloodstream to Nanny's—I will crack our family history wide open. Gene A, bequeathed from Grandpa Neves to Ralph, swims through the viscera of his body, colliding at every turn with Gene B, one he got from Fat Gramma. Every time these two particles collide, a wave is created. Waves, according to physicists, don't follow the ordinary laws of physical reality. Nanny comes along and spends decades in close contact with Ralph, arguing with him, birthing his offspring, laughing at his jokes. With every intimate moment, the wave created by the collision between Gene A and Gene B swirls through his aura and into hers, until his Port-a-Ghee blood swims in her too. Now multiply this by the billions of DNA strands in the billions of cells in both their bodies and multiply that by all the billions in the bodies of their children, and their children's children.

If I can do this, I will be close to an explanation.

Any science textbook will tell you my plan is ridiculous.

The way it really works is that the nucleus of every cell in my body contains chromosomes, tight packages of DNA I inherited from my mother and father. These packages unwind so the sequence of proteins that compose them can copy itself and transmit tiny messages within my internal milieu. This is how genes govern the development of an embryo, or any other organism.

But governing is not the same as determining. The race to "map" the human genome was reported as though it would tell us everything about the meaning of life. Big surprise: it didn't. It turned out human

DNA is composed of fewer genes than anybody thought—between twenty and twenty-five thousand, hardly more than primates and less than twice the number in a fly. You can't just find a given gene for genius or cancer. Biology, as usual, turns out to be messier than this. The meaning of a gene depends on its place in the sequence and the environment in which its tiny messages are expressed.

99.9% of a human being's DNA sequence is exactly the same as every other human being's—and we share 98% of it with our closest primate relatives. Small differences in sequencing account for vast differences from one individual to the next. Within a family, there is significantly less variation. A child splits the .1% of the DNA that makes him unique with his mother and father.

That means we share about 99.95% of our DNA with each of our parents, and they share the same with their parents. There's always a story in that remaining .05%. These stories have many beginnings. One of ours was the moment Ralph pulled his slick car into the Sacramento drive-in where Nanny was working as a car hop. The youngest of thirteen children, she had always worked. Ralph, already a famous jockey, was training for the cavalry. After a few visits, he asked Nanny to marry him. She refused. Next time, he arrived married. Right in front of his new wife, a cute redhead, he asked Nanny if she'd change her mind. She refused. Three weeks later, he was divorced. A few weeks after that, he was thrown from a horse and broke his back. Nanny found herself at his bedside. When he recovered several weeks later, they married.

"Biggest mistake of my life," she liked to say, but they stayed married for twenty-three years, replicating a lot of DNA in the process.

5

SKIPPING ON PINK RIBBON

After the metallic brown car, I have two kinds of early memory: the ones I believe I actually remember and those implanted by adults repeating stories of my early life until I remember them like they're my own. Both memories come in hazy bubbles, a nearly palpable aura that acts like gentle force field between me and the world. The haze helped me cope; it distracted me from the people around me and enabled me to live among them.

The haze is kind of like physicist James Clerk Maxwell's ether. A century and a half ago, Maxwell postulated that Newtonian matter was composed of microscopic electromagnetic waves. Light, he suggested, was made of waves of oscillating fluid called *the ether*. This fluid was both a bridge and a wall between physical reality and the invisible heavens. Gravity and substance, Maxwell thought, were products of constant collisions between matter and ether.

But nobody could find the ether, and Einstein simplified things, demonstrating a direct relationship between mass and energy. Ether, the middleman, was cut out, disqualified by scientific observation. Protons and electrons were all we got.

I hold onto the idea that ether may be real, that I might have been floating in it when I activated the hazy force field that insulated me from the worst of it. It felt physical, not just psychological or metaphorical, like a subatomic transaction between my body and its environment, something like the blur of lights that go off as a pinball bounces around inside its machine. I always thought of the force field as separating me from my mom, her boyfriends, and everybody else, really. But instead, it helped me live with them. It was a connective tissue that bound me to the family organism.

My cousin Nichole and I are running rings around the trunks of the mythic redwoods of Big Sur. Our moms are nineteen and twenty-one, both single now. They've dropped acid with a bunch of other people. They've played a trick on their brains.

Nichole's two, born seven months after me, the closest thing I have to a sibling. You could fit hundreds of us inside a single tree. Through the treetops, the stars squint and glimmer. We hear acid-heated yelps erupt into laughter. We hear them dancing and shouting and fucking and plotting revolution.

The redwoods are a hilly maze. Nobody notices that we've wandered off until Nichole starts crying, loud. I look at her funny, like, *Why are you crashing my party?* Her face is mashed up, all red and wet. She's got sticks in her hair.

We hear the cracking of sticks, the fall of a body slipping on the leaves, and a half-scream, half-giggle, "Oh shit." Then the clearing of a throat and footsteps. "Boog, Nichole. Boog, Nichole." My mom goes straight for Nichole. "Ssshhh, honey, ssshhh. Auntie Cathy's here. Boog, she's pooped her pants. Come on."

I've always been sure the core of this one is a genuine memory: the tree, holding hands, my mom finding us. For years afterward, my mom will tell this story and Jennifer will swear we never wandered off at all. But a story denied is as potent as one told, so Nichole and I grew up believing it.

I'm wearing my navy overalls, with a black T-shirt under them for the special occasion.

"Boogie, do you understand?" my mom asked before we left. I couldn't answer.

"What?"

"He's your dad. He did a bad thing, so he's in jail. But he's not a bad person." She isn't convinced, but her resolve is firm.

The thick Plexiglas (is it bulletproof?) warps his image a little. He's wearing denim too, holding a telephone.

"Hi," he says, first to my mom. Then: "Hi, Jason."

She picks up the telephone on our side. "Hi," she says, holding the phone to my face. "Say hi."

"Hi," I say.

"How long are you here?" my mom asks.

"Maybe a week. I've been extradited. They're taking me back to Washington."

"How long?"

"Maybe a year."

"Do your parents know?"

"I don't know."

Talking on a telephone to somebody only twelve inches away is fun, but I can't think of anything to say. The phone and the Plexiglas make the visit an outing.

I never say, "Hi, Daddy, how's jail?"

He never says, *I miss you, son. I'm sorry that I've left a blank in the middle of your life, that I will never send child support, that I impregnated your mother before she was a grown-up and now she has to figure out how to be one.*

"What's it like?" my mom asks. Never "Fuck you. Thanks for ruining my life."

"The food is shit," he says. His body is clenched and rigid. His quiet is inviting though, locked up behind the glass.

A memory is not a thing but an electrochemical process.

The front seat of a brown metallic car, the giant trunks of redwoods, that Plexiglas window. The images of my earliest memories are durable. They've outlived most of the experience I've had since and still rise to consciousness regularly. They'll probably outlive what happens to me today.

Brains don't store memories like these whole and intact. Instead, the nervous system registers experience and is altered by it. The alterations are constant. When something happens to you—like seeing your father behind Plexiglas—multiple senses, emotions, and cognitive functions process it, in overlapping tracks. Neural networks that comprise each track communicate with each other, strengthening their previous connections. In the process, neuromodulators reshape brain chemistry *and* structure, subtly but permanently. You've shape-shifted.

An *engram*, in the words of psychologist Daniel L. Schacter, is "the enduring change in the nervous system (the 'memory trace') that conserves the effects of experience across time." This engram is not something you can locate or look at. It's the strengthened connection at the points of intersection among neural networks. It goes into remission when you don't need it.

To recall the trace, you'll require a retrieval cue. Unfortunately, retrieval cues are everywhere. Dazing out in front of the TV, I click past an episode of *Law & Order* with loved ones visiting a guy in prison. Before I can get to another channel, the retrieval cue has reconfigured an engram for the moment when Charlie and I confronted each other across Plexiglas. The memory is an approximation, because an engram will never reconvene in its original form, with all members present in their exact configurations. Things change. Cells die, or grow apart, or just get too busy or distracted. In this case, a trace of *Law & Order* is added, the wrenching memory and the stupid TV show melding with no regard for good taste or relevance. This is why a story recounted repeatedly, ritualistically over holiday meals, can become memory. Individual experience can become collective memory because stories resemble experiences enough to trigger identical neural systems. Story and experience become indistinguishable.

The block party is an annual event, timed to coincide with racing season and the fair, but this year it's also our going-away celebration. We're going to live in Hawaii, where Gary's already living with Bryan and Trever. "It's better than California," he says. "Better waves, warmer water, groovier people."

Nanny's wearing big oval Jackie O. sunglasses, with opalescent grey frames and periwinkle lenses. She and Doug sit on an India-print bedspread, sipping beer in glasses with salted rims and floating lemons. Nichole, in a bikini top, is grasping Craig's leg on the lawn next to them. Craig sips beer from a can and smokes. A kid has a lemonade stand set up in the middle of the street. He sits behind a table, a huge lemon-shaped poster board dangling from it: 5¢. I'm with my mom and this guy Mopa, who's supposed to be my godfather, running in the street with no one to stop me.

"Want a sip?" Mopa asks, handing me his beer.

"Mopa!" my mom says.

"Just a sip."

"One sip," she says to me.

I attach my lips to the plastic cup and bend it a little to make a spout. The gold bubbles spill into my mouth and down my chin. Everybody laughs. I run, at least twenty feet, and then back. I do it again. On my way back the second time, I see a man with long wavy blond hair idling down the middle of the street, one arm around his girlfriend, whose long black hair is perfectly straight. They're pinballs in slow motion, bouncing off each other, moving away slightly and then back.

Faster now, like he's ringdinging a triple-score tunnel, the man bends to my height and picks me up with his free hand. He lets go of the girl and looks me in the face. "Jason, meet your daddy," he says.

My mom is the slow motion one now, turning when she hears the voice. "What the hell?" she yells.

"Whooaa," he says. "Hold up. I'm just sayin' hello to the kid." The black-haired girl stares at him and me like we are her future.

"Put him down right now," my mom says. "Now."

"Don't get nasty," he says, slurring a little.

"Take it easy, Charlie," I hear Craig say. He and Nichole have joined the circle forming around us. "Give him to me."

"Hey, Craig, you didn't tell me things were gonna be so heavy."

"You told him, Craig?" my mom says.

Craig reaches for me, but the man backs up, stumbling a little. The black-haired girl giggles.

I feel two confident arms reach around him from behind and loose me from his grip. It's Doug. He squeezes me to him for a second and hands me off to Nanny. The man launches a wobbly slow-motion punch at Doug, who ducks it and delivers one in return, right in the stomach. The man leaps on Doug and they fall to the concrete, punching, rolling, two steel balls grinding at each other's polish. It takes less than a full minute for the man to surrender, scratched all over, his nose spouting blood. They both stand up. Game over. The man says to Nanny, "What do you think of your tough guy boyfriend now?"

Nobody says anything. The comment doesn't make any sense. He grabs the girl's hand, holding his nose with the other as they swagger back down the block.

My mom runs, regular speed, to where I'm standing with Nanny. "You okay, Boog?" I put my head in the crook where her leg touches Nanny's. "Thank God we're getting out of here."

"Didn't you hear?" Craig asks.

"About what?" my mom replies.

"That Charlie was out," he says.

"No. Where would I hear *that*?" she responds, the Sarah Bernhardt touch earned this time, putting her palms over my two ears and rubbing my hair up and down.

"Around. He's been sayin' he wants to see Jason."

"You talked to him?" She catches Nanny's eye for a second, before Nanny grabs my hand and leads me toward the India print spread on the lawn.

"He's my buddy," Craig says.

"After what he did to me? And Jason?"

No reply. Nichole runs to Nanny and me on the lawn, a cup of lemonade in her hand.

A few days later, I decide to get out of here. This place isn't for me.

The sounds of the ocean and the cars on 101 are my compass. There are only ten blocks between me and Nanny. I walk happily, careful not to touch my toes to the cracks in the sidewalk. *Step, crack, step, crack*. I'm surrounded by lawns and daisies and morning glories. Birds chirp. It all smells like ocean. I know the way, more or less.

I don't see the problem until I arrive. I'm standing on the sidewalk, dead center between two cracks, staring at a row of identical dark-shingled, two-story terraced condos with sliding-glass doors and matching front lawns. I have no clue which is Nanny's.

A woman Nanny's age, in an apron, her gray hair in a bun, slivers her curtained sliding-glass door and walks onto her terrace.

"Hello," she says.

"Hi," I say.

"Would you like some cookies and milk?" she asks. "I just baked these," she says, sitting me on her sofa with a plateful of chocolate chip cookies. The skeleton of her house is just like Nanny's. There's the champagne carpet, the golden fridge and stove, the kitchen overlooking the living room. But Nanny's condo sparkles with heavy ornate frames on original oil paintings and proportionally bizarre antique chests and curvy-legged sofas and chairs.

"What's your name?" she asks, handing me my milk. I tell her. "How old are you?" I hold up three fingers. "Are you lost?"

"I'm going to Nanny's. She lives on this street."

"Does Nanny have another name?"

"Midge." She goes to the phone.

"I guess you like the cookies," she says when she returns.

Ding dong.

"Surprise," she says. Nanny walks through the door, her hair especially silver and her eyes especially blue.

"Jason, what in Jesus's name are you doing here?" she asks, more entertained than worried or annoyed.

"I came to see you."

"You almost made it," Nanny says. "Almost," she repeats, with signature sarcasm. "Thank you," she says to the lady. "You are an angel."

"My pleasure," she says, scruffing my hair as Nanny shepherds me out the door. On the sidewalk, we pass condo after identical condo, like we're on a conveyor belt. Nanny says, "Your mother will be worried sick."

I've made it. I'm sitting on Nanny's overstuffed loveseat dotted in orange and olive flowers, happily lost in a forest of objects: the tall, narrow apothecary's chest with ceramic knobs and twenty drawers; the round dining table, its thick columnar base carved into four lion-like curves and its top stained in sections of chocolate and caramel; the green and gold chest with skinny legs taller than me; the brass eighteenth-century couple, she carrying a basket of flowers he with his trouser cuffs rolled up and his shirt draping open at the neck; the merry-go-round music box, its brightly-dressed riders undulating to the sounds of "I Left My Heart in San Francisco"; the green birdcage; the high chair; the wicker barstools; the three-foot-high porcelain giraffe with its legs tucked under its body. The paintings—Paris at night and by day, the Spanish doll lady, the interior of a museum, the fishing villages. They're all just outside awareness, props. I don't know then that Nanny will have to sell most of them to survive, or that the rest will burn in a fire thirty years from now.

My focus is on my favorite painting, of the kid in the field, which hangs above the loveseat. The kid is on a bench, planted in overgrown grass. The canvas is thick with paint chunks, but the image is all hazy outlines, the kid's hair the same soft green as the grass and the bench. The kid wears a smock painted in lavender textured with inky purple shadows. The view is mainly of the kid's back. No eyes, no features other than an ear and a cheek. She's a girl, but sexless in the way that only orphans from another era can be. If you were to walk around her and look her in the face, you'd see her staring into the grass, looking at the spaces between its blades. The kid is suspended in a green and purple haze, her own ether force field. The frame, both rough-hewn and ornate, traps her. If I stare hard enough, Nanny and I and the whole room might float through the dissolving frame and lie around in the grass with the kid.

The painting will always hang in the most prominent space in all of Nanny's many houses. By the time I am nine, when I am old enough to try on Nanny's sarcasm, I will say to her, "When you die, I inherit that painting."

"Killing me off already?" she will reply.

"Yep."

Of these early memories, the dream is particularly vivid, maybe because it was recurring, whereas real events happen only once.

I'm skipping on a road made of pink ribbon winding through outer space, in the body of the kid in Nanny's painting. My hair is long again, thin and green like hers.

I skip along the ribbon at a clumsy glide, wearing the smock dress, purple in the painting but green in the dream. I have her skinny legs and expressively still face. I'm fragile but tenacious. I'm Christopher Robin. I'm the Little Prince.

I'm skipping in pure, calm terror. I know I can't keep this up. It feels like my body might shatter into atoms and become floating debris. So I change my pace, to a frantic run. The running is chaos and feels almost like spinning, but less graceful, more agitated, like I've lost my footing, permanently. It's excruciating but preferable to the calm terror of the skipping.

I start to realize that I know what scares me. It's something like God, more remote than Satan but no less powerful or frightening, an omnipresent but disembodied male figure somewhere in space. He has in his hands a large nuclear bomb and is planning to drop it on me. The force of the threat propels me. I can't shake it. I can't outrun it. All I can do is alternate between the skipping and running, hoping the combination will keep my fear from killing me before he can. *Skip, run.*

The pink ribbon road has no surface, so I never feel it when my feet hit the ground. There is no ground. I skip, for minutes at a time, then run, slow to a skip, and break out running. I will do this eternally, as long as sleep persists. *Skip, run. Skip, run. Skip.*

I had this dream so often that the calm, pure terror became a permanent element in my life. I called it the dream feeling. It still sometimes seeps into waking life, but it did so regularly when I was a kid—at my mom's weddings, alone skipping rocks at Lake Hodges, in a crowd at a dance in high school. It neutralized me each time.

I couldn't tell anybody about the dream, because telling brought up the dream feeling. Before I knew it, not telling became a way of life, a personality trait. I spent a lot of time around Nanny's painting. My comment about inheriting it was a running joke between us, but I never told her I needed to inherit that painting because it was a version of me I was afraid of.

Of course, I'd never heard of Sigmund Freud or Carl Jung, the most influential dream theorists of the twentieth century. If I'd been a patient—and they were both fascinated by the minds of kids—they'd have coaxed the dream out of me. They'd have put it under the microscope of their competing theories and diagnosed my terror.

Freud and Jung disagreed about the nature of dreaming. Freud argued that dreams fulfilled wishes repressed during waking life. Through dreams, he believed, the more primitive, socially uninhibited self makes its presence known. Jung agreed that dreams are expressions of the unconscious, but he argued that their function was more positive, that they compensate for psychological imbalances and create mental harmony. My dream did both. It put me continuously in touch with a father figure who terrified me, but it also took me outside time and place—which is what I wanted more than anything as a kid. The dream made me think about a father I wanted to pretend didn't exist and it gave me a new place to live, where I could battle his giant ghost.

But there's more to it. Children dream differently than adults, and according to psychologist David Foulkes, dreaming is integral to development. Dreams help build minds and selves. According to Foulkes, children between three and five dream in isolated, static images, and they report a lot of dreams involving animals and few about people. Between seven and nine, a dream self develops, becoming a hinge for the images in the dream, and emotions become associated with these images. The images begin to form stories. After nine, the dream self becomes active, and dreams become emotionally charged scenarios involving other people. I'm sure I had this dream before nine, and I'm convinced that it changed very little over time. Still, I think Foulkes must be right when he argues that dreaming serves a *cognitive* function (as opposed to Freud's *psychological* function or Jung's *metaphysical* function)—that dreams help build our minds. If Foulkes is right, this kid in the dream wasn't just a product of my imagination. That kid gave me somebody new to be, somebody who could live in Nanny's painting and in outer space while the rest of me lived in a string of tiny houses my mom was fixing up, houses where we might start over after the disaster that was Charlie. And then after the disasters that replaced him.

Maybe someday you'll be able to put a kid like me in a scanner while he sleeps and reconstruct his neural connections, trace the origin of his dreams. In doing so, you'd be seeing my response to Nanny's painting, my running away to her house, the fact that God in this dream is also Charlie, my absent father threatening to steal me back, my decision to become mute about the dream and anything else I felt. Could a researcher stand before this kid, white lab coat precisely pressed, and ask just the right questions, the ones that would get the kid to offer up his mind so his brain might be visible?

Probably not, I guess.

6

STANLEY AND CATHY, I PRONOUNCE YOU

I'm in the air, spinning. Stanley, my mom's new boyfriend, is making a man of me. He brags about it. After Charlie showed up, my mom moved us to Hawaii, where Gary lives. We were gone long enough for Charlie to lose our scent. And for Stanley to find it.

Stanley's face is a red balloon. Mine's a pink tetherball. My body is the rope, and Stanley's is the pole. My features are out of whack, streaked with tears. I feel taut, hard, inflexible. I plead, "Stop. No. Stop. No." This cracks Stanley up. He swings me harder, grinning beneath his moustache. The red of his face travels up his balding scalp. You can see it through wisps of stringy hair. Sweat makes it cling to his skin. Stanley is a Southern California Jewish hippie. His dad works for Greenpeace. He has a big nose, hairy chest, and a bright smile.

Stanley's son Aaron, a speedy pinch-nosed three-and-a-half-year-old towhead with blue eyes, is sitting cross-legged on the floor in front of us, literally pointing and giggling. My mom shakes her head. "Stanley, be careful," she says. I take this as a cue to scream louder: "Stop. No. Stop. No."

"You two," my mom says, coughing.

We're living on the second story of a white, two-story house. The place has a treehouse feeling, with steep outdoor stairs. When they start to creak, Stanley says, "Somebody's here. Lucky break for you." He lowers me to the ground, my body stretched between his two hands.

"Knock knock," Doug calls. "We're here."

The door cracks open, and I crane my eyes, to see Doug first and then Nanny. Doug's wearing rounded-off rectangle sunglasses with gold frames and brown lenses. His blond hair is a little thin on top but still hangs over his ears. Nanny wears jeans and a ribbed sky-blue turtleneck sweater, to match her eyes. Her hair sweeps in big silver curls across her head. Her sunglasses are red globes.

"Jesus, what happened to Unigagin?" Nanny asks, looking at between me and Stanley.

"We were just havin' a little fun," Stanley grins.

"Where's Cathy?" Doug asks.

My mom walks in, a mask over her mouth and nose, translucent wintergreen plastic bag dangling like an inflated balloon on a stick. "Jesus, Mary, and Joseph," Nanny says.

"The doctor says she has to do this three times a day. I said it's bullshit."

"Cathy, you look like a Martian. Suits you," Doug says.

My mom removes her mask and says, "For your information, Doug, it's called *bronchiectasis*, and it is very serious. Dr. Chang said I could die from it."

"She's not gonna die. She likes the attention," Stanley says, pinching Nanny's upper arm and winking at her. Stanley's wife died of cancer, and now his new girlfriend has a rare and potentially fatal lung disease. Nanny shakes her head, grinning along with him. Stanley, she has to admit, is a lot like Ralph, down to the cheerful denial of everything real.

My mom points to the huge loom in the corner. It looks like a square harp, a swath of violet-maroon woven yarn dangling from it. "She can weave while she's doing the treatments," Stanley says. "She's making me a wall hanging."

"For the bus?" Nanny says. Stanley lives on a converted school bus.

"What, you don't think you need art in a bus?"

"Sarah Bernhardt here has always been very creative."

My mom flips her middle finger at Nanny. Doug and Stanley laugh.

My mom coughs twice, feebly and high-pitched. Then again, this one deeper. They just keep coming, one cough deeper than the next. Tears drip out of her eyes.

"Here, sit down, Cathy," Stanley says, leading her to a chair next to the window. "Ride it out, like the doctor said." He's rubbing her back. Her head is down, back arched, body heaving, like the coughs are heavy winds pummeling her frame.

"I can't stand this," she says.

"Jesus, Cathy," Doug says. "This is for real."

"I've been trying to tell you."

Twenty-two spinning sessions later, it's wedding day. Charlie has vanished. Probably back in prison. Aaron's mother has died of cancer. So nobody objects.

Nichole, three inches smaller, lifting Jason seven inches off the ground. The cousins face the camera. She's wearing a red velvet mini dress with white lace cuffs, and he's got on a navy Mexican shirt with a Mayan bird embroidered on the pocket. Her half smile betrays the effort it takes to lift a boy seven months her senior.

Cathy and Stanley at the altar, the service just over. Cathy chasing a bouquet in midair, a satin border the only ornament on her white cotton dress. Stanley grinning, all moustache and thinning hair. Behind them is an arch covered in blurry bougainvillea. You can't see the ghost of Aaron's mother, but if you look closely, you can see the fallout of her cancer in Aaron's smile stretched too tight across his face.

Bride and groom with the parents. Stanley and Cathy are in the center, fingers entwined. Cathy's hair is tamed with baby's breath.

Sam and Sylvia Messin look like New York Jews dappled with Southern Californian sun: erect postures, heavy glasses and dark suit for him, matching orange lipstick, hair, and African robe for her. Doug's in Qiana, of course, the gold nugget on his right hand catching the sunlight, his smile pure and relaxed. Midge's smile looks genuine but bemused, as if to say, "Oh brother, here we go again."

Mr. and Mrs. Stanley Messin, alone, under the bougainvillea altar, beaming, their heads titled slightly toward each other, like they might kiss. You can tell there is a gentle breeze by the way the violet petals of the bougainvillea lilt upward. You can tell the sun is strong by the way it reflects off the sheen of sweat on her cheeks. You can tell they've had champagne by the way their eyelids droop. You can see Midge's view of Bird Rock behind them through the lattice, the rocky La Jolla shore, waves pounding, sea stretching to the horizon. Just in the corner of the frame, you can see Jason leaning on the stone wall that protects people from falling off the cliff. His legs are bent under him and he's examining a blade of grass.

Stanley swears he'll adopt Jason, make him a Messin. The words "I now pronounce you father and son" were not part of the ceremony. Without thought bubbles, you can't tell that Stanley's off-balance grin expresses his sincere belief that this boy just needs some men in his life. You can't see that in Jason's ether world, the next frame shows Stanley broken and bloody on the cliff below, the sea view behind him a sacred backdrop for his last moments of life. You can't taste the salty breeze that is Stanley's last breath.

7

STANLEY'S MAP

The Messins are an experiment. By 1974, Ralph has a new wife and is long gone. Midge is living in La Jolla, surviving on sporadic alimony and the sale of an antique or piece of art now and then. The Neves children—Gary, Craig, and Cathy—have dropped out. How might a generation of Southern California hippies change the world by raising kids on sea and sun instead of plastic and microwaves?

The Neves wealth and celebrity elevates them beyond the establishment, so dropping out comes easy. Their friends raised in traditional homes send chills through their family trees when they announce their plans: play rather than work, expand the mind with drugs and explore the body through sex, grow hair until it tickles the ass, reject the tract home futures springing up alongside San Diego highways. The dropouts are joining communes, renting fixer-uppers full of character and potential, and renovating school buses into roving homes. They'll cultivate a generation never hampered by the bullshit rules, fear, and dogma that have led the world into war, conspicuous consumption, and soul-numbing conformity. Gary, Craig, and Cathy associate luxury with the aforementioned bullshit, even though it rescued them from the status quo.

We, the Messins—Stanley, Cathy, Jason, and Aaron—are scions in the experiment. We'll live aboard a school bus, which Stanley has converted into a home on wheels. We'll travel Stanley's map of the world, which starts at Baja and runs up the California Coast to Big Sur, through Santa Cruz, and ends in Portland, Oregon.

The Pondo, short for Ponderosa, is a key point on the map. Anchovie, the prince of the place, has invited him to park (meaning live) on his big rocky hill of dry dirt named after the ranch on *Bonanza*—pure desert just two miles from the sea. Everybody knows the Pondo. The house, white paint flaking, tin roof rusting, sits at the top of the hill, shaded by a giant pepper tree, branches dangling like the tentacles of a tired octopus, pink peppercorns swinging with the wind. We park here when it gets chilly at the beach.

Anchovie's love-ins are living mythology. The Pondo is his Olympus, haunted by the soaring psyches, liberated souls, and naked bodies who have gathered to mark the coming of the Age of Aquarius. You can sense them in the landscape, spirits whose ecstatic reception of an enlightened future has left an indelible imprint in the rocks.

But life is not one long love-in, not when you've got a kid like me, who keeps pissing the bed. Stanley's going to put a stop to this.

Santio, Aaron's cousin, has been saving up a milk jug of pee for a week now. His family lives on a bus, and they're parking at the Pondo too. Ozie is Anchovie's son and lives here permanently, so he's in on it too.

Santio's got a contest planned. Who can drink the most? He'll win. He wins everything. This mixture of pee—Santio's, Aaron's, Ozie's, and mine—has been sitting in the sun behind the outhouse. It's light yellow. It looks pulpy like lemonade.

"Let's make a pact," Santio says. "Repeat after me."

"We four swear," he says.

"We four swear," we repeat in unison, Santio chiming in with us. "On our lives…"

"That we will drink…"

"The sacred pee…"

"From the milk jug."

Ozie gulps, almost pukes, hands the jug to Aaron. He gulps longer, spits the pee down his front, hands me the jug. I gulp, gag, throw up into my mouth, and spit. "Gross," Aaron says, "he's puking pee. He's always puking." Santio grabs the jug from me, raises it, and gulps. We watch as the pee disappears into his mouth and snakes an invisible tunnel down to his stomach.

Raising the jug from his lips, Santio declares, "Four inches. I win!" This is life at the Pondo.

"I want to go to school," I say.

"No way," Stanley says. "No school. We're goin' on the road anyway."

My mom is sitting on the edge of the steps to the master bedroom, her head between her knees, purple curtains draping at her sides. "I'm not supposed to talk," she says.

"You look like a circus freak."

"Thanks a lot."

"What's the fuckin' point of livin' on the road if you send 'em to the brainwashing factory?"

"What's your mom going to say?" she responds.

"It's none of her beeswax. Don't you mean what's *your* mom gonna say?"

"They need to read."

"We don't need no education."

"And write. I mean, I hated the nuns, but they taught me—"

"We don't need no thought control."

My mom lifts her head. "It's not a joke, Stan."

"I want to go," I say again, even though I know there will be consequences.

One morning, my mom wakes me up early. "Put these on." She's whispering, throwing my best rust cords on the bed.

She borrows Anchovie's car. After a ten-minute drive, we park and enter an office. Inside, a woman sits at a desk. She greets me with a smile. "I'm Principal Fletcher." I don't know what a principal is, but it doesn't matter. She ushers us outside and across some asphalt. She opens the door and signals our entrance. The room is cluttered with kids and plastic toys.

The teacher leads the class in a unison greeting: "Welcome, Jason." I meet Stephanie, who invites me to play with her Tinker Toys. Her clothes are bright and neat. Her hair is in two tidy black braids. Her skin is whiter than I've ever seen, precise beige freckles on her nose.

My mom is gone. I'm alone here. Playtime ends. We gather around a television and watch *Romper Room*, singing and playing along. I've hardly ever seen TV.

Every day my mom borrows Anchovie's car before Stanley wakes up and drives me to Romper Room, where I play with Stephanie, the angel of kindergarten. When I get home, she teases me about Stephanie.

"How's your girlfriend?" she asks me. "Every day he marches right over to this really straight little girl," she tells Stanley. This is her argument for my education. My mom's trying to give Stanley the chance to imagine me as Jason, the boy who seduces girls in kindergarten.

Stanley has lost this battle, but he's got plans. We're going on the road.

They can't see her, but Stephanie is here in the bus with us, eating her vegetable pie with a knife and fork, blushing as she says "please" and "thank you," her voice like a quiet bell. She wipes her chin with the white cloth napkin she brought. I follow her lead and do as she does.

Mexico is just a border away when you live on a bus. Baja is on Stanley's map of the world. The rest of Mexico is blank white space, but not scratched with black marker the way most of the U.S. is. "Bores and Prigs" is scrawled vertically along the East Coast. The

Midwest is a mass of messy black smiley faces with blocky horn-rimmed glasses. There is just enough of New England showing for me to imagine where everyone is educated, rich, well-mannered, and snobby. It scares me to think about, but I picture living a clean, luxurious, snobby life there. Instead, I am absorbing the soft desert sand, chipped paint, and scrubby vegetation of Northwestern Mexico.

No one can explain how, in 1975, a bunch of hippies and their stringy-haired, dirty-faced kids on a school bus are not detained every time they cross the border. Usually we aren't, but today we are.

"Pull over to the side, please." Stanley puts the bus in reverse and backs up at an angle, trying to maneuver through the small detaining lot. My mom is wheezing. A car honks behind us. "Shut the fuck up!" Stanley yells. "What the fuck is going on?" he asks JP, a friend who tagged along for the trip.

"Goddamn pigs are harassing us," JP replies.

JP is six three, three hundred pounds, with black hair. His initials stand for James Polk. His great-great grandpa was president of the United States. He never stops laughing. "That JP is a character," Nanny likes to say.

We are escorted to a beige linoleum waiting room with hard plastic chairs. Ominous female heads ignore us from behind a high counter. Aaron and I are seated next to each other. The adults disappear through a door. "Everything will be okay," my mom said between coughs as they were escorted out. Hours pass. My butt hurts.

"Just sit tight," one of the ominous heads says at one point.

Finally, my mom and Stanley emerge through the door behind the beige counter. JP's staying. He *stashed*—Stanley's word—a trash bag full of pot in the storage container under the floor of the bus. He's going to jail. Miraculously, the police are satisfied that my mom and Stanley didn't know anything about it.

"I can see confiscating a man's vehicle," the cop tells us. "But I can't see taking his home."

We're in Santa Cruz, three hundred miles north of any place I've ever been, and I'm soaking in my own pee. After the border incident, Stanley decided it was time for a trip north. He'd been wanting to do it anyway, and it seemed like a good idea to put some distance between us and Mexico. My mom had to agree, so they pulled me out of school. I was there for less than two months.

To break me of the habit, he hauls me out of the bus each morning before dawn and forces me to bathe in the coldest water he can find. I lie in my piss, checking now and then to see how much there is, how wet the sheets feel. They're drenched. I practice my evaporation skills. I conjure my ether force field and think myself inside it. But thinking so hard keeps reminding me that I'm here. When Stanley gets up—to take his own piss outside, like a normal person—I am ready.

He strides by and runs his hand over my sheets. "Fuck. You fuckin' baby. He pissed the fuckin' bed again." He's loud. "Get up." I just lie there, my body tight like a corpse.

Stanley grabs me by the neck, the way he grabs kittens, and yanks me out of bed. I'm filthy in my own piss, disgusting to touch. Stanley climbs down the stairs of the bus, and I feel the burn of cold air on my face, feet, and hands. "You've gotta fuckin' learn. Hear me? Huh?"

"Yes," I say.

Stanley has to walk down a hill slippery with frost to get to the stream. He dunks me a couple of times. "Wash," he demands. The water is icy. I hate him. "Take off your pajamas. Wash them." I whoosh them around in the stream. I'm shivering, but I keep busy.

"Do you think it's any Goddamn fun for me to go outside when it's freezing cold?" Stanley asks. "Do you think it's fun for your ol' lady to clean the Goddamn sheets every day?" He knows that if he's consistent, I will stop the bedwetting. He's right.

Here's where I use neuroscience to get back at Stanley.

A *perceptual signature* is the unique way an individual brain processes sensory input. Our signatures create the world in our heads, like Stanley's map. He didn't even know about it, but it shaped his world, and therefore my world.

Genes predispose us to our perceptual signatures, but people who spend a lot of time together will pick up each other's habits. Genes plus habit make for shared perceptual tendencies among family members. You can pick out common ways of seeing, thinking, and feeling within a family. It took me a long time to admit it, but my fascination with the almost seen—vanishing sand crabs, Anchovie's love-in ghosts, the ether world—is a product of my hippie childhood. I learned to trust hallucinations.

Signal and *noise* are basic concepts in cognitive science. Neurons send constant signals, whenever they are electrically stimulated by the chemical message of another neuron, as much as several times every second. The neuroscientists call this constant random firing *noise*. A meaningful *signal*, they postulate, is one that breaks through the noise and becomes perception. Thought is the ability to synchronize the electrical activity of the brain. *How* we synchronize depends on our perceptual signatures. For Stanley, the coast from Oregon to Baja was signal and the rest was noise.

My New York apartment, where I'm typing now, was so far off the map it may as well have been another planet. As I type, I glance to my right, out my apartment window, and focus on the four black-capped towers of the power plant near the East River. I hear a faint siren. Then I'm distracted by the geraniums on the windowsill. The big one is in a green pot and the little one, originally a cutting, is in glass, its roots visible. They both sprout magenta blooms. I'm surprised to see that the cutting has grown enough to bloom. Their leaves strain toward the light, so my view is of their undersides, bright green like grass in full sun. The petals give the illusion of transparency. But my aesthetic meditation shares space in my head with Stanley's image. I'm recreating him by writing about him, giving him a new kind of life when what I really want to do is kill him. Let's face it: he's signal for me, not noise. My perceptual signature was shaped by and through him at a crucial moment of development. I'll never escape that.

Each of these perceptions—the black-capped towers, the sirens, the light through the leaves and petals, the specter of Stanley—cuts through my mental noise to become a signal. Why? Maybe because my brain, fatigued from an intense focus on finding language to describe itself, was looking for a distraction that would give it time to rest. But another part of my brain, the conscious motivator, overruled the impulse to rest and transformed my daydreaming into an illustration of the idea I was already writing about. An idle perception is not noise; it's a signal without a clear motive. Neuroscientists postulate that the constant random firing of neurons is functional: a neuron already in motion will react more efficiently when it's needed than one at rest. Those signals often produce order by accident and come to feel meaningful. As I write this thought, I'm aware how much life with Stanley primed me to think it.

Living on a school bus was an education in accidental order. Mornings became afternoons became nights. Stanley drove, parked, drove. We slept, woke, ate, swam, argued, laughed, slept. We stayed in some spots for weeks, others for hours. The bus was the roving center of our universe, the place from which we looked out onto the world, the place we went to escape it.

8

APLYSIA CALIFORNICA

We made it all the way to Oregon, where Stanley spent a summer helping some people build a boat. Aaron and I got ringworm from cats. My mom did her lung exercises every day and perfected her no-bake cookies.

Now we're back in Cardiff, for the winter I guess. Hours pile up into days and weeks on Southern California beaches. There are no rules, except don't be a sissy. I love rules, but I keep breaking the only one I have. "Your life is most kids' dream," Stanley says. "You live on a fuckin' school bus and hang out at the beach every day." He forgets that my dream life also includes almost no sugar, no TV, and him.

My mom, Stanley, Aaron, Santio, and I are walking to San Elijo for a change of pace. We have to walk from the parking lot at Cardiff Beach. We sneak through a private campground and descend steep concrete stairs, slippery with sand, down the cliff to the beach. I hate this.

Now that we're back, Stanley wants Aaron and me to try surfing. The far right end of this beach is called Pipes because the waves there rise high and break slow, like animated sculptures, their frothy heads sloping high and wide for the surfers who want to lose themselves in pockets of air between a wave's summit and its base. "We'll get some of these motherfuckin' beach bums to give you a lesson," Stanley says. I hate this.

We spread our towels and settle in. There is too much seaweed, the brown kind, darkening the surf and scattered in big tangled piles all over the sand. I'm wrestling with my Snoopy towel, trying to get the corners flat and smooth out the folds that make his sunglasses look like they are specially designed for a one-eyed beagle. I plop myself down.

There's a family of three about twenty feet down the beach: a girl in a pink one-piece with yellow palm trees on it, her nose white with zinc oxide, eating a bologna sandwich while her mom and dad read. They're pale, and they treat the beach like Disneyland, a place good for a few hours of tanning and sandcastle building. That girl doesn't know anything about body surfing or sand crabs. She doesn't know what it's like to live on a school bus. Her life is not a blur of gray, foamy Pacific Ocean, breaking waves, and abalone sandwiches, tans everywhere, all year long, and scrambling to make the public showers during regulation hours or sneaking them otherwise.

I see their wet heads first, seven or eight guys rising up out of the seaweed, strolling toward us on their way to Pipes. All tan, some of them preadolescent but others with fine blond hairs crawling their forearms and stomachs, surfboards welded to their torsos, puka rattling on their collarbones.

"Hey," one of them says to Santio as they pass, "aren't you Mike's kid?" He's yellow-haired with white eyebrows and more yellow hair on his stomach. Probably thirteen.

"Santio's Mike's kid," Stanley says.

"I know your dad," the kid says.

"He's my brother-in-law," Stanley says.

"Oh," the kid says. "I told your dad I'd let you use my board sometime," he says to Santio. "He loaned me his wetsuit the other morning. It was like sixty degrees out, but the waves were rad. You want to try my board in a little while? My girlfriend's gonna show up pretty soon anyway."

"Sure," Santio says. He's only six, but he knows how to surf and how to talk to surfers.

"Hey," Stanley says, "how 'bout you guys give all three of these kids a lesson? For Mike?"

The yellow-haired surfer nods at the rest of them. One of them says, "The chicks will dig that shit. Surf lessons." Another one grabs his balls and makes a screwing motion with his hips. Aaron and Santio look at each other and giggle.

"So when the chicks show up, I'll send the boys over," Stanley says. "What's your name?"

"Leaf," he says.

"Cool, Leaf. It's a deal."

The flock of surfers migrates south. We watch them descend into the seaweed as they round the curve of the cliff, barely visible when they float their surfboards into the brown sea and glide out past the breakers. I'm all waiting now. Waiting is okay because it's not the thing I'm waiting for. I can almost convince myself that the waiting will last forever, that I'll never have to get on a surfboard in front of all these guys. At one point, my mom says, "Surfing's fun, Boog. If you learn, you can go surfing with your cousins. Bryan and Trever surf."

"Why the hell d'ya call him that all the time?" Stanley asks.

"Why not?" she asks.

"You're gonna turn him into a wuss."

If I can learn to surf, I will enter the universal brotherhood of Southern California boys flouting authority and oozing sex from every pore. I pretended not to recognize the screwing motion that kid made when they were talking about the girls, but I did. It made my insides feel squirmy, like there were jellyfish in me. I know who these guys are. They surf all along the coast, from Torrey Pines to Solana Beach. "Just one killer wave, that's all I want," they say. When the waves don't show, they smoke joints on the beach and talk to girls.

I sit and think about the waiting until my skin feels hot. Then I become a bullet and shoot into the surf. I can hear Aaron and Santio pounding behind me. Seaweed wraps its snaky arms around our ankles. The surf is pretty strong today, so we have to weave sideways, wrestling with the residue of broken waves, to get out far enough to ride some. "No farther," we hear my mom yell. "That's deep enough."

"I got this one," Santio shouts. We all three freeze into position, waiting for the wave to find us. One, two, three—we all push off, heads and shoulders pointed diagonally at the sky, three slick bodies skimming weightless, both inside and above the wave.

Riding a wave takes you outside time. The wave becomes your universe, and the ride is all the time there is. It lasts forever. Every day delivers a different kind of wave, some gentle, some rough, some even, some rocky, some with little dips, others with steep cliffs.

The first wave is always an education. It teaches you the shape of the set. This one's got a second crest and a second dip. We ride the first dip, a quick slide down to the surface of the water, and after skimming for a few seconds, dip number two, a steep dive under a strong foamy crest. We all three go under. My limbs are wrangled in four distinctly different directions, the sockets of my shoulders and knees stretched way past comfort, my chin skidding on the sand. I'm sucked into the ocean sound, like the one you hear when you listen to a shell, but times a thousand. I know this world. It's confusing, and the banging hurts, but I love its directional chaos, where up or down, surface or floor, shallow or deep no longer have meaning. I'm there for a few uncountable seconds before I feel my head in weightless air, my up and down coming into clear focus, Stanley and my mom a salty blur on the shore.

"I got totally sucked under," Aaron shouts.

"Me too," I shout.

"Me three," Santio shouts.

We run through the seaweed, our sideways paths quicker now that we know what we're looking for. I'm a succession of take-off positions, risings, skimmings, glidings, and occasional plummetings. The three of us are doing this together, but wave riding is solitary, which is why we have to tell each other about our nearly identical rides every time we pull up. I've forgotten that I'm waiting for a gang of surfers to expose me.

"That one was smooth," I say. Santio and Aaron don't have time to respond.

"Check it out," Stanley yells. "Their chicks are here. They're paddling in, like little duckies."

"You guys ready?" my mom asks.

"Yeah!" Aaron yells. Santio and Aaron rise like little rockets. I try to be quick like them, but my force field is activated, and I'm trudging through ether. It'll look weird if I'm too far behind, so I try to run. Then Stanley comes up behind me and hurls me into the air. I don't have to do my own walking. He carries me like a surfboard, bouncing like an under-inflated balloon to the beat of his stride. When he reaches Aaron and Santio, he hurls Aaron up with the other hand. He's delivering us to the surfers.

"You cats ready?" he asks when we reach Pipes. There are more surfers there, some of them as old as nineteen. They're looking at Leaf, their pink eyes asking, "What's this old guy want?" There are about a hundred girls in bikinis, four or five for every surfer.

"Hey, who's gonna help me teach these kids how to surf?"

It takes a few seconds, but a kid about twelve, wearing red trunks, his golden, feathered hair almost dry, says, "What the fuck. I will." You can tell his hair would be brown if he didn't spend every day at the beach.

"Gotta train 'em young," another guy says. He's probably fifteen, white trunks, half-Mexican looking, with a darker tan than anybody and straight dark hair streaked reddish.

The half-Mexican guy takes Aaron. The guy with the golden, feathered hair takes me. "I'm Jake," he says. His hair is longer than short. His skin is the color of light coffee, and he has a few golden hairs circling his belly button. The ones on his arm are so bleached they're transparent. I've seen him before. Everybody knows him. He hangs out with guys a lot older. I guess because he's so good.

The hierarchies of the outside world, the ones you're supposed to leave behind when you commit to your hippie lifestyle and live on a bus, find their own forms at the beach. The secret society of surfers requires an attitude, a healthy disregard for fear, and some skill. Santio is already in. Our connection with him grants Aaron and me an audition. If you can surf, you can be an instant teenager. If you can handle the sea, you're ready for beer, pot, and girls. I have the genes for this. My uncle Gary's surf shop, S&N, is legendary, one of the first, way back in the sixties. During my freshman year of college, I will learn about fifth-century Athens and realize that S&N is the surf culture version.

Jake and the half-Mexican kid lead Aaron and me into the breakers. "Hop on," Jake says, guiding me onto the board. It's twice as long as I am. Jake is only twelve or thirteen, but like all surfers he moves like a man and is treated like one. His body, molded by hours and days and weeks tussling with ocean currents, has bypassed adolescence. I smell the pot when Jake starts fiddling with my body, feel it sweetening my force field. "Like this," he says, showing me where my limbs should sit, how my muscles should feel. His breath is weirdly hot on my cheek. Waves sneak up on me and bobble me forward. I can ride them fine, lying flat. I have a lot of experience with boogie boards.

Then comes standing. Jake shows me how to stand on shore, fixes my legs in place and bends my limbs to strike the pose. I can do this on the sand, no problem. Out in the water, it's impossible. Wave after wave, I feel myself move and crouch. I stare at the shark head of the surfboard and imagine it skewering me. I chicken out, lying flat every time.

"This kid can't ride a wave," Jake says, mistaking waves for surfboards. My fear of him, this sport, my whole life, is a tangle of seaweed that trips me as I climb off the surfboard. My forehead just misses the board's shark fin when I fall, grazing flat fiberglass instead.

At least the waiting is done. I walk pretty slowly back up through the seaweed to where Stanley and my mom are. I can see them reaching over the sand between their two towels, kissing. The zinc-nosed girl and her parents are packing up. People like them stay at the beach for a couple of hours at most.

"You chicken out?" Stanley asks.

"He's too uncoordinated," my mom says in my defense. *Lack of coordination* is a euphemism for the fear and longing that makes it impossible for me to stand up while Jake watches me.

"He chickened out," Stanley says. Zinc-nose and her parents are walking toward the steps that lead up the cliff and out of the beach. Her pink buns reminds me of the girl with pigtails in the Coppertone billboards, begging as they bounce to be snatched by the jaws of a yappy little dog. But there are no dogs allowed on San Elijo.

She's not the Coppertone girl, and I will never be a surfer. I won't smoke pot at seven, have sex with girls, wear wetsuits all winter. I won't master the skill and strike out on my own, heroically, to become a new kind of surfer, one who masters his fear but feels it, one whose expertise makes him sexually irresistible to your more regular surfer. Everybody sees the failure. "Jason doesn't surf." It sounds like no big deal, but the sentence reverberates and the failure is definitive.

I can't sit here basking in it while my mom and Stanley enjoy each other. I need a way to eradicate them from the beach. Between bouts of surfing, I can see Santio and Aaron throwing seaweed at each other and anybody else who won't kick their asses for doing it. This makes the difference between me and them, the difference that infuriates Stanley.

Pouting, I wander through the seaweed, gritting my teeth and half-thinking. I am an expert pouter, feigning indifference but courting attention. *Don't notice me because I hate you*, I scream with contorted, too slow gestures and backward glances. It isn't working. Nobody gives a shit. Killing time, I experiment with designing myself a seaweed outfit—a wreath for my head, a stole around my neck, a hula skirt. I untangle yarns of brown vines and select strands on which the poppers are still inflated with water. I am risking Stanley's derision, and I know it. Maybe I want it.

Then everything changes, the way it does when you see something you don't understand, a sight so inexplicable that just trying to process it transforms you.

Among the seaweed, I see a shiny sparkle of light too slick and too long to be a bead of water. For a second or two I'm not sure what I'm looking at, but gradually the shine takes shape, and I see a slimy mass camouflaged in the seaweed. It's about eight inches long and four wide, curvy, solid, heavy—the same mottled dark browns as the darkest strands of seaweed. It has antennae and eyes and a gill-like tube poking out of his back. It coils around itself on the underside. I poke it and watch it quiver, tightening the coil. I pick it up and after a few seconds the coil loosens. I've heard of sea slugs, but I've never seen one.

"Hello, Mr. Sea Slug," I say, peering into the coil. I am somehow so sure he is a Mr. and not a Mrs.

"Those squirt poison," I hear Stanley say. "They do." Santio and Aaron are fading. "What are you doing? Be careful." My mom is wasting her breath. I don't even hear her asking Stanley if they really do squirt poison. Stanley, the guy who gleefully warns me of the sterilizing power of oleander every chance he gets, says, "Yes, yes they do."

My new friend has a complicated organ on his underbelly, beneath the coil, also dark brown, shaped like a little human heart. "Poison, poison, be careful. Don't touch it." "What the fuck is he doing?" He needs water. He seems lethargic. With every poke and every second he seems to move with less strength. He pees purple stuff all over me. That must be the poison, I think. It doesn't sting. *They don't know anything.*

He's drowning in air, drying out. The tide will rise too late. So I carry him, out to my waist in ocean and seaweed. I wait for a break in the waves and hold him under the water. He seems to loosen, blossom. "What the fuck? I always said that kid of yours was a freak." I cradle him in both hands. He has eyes, but his expression seems to be in his coils more than his face. His demeanor says calm relief. He isn't rapturous, just content, regaining equilibrium. He isn't quite grateful, just glad. "Poison. Freak. Fuck." We understand each other. I slide my hands out from under him, careful not to jostle his body. The water catches him and he floats, relaxing into the current. Three seconds and I can't see him, only seaweed.

I wade back to shore. Santio and Aaron are out in the surf with boogie boards now, Stanley and my mom kissing. The surfers are way out deep, having left the little kids in the dust. I'm shocked to find that nobody's paying attention to me.

Back in the seaweed, my eyes now open, I can see dozens of slugs, boys and girls, adults, teenagers, and toddlers, maybe hundreds of them, all varieties of sea slug fighting for their lives among the kelp. I'm in motion, more focused than I've ever been. But I'm not quite conscious or in control. I discover my autopilot. Without even thinking, I step up my rescue mission. I carry slugs in twos and threes and return them to the sea, taking only a few seconds to cradle them before slipping my hands from underneath their heavy little bodies and watching them disappear under the water dyed red with so much seaweed. I root them out of the most tangled piles of kelp. I move methodically, in inches, combing every strand. It feels wrong to do any less. If I save one slug, they all deserve to be saved. I don't want those left behind to think they are somehow inferior and deserve to die. Simultaneously, I guard incoming waves diligently, watching for new or repeat wash-ups.

My task turns out to be harder than I thought. Nobody interrupts me or asks me to stop, but I just can't save them all or stop them from washing up again. In my new slug-induced state of mind, the cumbersome physical loses its solidity. The slugs take precedence. I hunt and return the slugs all day. I spend a little time talking to each one. "Hi there. It's gonna be okay. Don't worry." I examine its contours, its firm, brown balloon body, waiting for the tide to pass.

I feel the individual presence of each slug. I poke and caress them all. Like the original Mr. Sea Slug, they recoil, but seem to calm as they acclimate to the world of my cupped hands. My force field has achieved equilibrium, dissolved gently into salt air around me.

But I can't save them all. I regret it even now.

The *Aplysia californica* is a star in the history of neurobiology. The common Californian sea slug has played a major role in the science of memory.

The sea slug is an invertebrate, a distant relative of oysters and escargot. Humans often say they're gross. Neuroscientists tend to apologize for their unattractiveness, but celebrate their unique nervous system nonetheless. Few people appreciate their aesthetic charm—the glistening brown skin, the way their shapes morph when they move, those antennae wiggling for empathy. Not to mention their huge neurons, nearly a millimeter: easy to study. Their nervous systems traverses their bodies and do not center in their heads. This must explain their expressive bodies and relatively static faces.

The passages on sea slugs in John Dowling's *Creating Mind: How the Brain Works*—one of the first books I read about brain function—stunned me. I hadn't seen a sea slug in two decades. This was a reunion. Like me, Mr. Sea Slug was a californica. His relatives are about ten inches long, so he was undersized. He is also commonly called a sea *snail. Slug* suits him better. His purple pee was defensive ink. He was defending himself against me.

According to Dowling, my memory is inaccurate. It isn't Mr. Sea Slug's underbelly that recoils when touched. His coils are on his top side, with the gill poking out from them. The behavior is called "gill-withdrawal reflex." And he's famous for the fact that with each subsequent touch, his gill recoils with less force. It's called *habituation*. Neuroscientists see this behavior as a primitive form of memory, perhaps the foundation of even the most sophisticated forms of human memory. But if he is pricked too severely, as with a needle, the withdrawal is more extreme and lasts longer. The technical term for this one is *sensitization*. This doesn't seem like a revelation. *Duh*, I want to say, but I'm too busy grappling with the idea that neuroscientists have been collecting my Mr. Sea Slug's progeny and pricking them with pins. That's not the worst of it. They have been removing those little human hearts, called mantles, from their bellies. They shock them. I could never be a neuroscientist, I realize, letting go of the fantasy. But then, I could never make my rapturous discoveries if everybody else had been as squeamish and empathic as I am.

Habituation and sensitization fascinate neuroscientists because they indicate a form of learning, a long-term alteration of neural systems in response to environmental stimuli. There are thirty-three tiny neurons in a single fifteen-hundred-member ganglion (colony of nerve cells) in Mr. Sea Slug's abdomen, responsible for the coiling and loosening. Twenty-four sensory neurons do the feeling, the receiving—these are the neurons that spied on me when I first poked him. Six motor neurons do the moving—these are the neurons sent to negotiate with the intruder. Just three interneurons transport messages between the stimulus troops and the diplomat motors—this trio was responsible for telling the motors how to deal with me.

With repetition, *Aplysia californica* learns to gauge stimuli and thus either habituation or sensitization can have lasting effects, for up to a month. In the process, those thirty-three neurons—which are not, after all, spies, diplomats, and negotiators, but dramatically and morally neutral biological entities that exchange bits of chemical—are reorganized. They "learn" to exchange different chemical compounds in different patterns. The theory goes that long-term memory involves a similar reorganization of neural conglomerations. The human hippocampus consolidates short-term memory and makes it available for future recall, using mechanisms similar to those of my friend *Aplysia californica*. For both Mr. Sea Slug and me, the processes involve synapses, phosphorylization, Calcium (Ca^{2+}) and Potassium (K^{+}) ions, and neuromodulatory proteins called *kinases*.

Channels open and close; chemicals are released and ingested. Mr. Sea Slug recoils, then loosens. I recognize his fear and am bowled over by his subsequent trust, inspired to save his life.

The seduction, I like to think, was part of the species' evolutionary plan. I imagine a meeting of the elders, long ago in the early days of the *Aplysia*, just after they found themselves cast from paradise into the chaos of the seas. "Emotionally wounded human boys will save us from extinction. You must practice your habituation and sensitization. Without these skills, we will perish in beds of seaweed on dry shores up and down the California coast." And thus memory was born.

The *Aplysia* spent thousands of years evolving their primitive memory skills. Centuries stretched into millennia, until finally the prophesied moment of their peril came one day in 1975. There on the shores of San Elijo, while surfers languished in their pipes, the slugs habituated and sensitized me into a trance.

Imagine the complexity of the tiny neural patterns the slugs and I induced in each other as we reshaped each other's perceptual signatures—the vastness of the tiny synaptic responses, the multitudes of potassium and calcium secreted and ingested, the neural channels coaxed open. Think about the fact that neural structures had to be permanently reshaped for memory to result, in both them and me. Stanley, my mom, Aaron, and Santio faded from my neural structures as the slugs took possession of them. Overwhelmed with the power of their stimuli, I have spent a lifetime turning the slugs upside down, imagining their underbellies recoiling and their gills motionless on their backs. My faulty memory is no dishonor, though. After all, it's the sea slugs themselves who remind us that memory need not be accurate, just functional. It comforts me to think that the slugs and I were busy rearranging each other's neurons. We did this for our mutual protection.

When Stanley finally tore me away from my rescue mission, I resisted quietly until there was no more hope of delay. I snatched up my Snoopy towel and followed him up the stairs on the cliff, trying to squelch the knowledge that so many of those slugs were drying out in seaweed clumps up and down the beach. The sea slugs couldn't calibrate their coiling. At the first sign of danger, they reacted strongly, unable to hide their fear. Not me. I had to use my more advanced human powers of deception to protect the secret of our bond. When I felt my coil want to tighten, I loosened instead and walked quietly up the stairs, my hands stained with purple ink, dragging Snoopy in the sand.

9

DEL DIOS

Tectonic plates gnashed at each other beneath a few hundred acres of Southern California land, thirty miles inland from what would eventually become the coastal towns of La Jolla, Del Mar, Cardiff, and Encinitas. Escondido and Rancho Bernardo grew on either side of what would become Highway 15, a stretch of asphalt that divided and linked them, winding through strip-mall suburbs and scrubby hills until it reached downtown San Diego.

The plates pushed with patient force, like two well-matched wrestlers. Soil particles accumulated with slow deliberation until they formed hills. Sage, oak, and wild mustard sprouted, devouring the sun that baked the soil. Fresh water on its way to the ocean filled the crevices between the hills. In 1916, some white men, ignoring protests of the Kumeyaay tribe that'd been living downstream for centuries, decided to fight gravity and built a giant concrete dam to frustrate the forward motion of a river that had been gunning for forty thousand years.

The dam was finished in 1918. The result was Lake Hodges, a body of fresh green water shaped like two kidney beans laid end to end, providing drinking water for the county.

The hippies who settled among the dust and sage and moss and carp think the name *Del Dios* had something to do with them, but it had been used for years before their arrival. Like anybody else, the hippies liked to think about names, and as with any name, this one choked with barely noticed meaning. *Del Dios* commemorated a past when the valley had been Mexican territory, blanketing a forgotten era when the Kumeyaay tribe had names of its own, before Spanish was ever heard in Southern California. Now the name marked a stop-gap paradise on earth that ensured the temporary survival of the free lovers putrefying on the banks of the lake.

The settlers and their progeny swore to the existence of Hodgee, an LSD-fueled cousin of the Loch Ness Monster. The hippies didn't invent Hodgee. They inherited him. The Scripps Institute of Oceanography even lowered a cage into the lake in 1932 to capture the beast. They never found him, but hazy photos document Hodgee's buffalo-like shape and new sightings occur every decade or so.

Hippies had gone out of style by 1975, but enough brains had been altered that a place like Del Dios was necessary to quarantine them.

"Jesus Christ," Nanny says, as our pet geese lunge at her while she makes her way toward the porch of our newest house—on top of the highest hill in Del Dios, with brown trim to match the bus. "Can somebody please get these animals to stop honking?"

"Meet Lucy and Louis," my mom says. Stanley went out and bought chicks and ducklings—and two geese, for protection.

The screen door squeaks, and Stanley stands in the door sliver. Aaron squirms through his legs and crawls down to the porch. "Do you like our vicious guard dogs, Midge? Your daughter wouldn't let me name the gander 'Desi,' because he supposedly got loaded one night and aimed his shotgun at her."

JP, fresh out of prison, pops his head out between Stanley and Aaron. "Honk honk," he says to Nanny. He's going to build a shed for himself to live in behind our house.

"There he is," Nanny says. "The famous JP."

"Busted out," he says. "I had to get back to my one, true love. The silver fox."

"Oh, Jesus, Mary, and Joseph," she says.

"Hello." We hear a woman's British accent behind us. "I'm Brenda. I live across the street." We turn to see a large woman with a short Dorothy Hamill cut and volcano breasts wrapped in a turquoise short-sleeved sweater that stretches tight around their pointed masses. Aside from this detail, she's clearly a proper, middle-class woman, completely unlike the hippies that drew us to a life in Del Dios.

Later, after she leaves and nobody else is listening, Nanny will say to me, "Well, that was a surprise. How did someone like her end up in this Godforsaken place?" I don't know either, but Brenda is a relief.

"You'll have to testify in court," Stanley says.

We're having dinner at the Del Dios Store, across from Lake Hodges. My mom was going to cook, but she got wheezy working with her leather glue. Everything inside, the bar, the floor, the booths, the walls, the ceiling, is made out of beat-up planks of wood heavily shellacked. There's a giant deer head with antlers above the bar, and other taxidermic ghouls on other walls: a bobcat, a squirrel, a gopher with its teeth exposed like it died mid-attack.

"They'll just ask you a few questions," my mom adds, sounding labored because her breathing's still not right. "All you have to do is tell the truth."

"Like what?"

"That you want Stan to adopt you." I can see myself seated in a booth, three feet off the ground and enclosed in heavy dark wood, a handsome and official lawyer asking me questions: "If Stanley adopts you, he will be your legal father. How does that sound?"

I look out into a courtroom full of spectators and spot my mom, Stanley, and Aaron. "I don't know," I say.

But in the meantime, I'm still here eating dinner in this bar full of greasy heads, bloodshot eyes, and tanned hides. Most of the guys who sit here every day were in Vietnam. Sometimes you see one of them raving in the park across the street. "Another flashback," the neighbors remark.

"Your name will be Messin," Stan continues. "Like us." He means like him, Aaron, and my mom. But I don't want to be like them. I'd rather be like Brenda.

Jason Messin. Messy messin messed up mess. Gone messin.

"What do you think, Jas?" my mom asks, catching her breath.

"I guess," I say. *All messed up.*

"Stan is your father. He's going to take care of us." This sounds like a threat to me.

"Okay." *Messin around.*

"Stephen has been diagnosed with a learning disability." I hear Brenda's British accent on our doorstep. She's talking about one of her sons. "It's a perceptual problem with his brain. If Stephen looks at a tree in the distance, he'll see one leaf, but not the tree. The rest of us wouldn't see the leaf at all." I don't really know what she's talking about, but Brenda's accent makes living in Del Dios seem less horrible.

"Is there anything they can do about it?" my mom asks. Her lung disease was recently cured by a doctor who studied Eastern healing. Stanley calls it a Lucky Seven miracle, courtesy of Ralph Neves. Miracle or not, it's got my mom in the mood to search for cures, and I'm next.

"Well, the school has a new program, the Perception Center. He'll spend part of every day there. In a way it's a relief. We just thought he was slow."

"Steve is a great kid," my mom says. "He's so kind."

"Sometimes that worries me. He'll trust anybody."

"In the long run, that's better than not trusting anybody."

"I suppose so. Anyway, I just popped by to say that if you still need to me to look after the kids this afternoon, I can do it."

We've just finished the dinner Brenda cooked: cheesy Hamburger Helper. My mom's at Nanny's, Stanley's at work, and Aaron's with his grandparents. It's just me and the Lewises. Bellies full of cheesy meat and noodles, the family is scattered around the TV. Mr. Lewis is balding and quiet, but his English sounds educated when he does speak.

The news is on. There are fires in the mountains fifteen minutes from Del Dios. People have been evacuated, houses burned to the ground. The commercials are for Trix, Kool Aid, and Kit Kats. When the announcer comes back, the footage behind him shows a parade. Thousands of smiling people are marching through the streets of downtown San Diego. Technicolor floats carry very tan men draped with garlands that look like giant Hawaiian leis.

"Disgusting," Brenda says. "Homosexuals ought to be transported someplace. Get them out of society." She's vehement, almost vicious. For the first time, she scares me. Nobody in my world says stuff like this. Plus, the someplace she's talking about sounds like Del Dios to me. People move here to drip out of society. But by choice. Sort of.

The conversation turns, and the rest of them move on, but I'm vaguely aware that Brenda's disgust has something to do with me.

A few days later, I tromp down the hill to the Del Dios Store to get a Honey Bun. When I walk in, I see Brenda at the bar, with a beer and a lit cigarette in front of her. Brenda doesn't smoke. That's part of what sets her apart from everybody else in Del Dios. Hippies smoke.

I pretend I'm looking at the chips and watch Brenda. She sips the beer. A string of smoke weaves around her face. She puts down her beer, picks up the cigarette, and takes a deep drag. Her stare is blank. Something's wrong. There are people who smoke and people who don't, and the difference between them is clear and obvious. I'm sure of this.

I can see by looking at Brenda and her cigarette that she won't notice me no matter what I do, so I grab a Honey Bun and tiptoe to the counter. I slide my quarter and two nickels across, steal a sideways look at her taking another puff, and tiptoe out the screen door. In the park, under a eucalyptus tree, I think about whether I should tell anybody about Brenda smoking. I think about Brenda and her gross cigarette all day, turning the image around in my head.

Later, after dinner, while I'm helping my mom with the dishes, I find the courage to say, "I saw Brenda smoking at the store."

My mom looks at me funny. "She probably needed one." That's it. That's all she says. I spilled my secret, sure I'd get a reaction.

The image of Brenda inhaling smoke from a cigarette sticks. It's a piece I can't find a place for in my six-year-old puzzle. I should learn from this that there are people who smoke regularly, people who never do, and people who sometimes do, when they "need one." But instead I just carry the image with me. It bugs me, like a key that won't open anything.

10

MILLER SCHOOL

"Everybody quiet down. Listen up," Mr. Warfel says. "We have a new student. Say hello to Jason Messin."

Hearing Stanley's name attached to mine makes it sound like the teacher is talking about some other kid. I never stood before a judge, like Stanley said I would have to. In fact, no legal document certifies the change. When Stanley finally gave up, my mom just signed Aaron and me up for Miller School, two brothers with the same last name.

I'm standing next to Mr. Warfel, looking up at his loose African shirt. School has been in session for three months, and the kids he's talking to are shiny with familiarity. *Jason Messin. Messy mess. Messed-up mess. Messin.* But it doesn't matter, because I've made it to school, which is full of regular kids who live in real houses with upstanding parents. At least this is how it seems to me.

Del Dios is too small to have its own school, so we have to drive to Escondido, twenty minutes inland. Stanley likes the fact that Miller School is round. "If they're gonna get brainwashed," he says, "at least it'll be in a round school." The Lewis kids go here too.

The kids in Mr. Warfel's class have settled into each other during the weeks I've missed. Class is just about to start. The room is full of kids whispering in clumps. A kid to my left kisses a girl on the cheek and she starts screaming. This one kid, Paul, is writing very intently in a notebook and periodically holding it up for the perusal of four or five others. He seems to be surveying the room, now and then fussily erasing something in his notebook and then writing something new. I want to know what's in that notebook.

The recess bell rings, and everybody rushes out the door. Everybody but me knows what to do. The stampede is noisy and orderly. I feel the dream feeling float through my skin. It hasn't fully taken hold of my nerves yet, but it's tugging at me. I can't run. I can't brush it off.

"Jason, comeer." It's Mr. Warfel. When I don't move, he comes to me and kneels next to my desk. "I need to show you a few things. As a new student, there's a lot to figure out." His voice is commanding and his breath on the side of my neck is compassionate. I didn't know that these qualities could be combined in one person.

In five minutes, Mr. Warfel initiates me into the ways of public school. He defines the word "recess," shows me a bathroom pass and explains how it works. He gives me a notebook, like Paul's, and a set of pencils. "Now, go outside and play. Do you like tetherball?"

"The color you get tells you what group you're in," Mr. Warfel says, walking up and down the rows passing out circles of construction paper. I see his waist moving toward me, and then, snap, a grass green circle lands on my desk. It's easy to see who else has one: Theo (pronounced *Tay-o*), with the orange hair and freckles covering every inch of her face, this kid Robert with feathered hair, and Paul.

We have to write a story. We've all got our notebooks. Paul's in charge. We have to choose an animal, give it a name, and make up a story about it. We all have to write the story in our notebooks. "I say we make up a story about an anteater," Paul says.

"What's that?" I ask.

"Like an armadillo, but bigger. It eats ants with its snout."

"Paul reads the encyclopedia," Theo, who is a second-grader, tells us. "For fun." These kids are nothing like anybody I've ever met, and they are going to be my friends.

"What's our anteater's name?" Paul asks.

"Tony," I say.

"Okay, Tony," he says.

"How 'bout we say he's super hungry, so he eats a whole anthill," Robert adds.

"And then has a tummy ache," I say.

"How does it end?"

"There is a miracle, and he is cured," I add.

"Okay, we're finished," Paul says. "Let's race to see who can write it down the fastest."

Paul wins the race. Once we finish, he has another task for us, an encyclopedia of his own making. He pulls out the notebook. "Okay, we have to figure out where Jason goes."

"What do you mean?" Something about Paul's arrogance makes me brave.

"Where you go on the lists."

"There are three: IQ, income, and looks. IQ is how smart you are. Income is how much your father makes."

"Oh."

"Now, you didn't know what an anteater was, but you came in second writing down the story. Being fast is a sign of being smart." He looks at Theo and Robert. "I think he's twelfth, before you, Robert, and after Vikki." They nod. "Theo is third, and I'm second."

"Who's first?"

"Right now it's Diane. She's fat."

"And weird," Robert adds.

"Robert is first in looks," Paul says. "Where should Jason go?" he asks, looking at Theo.

"Fifth, right after me."

"I'm tenth, because I have a Czech nose," Paul says.

"The lists change," Theo offers, consoling me.

"How much does your father make?" Paul asks.

"I don't know."

"You should ask. What's his job?"

"We just moved here." The three of them exchange a glance.

"Okay, well, where do you live?"

"Del Dios." I can't see any way of avoiding this. "In a house," I add.

"No shit." Paul cusses, like Stanley, which seems strange given his encyclopedic personality.

"What's Del Dios?" Robert asks.

"It's that weird place by Lake Hodges. The school bus goes there," Theo says.

"Poor people live there. We'll put you twenty-eighth, before Casper. He lives on a farm. Did you smell him? They don't shower. If you find out how much your dad makes, you might be able to spend the night at my house Saturday."

It never occurs to me that Paul's lists might be strange or cruel. I don't live on a farm, and I don't smell. I've made a contribution. I'm working my way up the lists. Life is changing, and it suits me.

"Read it again," Mr. Warfel says, each breath a little warm cloud swallowing my neck and ear.

"I am Sam. Matt the Rat," I repeat. "I see Kay. Ann the fan. Tad is sad."

"Okay, now listen to me, "Matt the Rat. Kay I say. Ann the fan. Is that what you read?"

I can tell he wants me to answer this question for real, but I can't. I don't know if that's what I read. "Yeah," I say. "I guess so."

"Okay," he says, mussing my hair with his huge hand.

I glance over him to the book, open to the first page. If I stare at the letters, I can make them anything I want. I just need the right answer. *Siam Ams. Miamis. I am Sam. Sam I am. Maimas.*

I hear Mr. Warfel talking to my mom.

"He's seeing stuff that isn't there. He has several of the symptoms. The reading, lack of coordination in sports, difficulty with spatial relationships."

Stanley was right. I've been in school just a few weeks and they're already handing me a diagnosis, the first step toward brainwashing.

"He gets confused about right and left," my mom says.

"That's another one. And confusion with time. We had a seminar on dyslexia here at the school a few months ago. The latest theory is that the brain of a dyslexic exhibits a different pattern of cerebral dominance from the rest of us."

My mom's been cured, and I've been diagnosed.

"Cerebral dominance?"

"Meaning that no single hemisphere in the brain is in control. You've heard of right- and left-brained people?"

"Yeah—creative or business-like."

"Basically. Well, if Jason turns out to be dyslexic, he may be 'both-brained.'"

"Is that bad?"

"It is if he can't learn to read the way the rest of us do. Luckily, there is a great deal of awareness—and funding—when it comes to learning disabilities in California schools these days. I'd like to get him started on some cognitive therapy."

"What's that?"

"It's not as scary as it sounds. To him, it will just seem like playing games. Blocks, word games. Stuff like that. We've got a program called the Perception Center."

"I've heard of it," my mom says, smiling. "Our neighbor's son has a learning disability. We'd better do it. Can I help in any way?"

I've got a learning disability, like Steve.

"We need all the parent volunteers we can get."

"Sign me up."

"Thank you, Mrs. Messin, you've been great about this."

The potential of black marks on a white page to shape mental pictures, to build wholly imagined worlds or ideas, is a fact that deserves consideration.

For Steve Lewis and me, those black marks suffered from malleability. We were neighbors, but our lives—and our mothers—couldn't have been more different. We had little in common, except that for both of us, letters mutated. We were out of sync with Miller School's curriculum. Between us, we exhibited many cognitive phenomena that prompted leaders at the National Institute of Mental Health, in 1976, to invite an international group of educators, psychiatrists, psychologists, pediatricians, and neurologists to present their hypotheses about dyslexia—definitions of the condition, what causes it, what challenges it brings for those who experience it, and what treatments might help.

The researchers met in 1977 to discuss their hypotheses, but in the preceding year they were examining children and adults like Steve and me, devising and refining methods of gathering data, and forming a massive variety of conclusions.

Dyslexia just means "language problem." But research turned up by the NIMH's call made it clear that it was a mistake to assume dyslexia was a single phenomenon with a single cause that could be treated with a single set of therapies.

The black marks are shapes before they're letters. To read, you have to be able to perceive distinctions among these squiggly shapes. Look at these letters: F and E, U and V, M and W, C and O. The differences are obvious, but if you pay attention, which we don't usually do, you see how slight they are. Add variable typefaces and handwriting styles, and the subtle differences proliferate. Shape matters, and so does order. To see that *god* and *dog* are different words, you have to conform to the directional laws of your language. And to conform, you have to be able to stop yourself from trying out other directions.

To determine the causes of dyslexia, researchers began looking for correlates—other common cognitive peculiarities—in children struggling to read: delayed speech or speech impediments, lack of coordination, difficulty interpreting pictures or naming colors, trouble with spatial relationships, confusion between right and left. The tentative conclusion that emerged from the conference proceedings was that the neurology of dyslexia comes in three forms: a general language deficit (63%), a speech deficit (10%), or a visual-spatial deficit (5%). The remaining 22% defy categories. In every case, "the presence of social disadvantage" increases the likelihood that a child will exhibit reading difficulties.

I'd have been the kid with social disadvantage, and Steve would've have been the one without. Somebody could have done a study, using us as controls for one another.

I got my diagnosis. I got cognitive therapy at school. But do I have dyslexia? Is dyslexia a meaningful category? Might my six-year-old brain—or self—have been rebelling, or responding to poverty and abuse? I'll probably never know for sure, but I'm convinced I became a writer and a professor of literature because of my brain's atypical relationship to the black marks on pages.

11

NEVES SPELLED BACKWARD IS SEVEN

"Watch," my mom says. "Watch that one in the red, on the black horse. That's your grandpa."

I'm leaning against her right knee, and Nichole's leaning against her left. The horses run in a clump with a tail of stragglers at the end. You can hear the thump of hooves pounding loose dirt. All around us, people in the stands are yelling names and cheering. I track the red speck on the black horse edging out the other horses to take the lead.

"Ralph Neves on Black Sand, leading by a nose," a voice echoes over loudspeakers.

"He's winning," I say, proud of my grandpa.

"Goddamn Portuguese Pepper Pot," Stanley says, rolling his eyes up to Aaron, who's sitting on his shoulders clenching Stanley by the ears and cheering. My mom is bouncing and squealing.

"And it's Ralph Neves on Black Sand for the win. Hear the crowd roar for the Portuguese Pepper Pot."

"He won," my mom says. "He won. He won."

"Let's collect our fuckin' moolah," Stanley says.

"Grandpa won?" Nichole asks. There's something sad about her calling him *Grandpa*, this guy we never see and hardly know.

"Yes," my mom says. "Lucky Seven!"

Neves spelled backward is *seven*. The mantra has new meaning for me, now that I know I have a disorder that makes me mix up letters, spell words backward. I'm like Ralph. It seems to have worked out for him.

Ralph is twelve, living at the St. Vincent's School for Boys in San Francisco, whose enrollment is stretched well past capacity. There's a depression in the air, *the* Depression. Most of these boys got here through a petty crime, their own or their parents'. For others it was a parent's suicide or murder. For Ralph, it was his father's schizophrenia. When he was finally locked up for good, Ralph's mother couldn't handle both him and the two girls, so he became an orphan with two living parents.

In 1960, a reporter for *Coronet* magazine will describe the adult Ralph—at four eleven and 109 pounds—as "a trim little party with inky hair, snapping dark eyes, olive skin, and handsome Valentino features."

At twelve, Ralph is a tiny party writhing under the heavy hands of frustrated nuns. He's the ringleader, surrounded by a band of boys, a wad of tobacco longer and wider than his tongue stuffed between his cheeks. He hears Sister Agnes's bellow at the precise moment the dice spring from his palm: "Ralph Neves!"

He grins. "Want a piece of the action, Sister?"

"Spit that out," she replies, "immediately."

Ralph spits the contents of his tiny mouth all over the short-sleeved white shirt of the doughy blond kid next to him.

"That's it, Neves" is all Agnes says, yanking his arm. Ralph relaxes his body until it's just a pile of flesh, forcing the nun to drag him like a cadaver. The boys, including the doughy blond, watch with the fear that should be in Ralph's eyes. Ralph delivers a wide grin, not fixing on anybody in particular, making sure they all enjoy his triumph.

It was only a matter of time, and he wants to leave them with something to remember, so that night Ralph jumps out his second-story window, climbs a seven-foot wall, and wanders through a forest of oaks until he finds an empty shack, where he sleeps, living on bread and apples he coaxes from some local kids who play in the forest. The kids make a project of the runaway. He swears them to secrecy, and for six days they bring him food and reports about the police search for him. On that sixth day, there is no report. It's odds enough for Ralph, and the next day, when the kids find the shack empty, they agree the scrawny runaway must have wandered off to die.

We're a clump on the doorstep, my mom in the lead, finger on the doorbell.

The door glides open, revealing white carpet and a woman in wide-legged slacks with a precise crease down the front and a lavender silk blouse that ties at the collar. Her hair is brown turning quickly gray, arranged in a bun on top. "Cathy," she says. "So good to see you."

"Hi, Kay," my mom says. "You remember Jason? And Nichole?"

"Hello, Jason. Hello, Nichole. So good to see you."

"And this is my husband, Stanley, and my son, Aaron."

"Come in, all of you. Ralph is just getting dressed."

We race our clump across the carpet into a living room full of orange couches and chairs with gold embroidery.

"Sit," Kay says. "Have a seat. Would anybody like a cocktail?"

"Whattaya got?" Stanley asks.

"What would you like?"

"Vodka tonic?"

"Coming right up. Cathy?"

"Sure. And the kids would love a ginger ale."

"Goddamn if it isn't little Cathy Neves," a voice bellows from the hall. It sounds cheerful and mad at the same time. "Goddamn Cathy Neves cute as a button."

"Hi, Dad," my mom says. "Long time no see."

"How long? Has it been that long?"

"Jason was only three."

"It's been that long? Which one's Jason?"

"Right here," she says, putting her arm around me.

"Shoulda known. Right next to Mama. And so I guess this is Craig's girl."

"Nichole," my mom says. "And this is my other son, Aaron, and my husband Stanley."

"Stanley, nice to know you," Ralph says, holding out a hand to shake. "Hello, Aaron. That your son, Cathy? He don't look Portuguese."

"He's Stanley's son from his first marriage."

"Then he's not your Goddamn son. He's Stanley's son. Ain't that right, Stanley?"

"You tell it like it is, Ralph," Stanley says.

"I sure as hell do."

"He always did," my mom says, suddenly sounding older, like Nanny.

Kay walks over, balancing a tray of drinks. "Ginger ale for the kids," she says, handing us each a glass full of sparkling liquid with a bright red cherry in it. "Vodka tonic, Stanley. And Ralph, an Old Fashioned for you," handing him a glass that looks just like what Nanny always drinks.

"That was some race today," Stanley says. "You kicked ass."

"You gotta. Fuckin' old-timers' race. If I wasn't so happy growing roses, I'd race the young guys and kick their asses."

"I bet," Stanley says.

Aaron's eyes are always wide and always light blue, but here in Ralph's rented condo on the beach in Del Mar they are as wide and light as eyes can get. He's quieter than I've ever seen him, slurping down ginger ale, sitting next to Stanley. Glasses get empty, cherries eaten. The sun starts to set outside.

"Guess what, Dad?" my mom says. "I'm cured."

"Cured of what, kiddo?"

"I told you, Dad. I had a lung disease. Dr. Brenner cured me."

"Can't kill a Neves," he responds. "I proved that."

"I told her it was her Lucky Seven genes," Stanley says.

"Goddamn right. So how are these kids?"

"Nichole loves horses," my mom says.

"That right?"

"Yes," Nichole answers.

"You oughta get yourself an old racehorse. They go cheap and they're good and strong. Well-trained. Get yourself a thoroughbred who doesn't race anymore."

"Jason had some trouble reading, but he's getting special therapy. He's got dyslexia. He sees words funny."

"I go to the Perception Center," I say.

"The Goddamn what center?" Ralphs asks.

"It's for my brain," I say. Mr. Warfel taught me about this.

"It's all in his head," Stanley interrupts, "if you ask me. There's nothin' really wrong with him. Just some mumbo jumbo they talk at that school."

"It's all in our heads," Ralph says. "That's one Goddamn thing I know for sure."

"It's in my brain," I say, hoping it's clear that I'm arguing with him and not agreeing.

"The fuck it is," Ralph says. I can't figure out from his tone if he's arguing or agreeing.

Nobody can find a response, so Kay jumps in. "How long's the drive to Escondido?"

"Del Dios," my mom corrects her. "About a half hour. It's a nice drive."

"Where the fuck is Del Dios, in the mountains?" Ralph asks.

"Almost," my mom says. "It's right on Lake Hodges. Really beautiful. Escondido is just a few minutes away."

"Well, I guess you'd better get going," Ralph says. "All them mountain roads to drive. Huh, Jason?"

I nod. "Uh-huh."

"Doesn't seem like there's nothin' wrong with him to me. A little timid, though."

"Don't be strangers," Ralph says as he's shutting the door. "Don't stay away so long next time."

We pile into the car. As Stanley starts the engine, Nichole says, "I love Grandpa."

In their Easter Sunday sermons, ministers in Des Moines and Saratoga Springs and Lafayette and Tempe stand before their parishioners and tell the story of the booter they couldn't bury—three times dead, told six times he'd never ride again, two lumbar vertebrae crushed, broken back twice, his skull cracked and partially replaced with a steel plate, leg fractured, hipbone smashed, ribcage caved in, lower body paralyzed, brain artery severed by a splinter of skull. Resurrection, the ministers intone, is a miracle for which we must rejoice.

At San Mateo's Bay Meadows arena, the ministers begin, one day in 1936, jockey Ralph Neves could feel victory in the way his mount carved the wind, hollowing a tunnel through which horse and jockey would glide to the finish line. A single misplaced hoof cracked the tunnel open and brought horse and jockey tumbling back to earth. Without time for breath, much less thought, horse and jockey were ground into the soft dirt of the track by the four horses that had been following most closely.

You could hear a rumbling gasp in the crowd and then quiet as everybody watched a circle of doctors feel the Pepper Pot's pulse, look for fractures, perform mouth-to-mouth, pound his heart. After fifteen minutes, hope was pointless. The quiet of the crowd was interrupted here and there by solemn statements of disbelief: *Not the Portuguese Pepper Pot. That kid had fire. Damn shame. He's only twenty.*

Forty minutes later, a voice lumbering with grief addressed the crowd: "Please join me in a silent prayer for Ralph Neves. Sadly, the Portuguese Pepper Pot was pronounced dead at Mills Hospital just a few minutes ago." The body was wrapped in a sheet and wheeled to the hospital morgue. A friend, Dr. Horace Wald, happened to be on duty and rushed to pay his respects. He unwrapped the sheet to get a final look at Neves's 109 pounds, still clothed in blood-caked silks. For reasons he could never explain, he had brought with him a syringe of adrenaline. He took out the needle and administered a pointless shot into the heart of the dead jockey, then sat watching for a miracle. When none came, he replaced the sheet and returned to his rounds.

"I knew I was in the cold room," Neves said later. "Something made me jump up and run out the door. That's all I know." Startled hospital staff noticed the apparition in jockey silks who slipped through the hallway, but he was out the door, hailing a taxi, before anyone found the bearings to respond. Two hours after his death had been announced, Neves galloped his two tiny feet down the track in front of the stands, a stream of jockeys, attendants, and Bay Meadows officials trailing him. The crowd gasped, then cheered, as Neves beat his arms at the wind—pounding for the tunnel he'd fallen through. When they finally caught him, Neves was incoherent, in a deep state of shock and delusion.

"Medically, you can't explain Ralph," said Wald. "Nonprofessionally, I'd say he's alive because he enjoys life too intensely to give it up. He simply refuses to quit." Medically, no, the ministers say on Easter. Resurrection is a matter of faith.

"What's my name spelled backward?" Neves asked Wald over a vodka martini. "Seven. Lucky Seven. God can't kill me. He's tried."

12

LEOPARDS EAT LEPERS AND DIE

"Nanny's here," I call from my bedroom. The purr of her Mercedes is threaded with chugs and spurts. She's here to see our new house. We've moved to Fourth Street, on the other hill in Del Dios. Nichole's our neighbor now, instead of the Lewises.

Nanny comes to a stop alongside the bus, parked in our dusty driveway. She looks at the ground with care and disdain as she opens the car door, annoyed by the rocks. "Hello there, Stanley." Nanny grins at him, almost flirting.

"If it isn't the silver fox."

Nanny performs a mock hair primp, charade-style.

"Well, come in. Take the grand tour. I'm Stanley. I'll be your guide."

My mom appears. "Hi, Mom. Well, what do you think?"

I creep out of the bedroom, where Aaron and I have been busy arguing about the fort we're building. He wants to destroy it, for the fun of it. I want to move into it.

"Nanny, Nanny." I run to her and she pats my head.

"Hello there," she says. I'm trying to picture her with Ralph, that tiny man with the dirty mouth.

"Hi, Nanny," Aaron manages to yell above the pathetic thud of plastic wheels toppling pillows and blankets.

"Come see our fort," I say to Nanny.

"Shut your trap," Stanley says. "She's not here to see your fort."

"It's coming together, don't you think?" my mom suggests. The house is unfinished inside, with splintery wood ceilings. It's dark in the daylight. Stanley's parents gave us the down payment. Nanny, whose owning days are over, advised us against spending $36,000 on the place. It's bigger than any place we've lived, and it has a big dirt front yard and a back yard with trees in it for our new pet geese, Lucy and Louis.

"Yes, Cathy."

"It was a great deal." Stanley is bragging.

"That's true. Let's see what you've done with the bedrooms." We tour them as a group. They have beds and dressers. Aaron and I have trundle beds. They can be adjusted for multi-level fort building. They also mean we sleep right next to each other.

"Those are fun," Nanny says. I'm monitoring her expressions and mannerisms for signs of her thoughts. *For Godssake, first a bus, now an overgrown shed.* I'm glad to have an ally, but it doesn't change the fact that I have to live here.

I am the only kid in my class who goes to the Perception Center. Nobody really knows what it means, but there is a vague association between my Wednesday trips and Special Ed.

There's something secret about the place, like it's in the depths of something, its unmarked door a magic portal to another dimension. Inside, it's small and dimly lit, with no windows. There are three or four other kids crawling through mazes, playing with big bright plastic puzzles, looking at picture books and answering questions. Sometimes I see Steve Lewis here, which is weird, because I hardly see him in Del Dios anymore.

My mom's here today. She has been volunteering since I started, leading kids through their activities, learning about my disability. She's fascinated. It's a connection between us.

"Hi, Jas," she says.

"Hi."

"Hello, Jason," Mrs. Lunden, the teacher in charge, says. "Come with me." She puts her skinny arm around my shoulder. My mom and Miss Johnston, the aide, sit at the desk near the door to talk.

"I have a theory, Mrs. Messin," Miss Johnston tells her. "I've been thinking about it, and I want to share it with you. According to the latest research, there are several distinct types of dyslexia. I think Jason has the kind that stems from a problem with visual perception. In cases like his, I like to say that the kids see more creatively than most. Literally."

"What do you mean?" my mom asks. "I don't get it."

"We're starting to learn that objects are recorded through our eyes and then translated—or recreated—by our brains. For Jason, the brain distorts the images more than most, particularly with words. But shapes and colors too. You have to remember that words are made out of shapes and colors. Most people don't think about that."

"That makes sense," my mom says, "if you think about it. I wonder if he gets it from me."

"Many dyslexics are very creative and above average intelligence. Einstein was dyslexic." I like the sound of that.

Mrs. Lunden sits me down at an apparatus that looks like a puppet theater, except the proscenium is a table with one chair on each side.

The stage is strewn with plastic in primary colors—plastic stars, octagons, circles, and hexagons. "Take one shape at a time," Mrs. Lunden says in soft-voice, "and put them where they belong." I have to place them into matching molds cut out of the stage floor. I'm getting better at this—*improving rapidly*, Mrs. Lunden says. After three rounds of shape matching, Mrs. Lunden says, "Great. You did great, Jason. I'd say you earned your lunch. Why don't you go a little early and I'll see you next Wednesday?"

"Okay," I say.

What would happen to my ranking, I wonder, if Paul were to find the secret door and pass into this dimension?

Honk honk. Honkhonkhonk. It's nearly morning but still dark. The honking becomes a wail, desperate and loud. By the time I hear it, Aaron's trundle bed is already empty. I step onto it and run toward the noise, in the backyard.

When we get there, everything is quiet. We stare at two Dobermans, bloody faces buried in white feathers, bodies almost invisible in the dark. They're smug, their black eyes glancing at us for a second and then returning to their feast. "Get," Stanley yells. "Get. Get the fuck out of here," running at them, his arms wide like he might fly.

"Motherfuckers," Stanley says as the dogs run off. "Get," he yells one last time.

This is not a good start. We've only lived here a couple weeks, and Lucy and Louis, our vicious geese, are dead. Their limber necks are severed, and now they're two mangled piles of blood and feathers, most of them stained orangey-pink like flamingoes.

"We have to bury them," my mom says quietly.

"Can we make headstones?" Aaron asks.

"Yes," she says.

"Go inside," Stan says. "All of you. I'm gonna clean this fuckin' mess up."

Inside, my mom says, "We might as well stay up. It's almost time for school. It won't hurt to get there early. I'm going in too, to work in the Perception Center."

It's maddening to know that my early memories are distorted by Stanley's abuse. And that I cringe when I type that word, *abuse*. Part of me still doesn't want to name it. Part of me just wants to think it was no big deal or that I'm remembering it wrong.

My mom married Stanley when I was four. The susceptibility of a child's memory begins to plateau at five. Before this, tell the child something happened, and he will be very likely to fabricate a memory of the event. By five, he will do this about half the time.

Memories of difficult, painful, or traumatic experience are even more unpredictable.

Child abuse can lead to memory so persistent that the past literally intrudes upon the present, or it can cause amnesia so profound it is impossible for subjects to believe in their own painful experience. This may be because *hyperarousal* and *dissociation* are typical responses to childhood trauma. Paradoxically, they are opposites. Hyperarousal is just what it sounds like: an intense focus on a real or perceived threat, activated by the flight-or-fight instinct. Dissociation is a withdrawal that prevents the child from perceiving the threat. Like other forms of trauma, child abuse can either excite or inhibit memory. Most child abuse will result in long-term symptoms that combine hyperarousal and dissociation. My best guess: that I experienced a combination of the two. I remember dissociating, walling myself in behind a shield of ether, but the strength and persistence of my memories suggests hyperarousal.

It was definitely abuse, but I'm not sure this was trauma. The Diagnostic and Statistical Manual of Mental Disorders (DSM-IV) defines *trauma* as an event "outside the range of usual human experience," one that involves "actual or threatened death or serious injury, or other threat to one's physical integrity." In the words of trauma theorist Cathy Caruth, trauma tests the "limits of our understanding." Because those limits are bound to vary from one person to the next, a trauma must be measured by its results, or symptoms: persistent nightmares, feeling of numbness, hyperarousal, unrelenting memories, or no memories at all. I admit that I recognize some of these symptoms, and reading them over, I wonder if the pink ribbon dream was about Stanley as much as it was about Charlie. But I banish the thought, because it would cast Stanley as my father. I've spent a lifetime denying him that.

Usual human experience is not easily defined. Nor are *the limits of our understanding*. Events are not inherently traumatic. It's all about the experience of the perceiver. I think Stanley's bullying and taunting had me walking an invisible border along the edges of the usual. When he swung me in the air, I was in the border's upper atmosphere. If experience is too far outside the range of expectations, the brain bends the subjective reality of the organism to a shape it can live with, for a while. The problem is this shape sticks, and it's not usually ideal for living later on. It becomes you. You become it. Your body responds to the world according to its rhythms. I think Stanley—like lot of the fixtures of my early years—was an education that made the borders of usual human experience seem ever-shifting, the limits of understanding a tightrope I was living on.

A bunch of us were screwing around at the lake. One by one, the other kids were called to dinner.

Once the last kid leaves, with the sun setting and the lake still, it's almost impossible not to think. I'm sitting with my butt in the mud and my back against a eucalyptus tree. It's dark enough that the leaves and branches above me look black, but the patterns of sky shining between them are bright. The trunks of the eucalyptus trees around me are peeled, two-toned. They remind me of leopards when things seem okay and lepers when they don't. I keep switching back and forth between thinking *leopard* and *leper*. *Leopard* means things are okay; *leper* means they're not.

If leopards eat lepers, do their insides melt and slough? I'm trying not to think this thought, but it's an invisible hand manipulating me like a marionette as I pick up a long stick and draw my name in the mud in giant letters. I try cursive, then all caps, cursive again. Just my first name and then all three: Jason Daniel Messin. *Messy Messin. Messin your pants.*

Once I let my mind wander, that's it. The water gurgles, leaves crunch. I'm spooked. I start to get the dream feeling, the skipping terror. How can a feeling from a dream come true? Where is it coming from? How can I get away? *Leopards eat lepers and die.*

I kneel and splash my face with lake water, which is a slight relief. But it doesn't last. I sense the guy with the bomb up in the sky.

I run toward Lake Drive. When I get there, I slow down. Someone might see, and besides, I'm out of breath. It's about a mile home. I can see this guy Newtie coming, with his huge dog Riley. His stringy brown hair is tied back in a bandana. He went crazy in the Vietnam War. Everybody likes Newtie and blames the government for his sad life. He grosses me out because he's so greasy and smells like cigarettes. I can see his huge mustache from here, covering his top lip and his nostrils. "How's it goin'?" he says when we finally pass. "Fine," I say, looking at Riley, an Irish Wolfhound who's taller than I am, whose silvery fur is oilier than Newtie's. I give him a pat on the head and he looks into my eyes.

Newtie and Riley behind me, I concentrate on each step. Don't touch cracks in the pavement. Step on every stick. Kick every rock. I walk until I reach our street, then run up our hill. The chaos feeling is a relief.

I stop when I get to the porch. Stanley sees me. He's there on the couch, hairy in boxer shorts. The light from the TV is blinking on his face and chest. His mouth is moving, like he's talking to the screen.

I open the door and walk in, looking straight ahead, at my room. He stinks, of course, like musty sweat and alcohol. *Walk. Walk. Walk.*

"Hey kid, where ya been?"

Walk.

"No hello for your old man. Would *Mommy* like that? *Mommy, Mommy, Mommy*. Fuckin' momma's boy."

"I'm here," I mutter.

"What was that? Huh? Whatever. You missed the fuckin' game."

"I hate football."

"Oh, fuckin' beats all. *I hate football.* Fuckin' wuss. Go play with your Barbies."

He's up, hairy and staggering toward me, red and grinning. "C'meeere. C'meeere. You scared? I just want to talk to you."

He picks me up. My body is stringy and uncoordinated. He shakes it. I start to cry.

"Whatsamatter, kid? I didn't do shit. Toughen up. Learn how to fight. Fight me. Fuck."

"I hate you," I say. He drops me. I try to stop my heaves. I rub my cheek on the floor to dry the tears. I struggle to compose my face. I can't stand that contorted crying face.

"Look, you Goddamn sissy-ass faggot. You want a fight? I got the belt. Look."

He's grinning but yelling too. Fun and fury are all mixed up in Stanley.

"Nobody ever teaches you a lesson. Your old man's a fuckin' loser. He's not around to teach you anything. That's your problem. I'll teach you."

I feel his foot nudging me, like I'm a dead animal he wants to turn over. I freeze. If I remain still, it will eventually end. I know this from experience.

It does end, sort of. We hear the engine. Then the headlights from my mom's VW Bug shine through the front window. She can see him, standing in the middle of the room.

"Oh, fuckin' great. *Mommy's home*. Run to Mommy."

She walks in, her Seafood Market apron still tied around her waist.

"Jesus Christ." For a minute she sounds like Nanny. "What is this? Are you a couple of babies? I can't even go to work."

Me? What did I do? Me?

"Jesus fucking Christ." She is starting to lose it. "Jason, get up off the floor."

"Fuckin' baby," Stanley says. "He got home late. He missed the fuckin' game."

"You're drunk."

"So are you. Been drinkin' with Cheech all night or what?"

"Oh, Jesus Christ."

I walk to my room. My body hurts all over. The dream feelings—both the terror and the chaos—are gone.

I shut the door behind me. Somebody opens it. I crawl into my bottom bunk and dig under the covers. I put a pillow over my head, but I can hear their stream of words: *Cheech, Jesus, faggot, work, hard, late, hell, drunk, work, fuck.* I push the pillow harder and harder. This feels like hours. I focus on my force field. It almost works. Eventually, though, I hear them giggling.

Leopards eat lepers and die.

After hours of this, I hear my mom walking toward my room. I remove the pillow. I assume my most convincing sleep position. She puts her hand on my head anyway. She brushes her fingers through my hair. Mentally, I shove her hand away, but physically I just lie there, sleeping. "Jason." I just breathe. "Jason, listen. Can you hear me?"

No, I say in my head.

"I know you can hear me. Stan didn't mean it. You'll see."

This seems like a chance to make it all go away, so I say, without opening my eyes, "Okay, I know."

"Kid," I hear Stanley's voice. "I just wish you'd watch the game with me once in a while. It'd be cool."

"Okay." I open my eyes and look at him. But I am not there. "Okay" means "I hate football, and I hate you." The force field is working.

"Okay, then," he says.

"Goodnight, Boogie." She brushes my head again. *Leopards eat lepers and die.*

The rain makes the Fourth Place house feel like the inside of a drum. I'm in the top trundle bed, Aaron in the lower. Neither of us is sleeping. It must be midnight. The phone rings. It's been ringing off and on all night.

"Hello," my mom says in a squashed voice that lets you know immediately that she's miserable. "Oh, hi." Pause. "What?" Pause. "I knew it. I knew it. I said it. I said he was screwing around. I knew it." Pause. "Was he drunk?" Pause. "I knew it." Pause. "Thanks. Okay, bye." The way she said bye made it clear that she was beyond politeness.

Outside the rain beats on the roof like tiny drumsticks, and now inside she is marching, offbeat, from one end of the house to the other. Aaron and I hear her slide open drawers, swing open closet doors, then march through the living room and slam open the front door. Then we hear her dump Stan's clothes in piles on the porch. Aaron and I don't look at each other. We've been here before and have a silent agreement to ride it out. "There," she screams, too hoarse to be high-pitched. "Take your fucking crap to her house." *Beat, march, swing, slide, march, slam, dump, scream.* She makes seven or eight full trips. "Take it. Take your crap to her house. Take it." She's on the front porch, the screams settling into sobs. "Take it. I should have fucking known. Take it. Goddamn you, take it."

The headlights fill the house, even our room. We hear Stanley's car door open and close, gently. "Very nice," he says. "Very fucking nice. How'd we get to this shit again?"

"You know. Or maybe you should ask Tina."

"Oh fuckin' Christ."

"I thought I'd help you move your stuff over to her place. I thought I'd get you started."

"I'm not moving my stuff any fucking place. Just calm down."

"I will not. I will," the sobbing takes over and she can't finish the sentence. "I won't," she begins again. "We're supposed to be a family here. We're supposed," the sobbing takes over.

"Fuckin' families don't throw each other's shit outside every three months."

"Fucking families don't get drunk every night and fuck whores. Fucking families—"

"You are a nut job, Cathy. You're a basket case. I can't take this shit."

"Stay away," she says. "Don't touch me. I'll call the cops this time."

"Don't worry. I don't wanna touch you. Get the fuck out of my way." Stan marches past her, swings open the front door, his footsteps a baseline for the raindrops. He swings open our door. I can feel him look down at Aaron, then me, then back to Aaron. "Come on, Aaron," he says. "Let's get out of here." He reaches down, scoops Aaron up, and marches back out the door.

I imagine the rain beating down on Aaron's pajamas. The car door swings open, then shuts. The engine turns over twice before starting.

I can hear my mom sobbing into the rain. I can picture her sitting in piles of wet clothes. I know what's coming. Her footsteps are quiet this time, falling into the empty spaces left by raindrops falling less swiftly now. She's standing in the doorway, right where Stan stood, looking down at me. I keep my eyes closed. "This is the last time," she says. "This is it."

Leopards eat lepers and die.

13

THE ONE YOU GET

The phone rings. "Hello." Pause. "Charlie?"

Pause.

"No way. I'm hanging up." Pause.

"I told you no." Pause.

"I trusted you before. Why should I now?" Pause.

"No. Why? Charlie." Pause.

"You've said that before. Why should I believe you?"

"I said no."

She hangs up.

Nobel Prize–winning neuroscientist Gerald Edelman was the director of the Neuroscience Institute in La Jolla, California, right down the street from Scripps Hospital, where the doctors sliced me from my mom's womb. Edelman's Theory of Neuronal Group Selection (TNGS), or Neural Darwinism, strives to explain how we become who we are.

Edelman's theory tells a story about the collaboration between Charlie and Cathy. Well, it's an attempt to explain the synaptic patterns that undergird each person's mind, and ultimately identity, according to the tenets of natural selection. Certain neuronal patterns or groupings, Edelman argues, get reinforced, or *selected*, because they are more functional than others. But the patterns of selection house stories. According to Edelman, there are three important brain functions that drive neuronal group selection.

ONE: DEVELOPMENTAL SELECTION. Cathy and Charlie's genes collaborate to form a patchwork, constraining the possibilities for my embryonic brain. At the beginning, the embryonic brain still faces a vast set of possible synaptic connections. Too many. Certain neural groups form electrical alliances with others. The more they work together, the stronger their overlapping point in the network becomes. Such alliances discourage other alliances. These alliances primed my physiology for certain traits. My father's genes said charismatic, prone to depression and rage, addictive, too sensitive, brooding, smart, irrational; my mother's said outspoken, creative, moody, fun-loving, prone to rage, irrational, novelty-seeking, too sensitive, addictive. I like to think my fetus got lucky at this stage.

TWO: EXPERIENTIAL SELECTION. Even as an embryo, my brain was developing in reaction to genetic codes and environment. The genes told the cells where to go, what connections to make, what structures to build, but the details of these structures and their links to each other were assembled in response to the environment of my mother's womb. Of course, the environment in her womb would have an indirect connection to the environment outside her body. What happened to the embryonic neurons during that drive to Mexico, in the clinic waiting room, on the table, and as she refused the abortion? Theoretically, my young mom's frightening experience, translated through stimulus to her nerve cells, concocted an emotional chemistry that influenced the migration and settling of neural cells.

THREE: REENTRY. Reentry is brain synchronicity. It is the way that billions of neurons, grouped into systems and subsystems, work together, across the expanse of the brain, to produce behaviors (my typing, my mom's laugh, Charlie shooting up) and states of mind (my obsessive memory, my mom's desire for junkies, Charlie's opioid peace). I imagine my brain, so much of it set up for me by my parents' genes and by the environments they created for me. Then I imagine reentry, sending constant impulses in multiple directions across the vast neural network. Again, the more certain paths are traveled, the stronger they become. According to Edelman, each brain's system of networks is a uniquely sculpted set of traits. A reluctance to display emotion, a tendency to perceive shapes oddly, a vigilance for potential threat, intense fear of disease, and empathy for animals are traits embedded in each other. It makes little sense to name one trait a deficit and another a strength because they shape each other. To enhance or quiet a trait, multiple strands in the network must mobilize, and therefore the entire system changes.

Reentry was my brain's chance for some say in how things were. I'm pretty sure this chemical communication pulsing in constant dual motion along network pathways exceeds the script of genetic selection and the performance of experiential selection. Edelman's reentry was where my brain, a physical object, became a mind belonging to a self, an intangible experience of being me that didn't belong to Cathy or Charlie.

"Kiss it. Kiss it."

"No way," I say, even though I want to do it.

Nichole is chasing me around our new house on Lake Drive with my favorite Shaun Cassidy record. She's living in Del Dios now, right down the block from our old house, where Stan and Aaron still live. Paul's here too, sitting on the floor watching, laughing less than you'd think. He and I have been best friends for two years now.

I'm almost nine now, finishing third grade. The divorce is final. When the new school year comes along, my name will change from *Messin* back to *Tougaw*. I wanted *Neves*, but we'd have to go to court for that. I have learned by now that the law is to be avoided.

We're still in Del Dios, but on the opposite end from Stanley and Aaron, "tucked away," my mom likes to say, in the last house on Lake

Drive. The new house is a compound, with a shack to the side, and another house, empty, behind ours. We have a dusty acre across the street from a stream that feeds into the lake.

"If you love it so much, kiss it," Nichole repeats. We're running circles around the living room. "Kiss it, kiss it." We're laughing too hard to hear the car in the driveway. Nanny pokes her head through the door. "Nanny!" Nichole says. "Nanny," I repeat, out of breath. Paul sits still.

My mom walks out of the kitchen. "Mom," she says. "This is it," gesturing to the house.

"This is it," Nanny sings, dipping her hips and swaying through the living room. "This is life, the one you get."

"Very funny, Mom," my mom adds. We all love *One Day at a Time*. Nanny loves to sing the theme. "It's our song," she says. "You can say that again," my mom adds. I watch the show at night when my mom's at work. I have a crush on Valerie Bertinelli. I like how Schneider always helps out whenever the ladies have a problem. I like to taunt Nanny by accusing her of having a crush on him.

"So that's the loft," Nanny says, trailing her eyes up the ladder. The loft is about half the size of the living room. We might get a lodger, to help pay the rent, depending on how tips are at the Seafood Market. "Pretty nice," Nanny says.

"I'll give you the tour," my mom says.

"That's my room, next to the kitchen," I say. "With the bunk beds." I love the fact that I can sleep on either bunk because I don't have to share with Aaron. The house is old but pretty nice, definitely the biggest house we've lived in, and technically it's a split-level. My mom's room is two steps higher than the rest of the house. We can barely afford it, but my mom wants life to be good after the divorce.

The adults' voices are trailing off, getting quieter as they make their way through the house. The record has ended, and Paul's fiddling with the player when we hear three knocks at the door.

"There's someone at the door," I yell. I'm talking to my mom, but I can't say *Mom*. I've stopped using *Mommy*, because she said I was getting pretty old for it. I can't get my mouth to say *Mom*. It sounds weird. Mostly I say *my mom* instead. Even though it's the same as *mommy* if you rearrange the letters, the effect is totally different. I can't say *love* either. The words have started to seem off-limits. If I say them, everybody will notice. They'll be able to look into my brain and see everything that embarrasses me. "Someone's at the door," I call out again.

"Well, see who it is," my mom calls back.

Paul trails as Nichole runs with me to the window. I'm picturing the exasperated dip Bonnie Franklin always does when she opens the door on *One Day at a Time*, because she knows a knock at the door always means fresh trouble. But it's okay, because somewhere there's music playing, and you can make it if you try.

The three of us crouch under the window and peek outside. I'm seeing JP through Paul's eyes. His black hair and deep tan make him look almost Mexican. His enormous belly looks like a steel balloon. He's wearing cut-offs, flip-flops, and a tank top with white hibiscus flowers on it. He's grinning at the door like it's a person.

"Who is *that*?" Nichole asks. Paul looks like he wants to go home. With Stanley out of the way, the coast seemed clear to have Paul over, but I'm regretting the decision now.

"Who is it?" my mom calls.

"It's JP," I yell, louder this time, because I know it's real news. We haven't seen him in a year.

"What?" she shrieks, running into the living room and throwing open the door. "JP! Oh my god, JP. Where'd you come from?"

"Well, I'll be damned if it isn't," Nanny says. I look at Paul, who's very still.

"Quack quack." JP quacks when words aren't enough. Paul's definitely not going to get JP.

"JP," my mom screams. "Where on God's green earth have you been?"

"Same ol' Cathy," JP says, wrapping his giant arms around her tiny bones. "Quack quack."

"Same ol' JP," she says. "Nobody has had any idea where you were. I was worried sick."

"You think I was back in the slammer or somethin'?"

"It crossed my mind. Sit down. Oh, JP, it's so good to see you." Her shriek is winding down.

"Kiddo," JP says, grabbing a handful of my hair as the adults walk to the kitchen. "Well, guess what, I *am* in the slammer."

"What? Shush your mouth, James Polk," she says.

"Don't try to stop the truth train," he says. "The truth train will run you down."

"What are you talking about? Are you on something?"

"Quack quack. I'm on truth."

The descent into Del Dios starts out sunny and bright, but it gets steadily darker as we enter the cave of oak trees that stretch over the top of the road. Our house is right on the edge of the cave. It's all brightness as we emerge, the air bleached so gold you can barely make out the white paint with green trim or the two women with a black Lab next to a VW Bug in the driveway. That's fine with me.

The bus squeaks, rocks, and stops. The women come into focus, and the accordion door squeezes open. The women wave at me as I walk down the aisle. They're shouting, pointing at the bus, then the dog, the bus, the dog. "Nichole," they're yelling. "Tell Nichole to get off too."

Nichole is sitting next to Cheryl Buffet, a girl with feathered bangs and buck teeth.

"Nichole," I say. "Nichole." She's looking down at something in Cheryl's notebook. "Nichole," I say in a cracking voice. She looks up. "My mom says you have to get off here."

"Why?"

"I don't know," I say. Nichole scrambles past Cheryl's bent knees and barrels down the aisle. We hop off the steps and climb the driveway.

"Check it out, you guys," Cheech says. "This is Mona," gesturing to the black dog whipping its whole body like a tail as it runs toward us.

Cheech works with my mom at the Seafood Market. She's Portuguese too. She's got the same shag as the Yourgales brothers who own the restaurant, except even blacker and more wiry. Her Portuguese skin is darker than ours and her nose is bigger. She could easily be a man. She talks like one. She and my mom hang out all the time now.

Mona jumps up and puts her paws on my chest. I pet her head. Nichole pets her head, and she takes her legs off my chest and plops them on Nichole's to get a good lick of Nichole's lips. Misty, our Siamese cat, is watching from the front step, the hair on her back rising like a disgruntled mohawk, her tail straight and swinging like it's motorized.

"We got her from the pound," my mom says.

"Really?" I say. "She's ours?"

"Yep," she says, putting her arm around my shoulder. "She's our new guard dog."

"That's rad," Nichole says.

I wriggle out of my mom's arm and run up the driveway, baiting Mona to chase me. Nichole follows, and we run laps around the dirt rectangle between our house and the empty one behind it. We hear a car pull up, and my mom squeals, "JP, JP!"

"He's here again?" Nichole asks.

"I guess," I say. We keep running around the rectangle. The adults go inside. Five minutes later, my mom yells out the window, "Come inside. You guys need something to eat. You can bring Mona."

JP and Cheech are already sitting at the dining room table. Cheech is smoking, the green pack of Salem Lights right in the middle of the table, next to the ashtray, which is already full of at least five butts. The smoke floats in my direction like a cobra. My mom is at the stove, stirring chili. "It's almost ready," she says. Mona is on one side of the table, and our cat Misty is on the other.

"JP," my mom says. "Cheech is moving into the house out back."

"That big green one?"

"Yeah," Cheech says. "Me and Randy."

"Who's this Randy character?"

"Cheech's boyfriend."

"Damn," JP says. "And I thought I had a shot."

"You don't want to mess with me, man," Cheech says.

"I could take you," he says.

"Let's go in the living room 'til it's ready," I say to Nichole.

"Just sit tight," Cheech says. "Your mom's workin' hard."

"We'll just be over there," I say, grabbing Nichole and marching for the living room.

From the living room, we can hear them talking in quiet grown-up voices.

"Cathy, how're you doin' on cash?" JP asks.

"Fine," I hear her say, hesitating between the "i" and the "n."

"Don't lie to JP," he says. "He reads minds."

"She's broke as fuck," Cheech says. "The gas goes off next week."

"Hopefully the tips will be good this week," my mom says.

"Yeah, right," Cheech says, "good fuckin' luck."

"Cathy, take this," JP says.

"JP, that's too much," my mom says.

"It's money," Nichole whispers in my ear.

"No, it's not," I insist, purposefully not looking back.

"It's only a couple hundred," JP says.

"A couple hundred more than nothin'," Cheech says.

"JP, you're like a brother to me," my mom says.

"It is too," Nichole whispers.

"Plus, I gotta do somethin' with it," JP adds. "I can't have this kind of cash on me all the time. You're doin' me a favor."

"Who's gonna come lookin' for it?" Cheech asks.

"Cops from outer space," he says. "Next time I'm deported. Pluto for life." Then he says, "That's more like it. Seriously, Cathy. How you doin'?"

"Okay, just broke," she answers.

"Tell him," Cheech says.

"Cheech!" my mom says, making a shush sound.

"Guess who's been calling here," Cheech says.

"Who?" JP asks. "You're fucking kidding me," he says, having figured it out somehow. "He's out of the slammer?"

"Yeah," my mom says.

"Who are they talking about?" Nichole asks.

"I don't know," I say, even though I do.

"It doesn't matter," my mom says. "We're not having anything to do with him."

If JP's like a brother to her, that makes him an uncle to me. Suddenly I have this new uncle who hands out money and worries about the police. And now the threat of a father who's out of prison and wants something to do with me.

"Want me to talk to him?" JP asks.

"No," she says. "Chili's on the table," she calls. "Come and get it."

As we walk into the kitchen, my mom says to JP, "You're good to us, you big fart."

Cheech is done smoking, and there is a sixth butt in the ashtray, still smoldering. "Milk or apple juice?" my mom asks.

"Apple juice," Nichole says.

"Milk," I say, because it's a better barrier. If I place it in the right spot and lean my head, I might be able to block my view of the ashtray.

My mom fills our glasses. "Cheese and onions?" Cheech asks.

"Yes, please," Nichole says.

"No onions for Jas," my mom says.

"This kid hates everything," Cheech says.

"I only hate onions and mayonnaise." I am developing a need to correct inaccuracy wherever I encounter it.

Nichole is scooping onion-covered chili into her mouth and gulping apple juice to wash it down. She doesn't even seem to notice the smelly ashtray. I'm ducking behind my milk, trying to find an angle that hides it, but the glass is too small. Plus, now I see that I've got the fork with the bent third tine. This fork is one of the grossest ones. All the tines are blackish-grey at the ends. I have my white bowl, at least. I knock my fork on the floor, and get up to take it to the sink. While I'm searching through the drawer for the fork I like, the stainless steel one with the black handle that Nanny gave us, I see the chili pot close-up. The black non-stick stuff is flaking off into the chili. In our whole house, there's only one fork, two spoons, one bowl, three plates, one frying pan, one pot, and four glasses I can eat out of.

I sit back down, nibbling chili and cheese, tasting used cigarette butts in every bean. "Eat up," JP says. "Don't you want to have a belly like mine one day?"

I look at the ceiling and make a show of taking as big a bite as I can handle without throwing up. "Thatta boy," JP says. My mom smiles. Cheech mutters something. Nichole scoops and gulps.

"Can I finish in the living room?" I ask, looking at my mom.

"I guess so," she says. "Whatever."

"Kids," JP says. "They got little minds of their own."

"You're a big kid yourself, mister," my mom says.

"Quack quack."

Mona follows me, her whole body wagging. I put my bowl on the floor and Mona dives in, swallowing it all in about three gulps.

"Gotta run," I hear JP say. "Gotta run."

"Why?" my mom asks. "Where?"

"Pluto. I'll be back, don't you worry. Soon."

"Christ," Cheech says as he walks out the door. "What's he on?"

It was a comfort to learn about the button boy. He was like me, but with a diagnosis and a set of treatments for his phobias. "The participant was a nine-year-old Hispanic American boy. He presented with his mother to the Phobia Program at Florida International University, Miami, with an avoidance of buttons." An avoidance of buttons is a sign of a specific phobia, defined by the Fourth Edition of the *Diagnostic and Statistical Manual of Mental Disorders* as "excessive or unreasonable fear of an object, place, animal, person, or situation." Like my fear of utensils, plates, and cooking pots, this boy's phobia was pretty debilitating. Buttons are everywhere, like forks. Buttons filled the boy up with disgust and fear, of hugging his mother, of brushing up against a schoolmate, of letting his own school uniform touch his body.

And so the button boy became a case history. In 2002, Lissette M. Saavedra, MS, and Wendy K. Silverman, PhD, published a case study about the boy in the *Journal of the American Academy of Child and Adolescent Psychiatry* because they had treated him successfully by going beyond conventional methods—which involved gradual exposure to the feared object. They noticed that fear alone did not drive their young patient's phobia. He responded to buttons also with an extreme *disgust.* He called them "gross" and "disgusting," though he couldn't pinpoint the source of their grossness, except to declare they "emitted unpleasant odors" (Saavedra and Silverman's words, not his).

The boy and his mother reported what they imagined to be the origin of the phobia. Four years prior, during kindergarten, the boy was working on a project pasting buttons to a board. He ran out of buttons and went to get more from a bowl on his teacher's desk. The bowl fell and the buttons poured all over him. The experience was "distressful," but it didn't lead to an immediate phobia. The boy's avoidance of buttons developed gradually.

This detail signals a controversy in the psychological literature on phobias. Some researchers believe a phobia is associated with a distressing or traumatic event. Others argue that most phobias are more complex than this, that they are formed out of a network of events and associations, often without any rational link between the fear and a single memory or experience. Saavedra and Silverman, by drawing our attention to disgust, want to shift the focus from *associative learning* to *evaluative learning*. Rather than predicting a danger attached to buttons, their young patient is evaluating a seemingly neutral object in such a way that he comes to perceive it as threatening, or disgusting. Disgust makes it reasonable to fear an object in the absence of any realistic harm associated with it. They make a reasonable argument, but I keep comparing him to me, wondering what network of events could have produced the boy's intense fear.

At first, the boy's treatment was behavioral. His therapists exposed him to buttons, sometimes just loose buttons, sometimes buttons on his mother's clothes while he hugged her. He rated his responses using a "feeling thermometer." When Saavedra and Silverman noticed his feeling of disgust increased with exposure, they decided to try a cognitive approach. They asked the boy to "imagine buttons falling on him, how they looked, felt, and smelled." Then they asked how the images made him feel. The boy's disgust ratings fell. His specific phobia "was in remission" at the six- and twelve-month follow-up sessions. By simply imagining buttons, repeatedly, in a safe setting, the boy learned to re-evaluate them. He had become desensitized through habituation. He no longer avoided buttons at the expense of living. This was a distinctly unpsychoanalytic approach. His cure did not involve any examination of fearful experiences that may have caused the phobia.

The same happened for me, but without the help of Saavedra and Silverman, the route was less direct and took years. Still, I finally—mostly—got over my phobias. In some ways, life is cognitive therapy, just less routinized and concentrated. Reading and writing about the button boy helped too. I wonder who and where he is now. I have a fantasy that he'll read this and contact me.

Nearly four decades later, I'm in Escondido's welfare office—technically Health and Human Services. I spent my childhood willing myself out of rooms where poverty congregates. But my mom fell, she's got thirty-seven stitches in her skull, and she's having trouble speaking, walking, and remembering. She can't afford food.

I spent ten years, from childhood into early adulthood, unable to speak the words *mom* or *love*. The words became a phobia, along with certain utensils, plates, pans, and cigarettes. Like the button boy, I've long since habituated myself into a mostly functional relationship with the words (and the rest of it). I love my mom. She needs my help.

Nobody can tell me what may have happened, or may be happening, in my mom's brain. They can tell me the surgeon removed a large blood clot—*subdermal hematoma*—from the left hemisphere of her cerebral cortex. The surgery was pretty successful, but she is haunted by a paranoid hallucination she had in the hospital. Several doctors and attendants surrounded her bed, wielding medical instruments. They were there to kill her. They talked about it right in front of her. She knows now it didn't happen, but she can't stop feeling it. She tells every doctor, nurse, therapist, and social worker who interviews her. She needs them to know. They don't know about the hallucination she had when she was sixteen and ate too much gypsum weed. Doug sat with her in a closet while she described the federal agents surrounding her bedroom, climbing from the roof through her bedroom window. Her brain is telling another version of the harrowing story, one of the set pieces in our family lore.

"I could have died," she says. "The doctors say they can't believe I'm doing so well."

"You're Ralph's daughter," I say. We laugh together. *Neves* spelled backwards is lucky *seven*. My mom is alive, despite the odds.

Sometime in my early thirties, I started to earn enough money to count as middle class. But it seems unlikely I'll ever earn enough money to support my mom, especially through a medical crisis.

My mom lives off a tiny Social Security check each month, and her health insurance premiums, deducted automatically, cut that just about in half. Billy, her husband, earns some money and gets VA benefits because he served in Vietnam. Their debt swallows most of it. Given how her injury went down, it's not clear she'll stay with Billy. Doug has called several times, urging her to leave him. My uncle Gary floats the idea of an intervention. My aunt Jennifer offers to let her move in. But my mom's in no state to make decisions.

I'm pretty pissed at Billy. My mom fell on a Saturday, went to the hospital Monday. They operated on her brain that night. Billy finally called to let me know on Thursday. His plan was that she would recover and he would let me know afterward.

Being Billy is exhausting and expensive. Partly because being poor is exhausting and expensive. If you're poor and you get arrested for driving drunk, you can't pay bail fees so you sit in a jail while your car sits in an impound lot, accumulating fees you can't pay when you get out. When you go to court, your penalty is fees and the loss of your license. If you get caught driving to work, more jail, more fees, the car back in impound. When you can't pay, the car stays in impound until the fees are more than the car is worth. You lose the car. In the meantime, late fees stack up on every bill you can't pay. You max out credit cards, get short-term loans with outlandish interest rates. You can't afford the fees that come with filing for bankruptcy. Life becomes about soaking up just enough debt each month.

I'm sitting in a waiting room built to house systems to help poor people live with the ones that punish. The social worker at my mom's rehab facility, where I spend my afternoons watching The Food Network with her, suggested my mom would be eligible for benefits she didn't know about. As a kid, I blamed my family for a lifetime of questionable choices. But their actions no longer define where I live or eat, so it's easier to see them as responses to a mess of systems built on systems. I want to help my mom navigate this mess.

This is my second of four visits this week. I showed up yesterday, but I only managed to wait two hours for some paperwork and the advice to arrive today at 6:45 am. The office opens at seven. Getting here early increases my odds of talking to a human being. Everybody has gotten this advice. The place is packed. We all wait around on new-looking office furniture for the rites of passage on the road to welfare. This means taking a number and responding when it flashes on a screen. This happens several times before you're granted an interview—the moment when the real work gets done. Nobody seems to know why, not even the people calling the numbers. These people, called consultants, are invariably kind, often apologetic. They ask questions, tap keyboards, and tell you what to do next, which is mostly sit back down and wait for your number to flash again. Everybody learns the routine or gives up. It turns out that persistence—the kind you need to earn a degree or launch a business—is crucial for getting welfare benefits.

Most people wait patiently. I notice the young mothers and pregnant teenagers, for obvious reasons. Their kids are me. I am their kids. A couple of them have men with them. These kids are not me. A couple my mom's age, apparently married, sits opposite me.

When something startling happens, most of us ignore it. A butch woman with scabs on her face and arms runs through the room, yelling the name of a friend she's looking for. Security guards chase her. She yells at them until she cries. A young couple is called to up to front desk, as we all are from time to time. As the consultant fiddles with her computer, the guy—his neck tattoo aggressively on display—licks his finger and sticks it in his girlfriend's ear. She doesn't react. He does it again as she begins talking to the consultant. Then he traces his finger down her neck and inside her bra strap.

What is in that girl's mind, or her life, that prevents her from reacting? It's not something I can know.

I've been sitting next to two cholo guys in loose chino shorts, long wife beaters, and flannels buttoned only at the top, their hair slicked back, their tattoos of their grandmothers. It's the same look guys like them have sported since I was a kid. There's something impressive and comforting about the fact that it's endured this long. One of the guys brought a bag of Jack in the Box tacos, so the whole place smells like the mystery meat and American cheese I loved eating when I was a kid. God, I loved those tacos. I didn't know you could buy them before 7 a.m. He must have at least twenty in the bag. After about three hours, one of the guys gets called for his interview. As he gets up, he tells his buddy, "If we get out of here early, want to hit up Walmart?"

When he's gone, his friend offers me the bag of tacos. "Bought way too many," he says.

I'm tempted, but I'm not hungry, I'm shy, and I'm not sure about Jack in the Box tacos that have been sitting in their own grease for three hours. It's recommended that you eat that grease fresh. I love that he broke the somber bubble of this clean place to make the offer.

When I finally get an interview, a few details work in my favor. My mom is disabled, cognitively and physically. Her neurologist cannot predict how long this will last. She'll regain of most her ability to write and spell, to walk and make sentences, but I don't know that yet. Our caseworker doesn't want to know. It's clear that she, and most of the people here, want to help. Helping means translating bureaucratic hurdles into workable solutions. If you want their help, you have to accept the hurdles they can't navigate. You have to show up four days in a row. You have to make endless calls. You have to enlist nonprofit organizations who have direct lines to human caseworkers because the official numbers connect you to robots with no knowledge of the lost paperwork stalling approval of benefits.

Our caseworker is interested in the couple who were living at my mom's house when she fell. Living there, as far as I can tell, mostly meant partying there. She hardly knew the couple. Billy, my mom's husband, was doing them a favor, but he was away on a job. I'll never know exactly what happened, except the couple neglected to take her to a doctor or hospital. She remained in her bed with blood clotting on her brain for forty-eight hours before anybody called an ambulance. By that time, Billy was home. The chronology is hazy.

"Neglect," the caseworker tells me, "is abuse. This is elder abuse." And this works in our favor. It also helps that my mom and Billy have been living without gas and electricity for the past few months. The home environment is not safe.

I leave feeling proud and hopeful. Our caseworker deputized me as my mom's official representative. She's promised to expedite the benefits. She's made it pretty clear my mom will qualify. I don't know yet that it will take months to secure these benefits, that I'll have to get myself power of attorney and find a nonprofit organization whose job it is to help me navigate the Health and Human Services bureaucracy—a system built on top of other systems—to track down missing paperwork.

Because I don't know all this, I can tell my mom truthfully that it looks like the benefits will come through. I can show her my folder stuffed with paperwork. She can report her good fortune to doctors, physical therapists, cognitive therapists, and language therapists who punctuate our days in the rehab facility.

It's pretty boring in rehab. One of our diversions is poring over the menus that allow my mom to choose breakfasts, lunches, and dinners for the week. Prime rib on Wednesdays reminds her of the luxury she grew up with. When the meals arrive, she wants to share them with me. The old phobias return. I can't get myself to eat off the plastic trays. I won't touch the weirdly small forks. I use the excuse that there's a great taco place a block away, in the spot where I had my first job, back when it was Froggy's Donuts.

My mom's doctor comes in once a week. She calls him Dr. J. We've known him for nearly twenty years. He treated Nanny during the early stages of her brain tumor. He confers with Sandy, the social worker, and she confers with me. During the last visit I witness, he says to my mom, "I'm going to ask you a question because I don't know the answer. Are you a drinker?" She says she drinks some. "How much?" he asks. "Just wine," she says. "Doesn't matter," he says. "How much?" She tells him maybe a bottle most nights. "That's called an alcoholic," he says. "You need to go to AA." These are words nobody's ever said.

After he leaves, my mom says to me, "I can't believe he said that in front of you." She hates AA, she tells me. Dr. J's sure she was drunk when she fell. She insists otherwise.

"He wants to help you," I manage to say. I don't have it in me to do much more. I can navigate systems built on systems, but I don't know how to talk to my mom about the possibility that she may be an alcoholic.

With power of attorney, I'm a new kind of son. I secure my mom's benefits, months after returning to New York. For now, she'll have medical insurance and a card that lets her buy $194 in groceries each month. We bond through phone conversations about the constant flow of new forms that threaten cancellation or promise new benefits, like free car services for trips to the doctor or pharmacy. But Billy's friends are still partying at their house when she returns home. The gas and electricity are still shut off.

14

POLICE ON OUR BACKS

Mona's barks are so frantic that we never hear the car in the driveway. The three knocks, when we hear them, are authoritative, steady, goal-oriented. "Go see who it is," my mom says.

I hold Mona's collar and peek through the window before I answer. It's two guys, both with moustaches, one with red hair, one with black, in square, pressed clothes, holding thick notebooks. I swing open the door like it's no big deal, Mona in hand, snarling. "Can I help you?"

"Who is it?" my mom calls, approaching.

"Will you get the dog under control, please?" one of the guys says.

"Boog, take Mona into your room," my mom says.

Mona keeps barking the whole time, even in my room. I leave the door open and try to listen, but I can't hear much. At one point, one of the guys, Red, says, "You are going to tell me that you don't know where your mother is?"

"We're not in touch," my mom lies.

"Was that the police?" I ask, after they leave.

"Sort of," my mom says. "The tax police."

"What did they want?"

"You don't know anything," she says. "Okay? Nothing. If I tell you, will you promise never to say anything?"

"Okay."

"Your Nanny hasn't paid her taxes. That's why they were here."

"They're not going to put her in jail, are they?"

"Let's hope not."

JP, a known felon, has moved into our shack, and Charlie, another known felon, keeps calling the house. But when the police come, they're after Nanny. This is life, the one you get.

"You're gonna be rich. You can buy all the Shaun Cassidy records you want," JP tells me. He's getting me a sheep for Christmas.

"Where do we get it?" I ask.

"From a sheep farm. We'll get it when it's just a wee lamb. That way you can raise it, and it will do anything you say."

JP disappeared for a while and returned with a new girlfriend, acting weirder than ever. Her name is Sue Ellen. They're both living in our shack. JP is our Schneider. He keeps saying he'll protect us from Charlie.

"Really?" I like the idea of a sheep who does anything I say because he loves me like a mother.

"Yeah, so when you take it to somebody's lawn, it'll eat quick. So you can earn more money faster. You can do all the lawns in Del Dios. You ever notice how many empty fields there are around here, full of wild mustard and weeds up to your neck?"

"I guess," I say.

"You can clear all those out. Plus, and this is the best part, you won't have to buy the sheep any food. He'll make you money feeding himself. It's the ultimate business."

"JP?" Sue Ellen emerges from the shed. She's tall, at least six feet, with a brown bob and bangs that don't quite feather but definitely curl. She wears no makeup and has strong, clear skin like a farm girl. "I'm from Peoria," she tells everybody. "That's in the Midwest." Her cheeks are pink, almost ruddy. Her teeth are big and white. You'd never know she was pregnant from looking at her flat stomach. But she is.

"I'm getting a baby sheep," I say.

"A lamb?" she asks.

"Yeah," I say. "To mow lawns."

"What lawns?" she asks. "Around here?"

"Fields," JP says. "All these Goddamn empty fields full of mustard—"

"And wildflowers?" she asks.

"Exactly," he says.

"Fantastic," she says. "I like a young entrepreneur."

"A what?" I ask.

"An entrepreneur," she says. "Somebody with good business ideas and the balls to make it happen. Say it with me."

"On-trah-pruh-noor."

"Excellent," she says. "Now, I have an idea. Just mow the weeds, but leave the wildflowers and cut them into patterns you can only see from the sky."

"From airplanes?" I ask, excited.

"Yes," she says. "You'll be the Michelangelo of Del Dios."

"She's getting all intellectual on us," JP says. "We're just trying to run a business."

Everybody but me knew what was up with JP. He'd OD'd. On PCP. It filled his head with dreams of lucrative sheep. I dreamed his dream, but ended up with a more mundane reality: a guinea pig. Which may have been fitting, because I was sort of a guinea pig in the big hippie experiment.

Smoking pot laced with phencyclidine, one joint, then two, then a half dozen, then five or six dozen over the course of a week or a month, is an experiment in brain ingenuity. PCP swims through lung tissue and surfs the bloodstream, crouching under the curl that forms as it approaches the blood-brain barrier and skimming right into the tube, no problem. Now one with the elements in the cerebral matter, PCP divides itself into multiple clone surfers and scatters. Surfers appear, as if from nowhere, in the posterior cingulate cortex, a section interconnected with the limbic system, pulsing at a theta rhythm matching output coming from the hippocampus, luring information destined for other routes into a detour. "Chill in here, bro. It's rad."

These surfers deal in fate changes. That particle of implicit memory they just liberated, whose day job had been to modulate the swing of a hammer for maximum efficiency—pretty square, right?—now lends its swinging arc to the pulsing feeling of optimistic melancholy the guy who smoked this PCP has been drowning in. Change the fates of enough particles, and the guy will start to flange and strobe. This guy smoking the laced joints has always been into rock, the freakier shit like Dylan, Pink Floyd, and The Moody Blues, but his world is becoming pure disco and he likes it.

Another set of surfer clones, stealth operators, travel an invisible path to the retrosplenial cortex, where they will fuck with his two-dimensional perspective. As days go by, this guy notices that he's starting to see himself from outside, like the real him, his consciousness or whatever, is out in the air, watching all the stupid shit he does: fucking chicks, building shit, dreaming up schemes and telling people about them. Even though a lot of what he sees seems pretty stupid, it makes him realize how perfect human beings are. Their stupid shit is all part of the plan, and it's when you resist that things get fucked up. Go with it. Enjoy the ride. He heard that somewhere.

PCP's surfer clones first found their way into human bloodstreams in the 1950s, when they were used as a disassociative anesthetic: they released patients from pain by releasing them from the selves who felt the pain. The surfers limit the reuptake of an array of neurochemicals. They also inhibit the action of glutamate by blocking NMDA receptors, which help cells die when their time has come. All this inhibition causes a glitch. The clones fuck with cell mortality, making vampires of cells who should have perished and let the system evolve in their absence. The vampires orchestrate PCP's notorious sensory shutdown, or, spun differently, sensory *concentration*:

the dirt yards and shacks and houses and people walking around on them and living in them distilled to a strobing essence that, from the angle of the consciousness in the air, adds up to one sublime stupid shit plan for universal convergence.

In 1965, when too many patients woke up schizophrenic, catatonic, or unable to spit words out whole, formal controls were enforced to keep the PCP surfers out of brains. So they went underground, found better settings and more willing subjects. The ingenuity of the PCP surfers lies in their clones and vampires, whose cerebral reconstruction smoothes an almost transparent layer of strobing, flanging reality over what had been there before.

If ether is real, JP has definitely fucked his up.

The second time the police come to the Lake Drive house, they're in uniforms.

It starts with a stuttered knock on the door. Not the cops—a terrified girl.

"Can I help you? Oh my God," my mom says when she opens the door. "Come in. Hurry."

The girl, in nothing but a torn T-shirt, arms wrapped around her chest, follows my mom to the kitchen. She looks like a bleached, tanned Leather Tuscadero, about nineteen, with shagged, bleached, permed hair. She's heaving tears. "He raped me," she says.

"Who? What?"

"Some guy." She points toward the hill, where there's nothing but sage brush and poison oak. "Back there. In a ditch."

"Jas, stay in your room," my mom says. I can hear the girl heaving and my mom talking quietly. The guy was giving her a ride. She didn't really know him. No, she doesn't want to press charges. She doesn't want any cops. I can hear the bathtub running. Something about it sounds really hot, the kind of bath that burns when you step into it.

"We really should call the police," my mom says.

"No," the girl says. "It's happened before. I turned the guy in. I had to testify, and he got off. He got the fuck off. I don't want any cops."

I can hear the girl stepping into the bathtub and more talking. Then footsteps. "Jas, you okay?"

"Yeah," I say.

"We have to help this girl." She walks back to the kitchen and picks up the phone. "I have an emergency to report," she says. "There's been a rape."

With the police, it's always those same three solid knocks. This time we know why they're here. Two officers in uniforms sit down in the living room with my mom and the girl, dressed in my mom's clothes, which are all too small. I know I'm not supposed to, but part of me likes these cops. They smell strong. The breath in their voices whispers protection, maybe even salvation. They have a fatherly quality, and though I don't know it, would never admit it, I want that.

By now, I recognize those three knocks. We put up a Christmas tree, and I've been busy all morning rearranging the decorations, so I'm right near the front door. It's two men, different ones this time. The blond one is in black shoes, green polyester slacks, and a white shirt, the brown one in brown shoes, black polyester slacks, and a yellow shirt. They've got those fat notebooks again. I'm worried about Nanny, but I like the way the police look. I like their confident authority.

"Can I help you?" I ask, copying the voice my mom uses to talk to police. Mona yelps like somebody's beating her. We have to keep her tied up out by JP's shed because she's been freaking out lately, attacking anybody she doesn't know.

"Hey there, Tiger. Is your mother home?" Blond asks. "That dog okay?"

"She's okay," I say, lying. "My mom's at Cheech's," I say.

"At Cheech's?"

"Right there," I say, looking toward the green house in back of ours.

"Hey Tiger, will you show us the way?"

"Okay," I say, not knowing what else to do, and start walking to Cheech's house. Blond and Brown follow, Mona straining at her leash, yelping herself into the air like she might fly.

"That dog should see a vet," Brown says. They follow me up Cheech's steps, but I run right in, leaving them at the landing, worried about Nanny, worried about Mona.

My mom is sitting with Cheech and Randy. Cheech is smoking, of course. "Well, hello, Jason," she says. "Don't bother knocking."

"Some police are here," I say, knowing the adults are going to freak out.

"Cops?" Cheech says. "What for?"

Three knocks. "They knock like fuckin' cops," Cheech says, walking to the door.

"Can I help you?"

"Is Cathy Messin here?" Brown asks.

"Sure is, but her name's Cathy Neves now."

"Can we speak with her, please?" Blond asks.

"Cat, it's for you."

"Ma'am, I'm Agent Brown and this is Agent Blond. Secret Service." They flash their badges. "Your dog seems to be in some distress." We've all gotten used to the yelping, but you have to admit the lunging toward the sky is pretty weird.

"I'm taking her to the vet," my mom says. I wonder if it's true.

"But that's not why we're here," Blond says. "We're here to discuss a Stanley Messin. We believe you were married to him."

"Yeah?" she says.

"Mr. Messin was heard making a threat on the life of President Ford."

"What?" my mom says.

They're not here about Nanny. They're going to arrest Stanley. I'm really starting to like police.

"Goddamn Stanley Messin kill the fucking ex-president?" Cheech says. "Now that's hilarious."

"We take these threats seriously," Brown says.

"Not this one, honey," Cheech says. "It's a fuckin' joke."

"Cheech," my mom says, shooting her a *shut up* look.

"Is that your impression, ma'am," Blond says to my mom, "that the threat is not serious?"

"Stanley just likes to talk. He gets drunk and talks."

"Thank you for your time, ma'am. We'll be in touch if we have further questions."

"Okay," she says, shutting the door.

We all go to the window and watch Brown and Blond pull out of the driveway, Mona's yelps deepening to a growl. At the side of the shed, we can see JP and his friend Sonny looking down at the ground like two archeologists who just found buried treasure.

"What's up with them?" Randy asks.

"JP is out of his mind," Cheech says. "He buy you that sheep yet, Jas?"

"No," I say, starting to think he never will. "I could have been making money by now."

"Don't count on it," she replies.

"Cheech," my mom reprimands.

"Well, he's out of his fucking mind. He shouldn't get the kid's hopes up. What the fuck are they doin', anyway?"

When we get down there, we see they're kneeling over a pile of dog poop. Mona poop. "What's up?" Cheech asks. What's up is that the poop is dotted with shreds of what looks like construction paper with colored patterns on it. "Oh, shit," Cheech says.

JP's eyes are wide like a toddler's. His mouth's a little open. "She found it," he says.

"What?" my mom asks.

"The acid Sonny buried."

"That was two hundred hits," Sonny says.

"What?" my mom says.

"That's it. In Mona's shit," JP says, pointing at the pile of dried-up Mona poop from which Sonny is prying little bits of mangled orange and blue paper.

"Goddamn dog ODs," Cheech says, "and the cat leaves another dead fuckin' rabbit at the back door."

Everybody looks. Misty's not around, but her gift is curled up on the back step, its tiny ear sticking up and its white ball of a tail. Mona's on her side now, exhausted, whimpering.

Mona wags her body down Lake Drive, a frothy rage growing out of the discomfort she feels with the freedom. JP and Sue Ellen were sitting on the porch, sunning their new baby, Jimmy Freddy. Mona had the same idea. When the sun is straight up at the top of the sky, it makes her black fur shine in this way she can feel beneath the skin. She likes to lie with her two front paws stretched straight out in front of her snout. The baby was right in her line of vision, on Sue Ellen's lap, naked, a pink ball of fat with droopy blue eyes. It was something about the squishy velvet of his skin. Mona pounced in one straight glide, her teeth bared so that all she had to do was clamp and she could feel her teeth sink in before Sue Ellen, screaming and hitting her hard on the top of her head, pulled the baby into the shack.

She can still feel the sun under her skin, and she can taste the baby's blood under her tongue, where some of it lodged. She passes Riley, whose lanky Irish Wolfhound gait and greasy matted fur intimidate her into snarling. When he just trots past, she releases a high-pitched bark, the kind that makes an animal sound like she's lost control.

She's just passed the mile point when she sees the cage—a wooden rectangle on stilts covered in chicken wire. She has to climb a bank of ice plant to reach it, but the fur poking through, a light grey dusted with cocoa at the ends, is worth the effort. Her paws get tangled in the vines more than once, but she just keeps her eye on the fur, which moves almost imperceptibly every few seconds, like good bait should.

The humiliation of the tangled ice plant still in her eyes, she reprises her pounce, diving straight at the cage and breaking one of the old wood posts that it holds together. The Angora inside is trying to adjust to the new slope in its floor when it sees Mona's snarl invade. Barking maniacally now, Mona goes straight for a mouthful of wide round eyes and droopy cocoa ears. The crush of bones and the stringy resistance of muscle become the sum of her reality while she chews the carcass, until she hears a scream a lot like Sue Ellen's, but deeper. She dives straight down the ice plant and lands hard on the concrete of Lake Drive. Her mouth is a matted mess of cotton-dry fur and salty blood.

I'm in the bunk, thinking about Mona and the leprosy sloughing between my toes and on my knees and elbows. Mona's gone to live on a farm. That's what my mom told me, at least. I'm picturing her running around with the sheep JP never gave me. I know my mom's probably lying.

I saw a movie about a leper colony, and now I'm sure I've got it. I think over each curve of each toe and each pore on each knee and each elbow. I think think think leprosy while the sun buries into the hills to the west, the stars climb the blackening sky and twinkle and just keep twinkling second after second. I think the leprosy away, realizing it's just my imagination, just athlete's foot, just dry skin, a wart at worst. I think the leprosy back to feeling real and fatal. I'm not sure if I'm awake or asleep. I'm not sure if I've slept at all. I think the leprosy until the sky fades lavender and eats the twinkle out of the stars, and I feel my mom's hand on my head. "Santa's been here. Boog, Santa's been here."

The bike is there, under the tree, a silver Schwinn with a black banana seat eighteen inches long, a big green bow on the handlebars.

There's another big package. "Don't you want to see what your dad brought?" my mom asks.

That's when Charlie walks in from the kitchen. His hair is wet. He seems nervous. He's early. Nobody else is coming until ten. JP said he'd protect us from this, but he also said he'd get us a sheep.

"Go ahead, open it." Charlie says this gently and slowly, as though I need coaxing.

I start wrestling with scotch tape and wrapping paper. I can tell from the shape and the heaviness that it's the electric racetrack I've been asking for. My mom said we could afford the bike or the race-track, but I got both. This puts me on a par with Paul. I've always suspected that kids with two parents get what they want. To them, bikes are not toys. You just have them. I'm ripping the plastic wrap with my teeth. I've got the box open.

"Wow," I hear myself say. "A racetrack! It's got everything. I wanna put it together before Nanny comes. Can I do it now?" This is not so bad.

"It's your racetrack," my mom says. "Whaddayou say?"

"Thank you."

"Want some help?" Charlie asks.

"Okay." We connect the tracks, following the diagrams with only a little trouble. The track is shaped like a figure eight, part of it raised off the ground. "You be blue, and I'll be red," I order. We learn how fast is too fast. You have to be careful to keep the cars from racing right off the edge of the track. Nanny shows up with my mom's cousin and her kids. Sue Ellen and JP come over and everyone coos over the baby. I hear them talking about Misty, how they hope she's on a hunting excursion and hasn't been eaten by a coyote. The turkey turns gold. Nanny makes the gravy and cranberries, whips cream with Grand Marnier for the pumpkin pie. I half notice that she stays away from the living room. We race the cars to the beat of the two records Nanny brought me for Christmas, Olivia Newton-John's *Totally Hot* and Andy Gibb's *Shadow Dancing*. We race the cars, then eat. Dishes are cleared away, food wrapped up into doggie bags for people to take home. Dishes are done. People get in cars and go.

Charlie looms but eventually leaves, with or without ceremony. I don't remember.

We get a few more phone calls. My mom sounds tense. She uses the word *heroin*. Then we stop hearing from him. At least when the police catch up with him, it's not at our house.

15

"HE REMINDED ME OF YOU."

July 16, 1995, 7:35 p.m.

Phone rings. "Hi, what are you doing?" my mom asks.

"Studying for my comps?"

"Your what?"

"My comprehensive exams. I have to know the entire history of American and British literature from the Anglo-Saxons to the present." I've been in New York two years. I came for graduate school. I knew right away I'd stay.

"That's over my head."

"The last fifteen hundred years."

"I've got something to tell you. I heard a rumor that Charlie's out of jail. He's looking for you." Just like he always said he would. "I think he's living with your grandparents."

"Really? Gramps is speaking to him?"

"I guess. I don't know, Jason."

"Well, he doesn't have any way to find me. How'd you hear?"

"He's been hanging out with Craig."

"What? Craig's hanging out with him? Why?"

"They were friends."

"That was twenty-seven years of prison ago."

July 16, 8:04 p.m.

Phone rings. It's Nanny.

"Did you talk to your mother?"

"Yes. I heard. I can't believe he'd show up now."

"Stay away from him, Jason."

"Don't worry."

July 24, 11:10 a.m.

Phone rings. Mom says, "Charlie called me. He wanted to come by."

"You're kidding. Why? What did you say?"

"He wants to find you."

"What did you say?"

"That you live in New York but that I wouldn't give him your information."

"Good."

July 24, 11:14 a.m.

I call Nanny. "She told him I live in New York."

"I don't know why she has anything to do with that imbecile. I tell Craig to stay away from him."

"Craig has seen him?"

"He came by here a few times."

"What? You saw him? A *few times*?"

"I told Craig I didn't want anything to do with him."

July 26, 10:45 p.m.

Phone rings. It's Nichole. "Hi, Toug."

"Hi."

"My mom talked to your mom. She says Charlie is out of jail."

"I know. She actually seems to want me to talk to him. What the hell is up with her?"

"I don't know. It's weird."

August 2, 2:00 p.m.

Phone rings. Mom. "Your dad came by."

"My what?"

"Charlie."

"Why'd you call him my dad?"

"Well, he is."

"That's debatable."

"He wants to see you."

"So I've heard."

"I don't know what to tell him."

"'Sorry, no.' How 'bout that?"

"Jason."

"Now you want me to see him?"

"I just want to know what you think."

"I wish he would disappear."

August 3, 11:12 a.m.

The phone rings. It's Nanny. "Now she wants me to see him. Can you believe this?"

"Your mother is cuckoo. She always was. She has no sense. She never did."

August 29, 9:25 p.m.

Phone rings. "Your dad's been coming by. I've been helping him out."

"With what?"

"He's clean. He's going to, what do you call it? Narcotics Anonymous. He goes to a psychiatrist. I think he's changed. Why else would your grandparents take him in?"

"I don't know. I don't know. I can't talk about this now. Tomorrow is the first day of comps."

"Your what?"

"My comprehensive exams. It's a big deal."

"All I'm saying is that maybe it would be good for you to talk to him."

"I don't think I want to."

"It's up to you. You don't have to talk to him, but I gave him your address."

"You did what? Why?"

"I wouldn't give him your phone number."

"Thanks. I've got to go."

October 3, 4:15 p.m.

A letter comes. It's addressed "Dear Jason" and the first line says something about "my only son."

I spend several sessions with Susan, my therapist, analyzing it. I object to the handwriting. The promises seem unrealistic. I feel manipulated. He just wants to be my friend. He knows he can't make up for the past. The letter is signed "With Hope, Your Father."

November 14, 6:30 p.m.

I call Nichole. "So you know?"

"What?"

"About your mom and Charlie?"

"She's been 'helping' him or something. She fucking gave him my address. He sent me a letter."

"So you don't know?"

"What?"

"They came into Nordstrom. I was stuck behind the counter. I met him."

"What? What? You met him? You talked to him?"

"They're going out."

"Going out?"

"I think he's living with her."

"What?"

"I know. You know what's weird? He reminded me of you."

"Really?" I am evaporating.

"He's kind of good-looking. He's like quiet and sensitive. He hunches a little, like you."

"I can't handle this. I can't believe you met him."

"She wants to bring him to Thanksgiving."

"No. What? Are you kidding? No."

"That's what she said."

"What did you say?"

"I don't know."

"Please, tell her no way. Please. This cannot happen. Everyone is going to sit around and eat Thanksgiving dinner with this guy. No. No."

"Okay, I'll tell her. Are you okay?"

"No. She's fucking crazy."

November 16, 12:50 p.m.

I call Mom. A man answers: "Hello." His voice is soft and slow-sounding. I hang up.

November 17, 6:41 p.m.

Phone rings. "Jason?"

"Nichole told me you want to bring him to Thanksgiving."

"He has nowhere to go."

"Who cares?"

"You are so cruel."

"*I* am? I—?"

"Can't you give him a second chance?"

"What? Why? I absolutely forbid you to bring him to Nichole's house. That guy is not having Thanksgiving with my entire family. It's not happening."

"Jason, I am a person who gives people a second chance. Isn't that the way I raised you?"

The conversation lasts forty-five minutes and involves a lot of screaming.

November 17, 7:30 p.m.

I call Nanny. "She wants to bring him to Nichole's for Thanksgiving."

"I won't talk to her. I told her that as long as she is with that man, I won't talk to her."

"She thinks we're mean."

"Does she remember what I went through to get her away from him the first time? Does she remember how he beat her black and blue?"

"Apparently not. She gives people second chances. That's what she said."

"Oh, bullshit."

November 24

I spend Thanksgiving in Connecticut with Dave, my boyfriend of two years. It's uneventful. I don't tell anybody but him what's going on.

November 25, 12:15 p.m.

I call Nichole. "Did she bring him?"

"She got mad and boycotted."

Nichole, I notice, didn't forbid his coming.

December 8, 4:40 p.m.

A second letter arrives. This one begins, "My childhood…" and focuses on how harsh and distant Gramps was when Charlie was a kid. There isn't a word I can type that will convey the massive swirling frustration mixed with sadness that is erupting out of my skin.

I try to figure out what to do. All I can do is ignore the letters. I draft a couple of responses. They're full of rage. Dave and Susan tell me not to send them.

March 3, 1996, 10:24 p.m.

The phone rings. It's Mom. She's crying. "Your dad is gone."

"Don't call him that."

"He's manic depressive. He gets so out of control. I don't think your grandparents want him there anymore."

"Why are you telling me this?"

April 13, 11:10 a.m.

"Hi, Nanny. Happy birthday. You're seventy-four today."

"Jesus Christ, Jason. Don't remind me."

"What are you going to do?"

"Your mother wanted me to come over for dinner, but Charlie's there again."

"He's back?"

"Apparently."

June 12, 3:12 p.m.

Phone rings. "Hi, Jason."

"Hi."

"I'm moving."

"Really. Where?"

"Lake Wolford. They have these cute little trailers, but they're not really like trailers. They have these California rooms attached to them. Mine's on a hill with a view of the lake. Your dad is helping me build a deck out of crates he got from a construction job. You buy the trailer and lease the plot."

Yes, I know how trailer parks work. "When do you move?"

"In three weeks. Your dad's helping me with the down payment."

June 12, 3:50 p.m.

I call Nanny. "The down payment? It's been almost a year. Can you believe this?"

"Auntie Florence is giving her most of the down payment."

"What? Really? How did—?"

"I don't know. I told her not to ask. I'm staying out of it. She'll be sorry. Florence doesn't like when people don't pay her back." Nanny knows this from experience.

July 1, 1:00 p.m.

Phone rings. "We're here. It's so cute. You should see it, Jason."

"How long have you been there?"

"A week almost. You should see all the work your dad is doing."

"Did you get a new phone number?"

She gives it to me even though I can't call it.

December 5, 8:20 p.m.

Phone rings. She's crying. "The police just came, Jason. I don't know what to do. I had to get a restraining order against your dad."

The conversation lasts an hour. She tells me he got mad because she didn't want to have sex. He said he doesn't know what his life has come to "when my old lady doesn't even want to touch me." She tells me, again, about how out of control he gets and how he is probably bipolar. She tells me she's worried Charlie's parents are mad at her. She tells me I should never have anything to do with him.

16

JUNKY

When Charlie died in 2011, we'd been in touch for several years.

With the death of my biological father, I learned that the State of California takes biology seriously. California has that much in common with William Burroughs, perhaps America's most famous junky, who wrote: "Junk is not a kick. It is a way of life."

Charlie had been shooting heroin into his bloodstream since before I was born. His absence was an inexorable presence when I was growing up. When he wasn't in prison, he'd sometimes get in touch, but more often he wouldn't. He never acted like a father. We rarely met face to face, but we haunted each other's lives. So it was a shock to learn that the State of California named me the person with authority over my father's remains because fifty percent of his DNA lived in me. According to the State, I was next of kin, more "next" than his mother or sister. My signature was necessary for the "final disposition" of his dead body. This was statespeak for what would be done with him.

Genes are not nothing. When I finally reconnected with Charlie as an adult, I learned that Nichole was right: many of my mannerisms were his. He looked like a cross between his father and me. His shoulders stooped a little, suggesting a spine bent like mine. He was soft-spoken and smart. He was wry in a dark, dry way that I recognized. I have some of him in me, and he had some of me in him. But genes aren't everything, either. My father insisted on refusing social graces. He fought with people. He seemed to insist on making others uncomfortable. He broke into houses and stole shit to get money for drugs. He spent a lifetime resenting his own father and redeemed himself by helping to nurse him through a long series of illnesses. This is part of what convinced me to see him after ignoring his sporadic letters for several years. When we finally met, he said to me, "Just before he died, I found out my father was not who I thought he was."

I'm not sure who my father was, but I learned about his death in a way that was as indirect and convoluted as my relationship with him. My husband, Dave, got an email from my cousin's husband, giving a phone number and asking me to call about a "family matter." Dave forwarded it to me, and I hesitated over it for a couple of hours. It was puzzling. My cousin had contact information for me. My grandmother had my phone number. None of them had met Dave yet. Why did he get this email? I don't know my father's family well, even though they'd always been kind to me. We had a formal, intermittent relationship. They couldn't have been more different from the people who raised me. Where my family went to happy hour, they went to church. Where my family listened to records, they read books and attended operas. Where my family lived from day to day, they had jobs, pensions, and insurance plans. I still don't know why they contacted Dave rather than finding me directly, but somehow that seems typical of a story about this family.

I dialed the first number, then another, then another. I got the story in pieces, from my cousin and her husband, my father's sister and her husband, and finally my grandmother. Charlie had been found dead in the parking lot of a drugstore on Sunday. It was Monday night when I received the email. I'd been in LA on Sunday, just a couple of hours from the parking lot where he died. I'd debated whether to see him that weekend, not knowing it was to be the last weekend of his life, and had ultimately decided against it. It turns out it wouldn't have been possible—or, if I had seen him, I'd have stumbled into the degrading scene of his final binge. I wondered how many of these degrading scenes he'd lived through. I found an image of the parking lot on Google Earth and stared at it, imagining Charlie's body in different spots on the pavement.

A few months previous, my grandmother had found him lying on the carpet with a needle in his arm. He was supposed to be clean. He'd been living with my grandmother for several years now. He wrote me letters addressed to "my only child." The letters helped me realize that I'd been just as much a ghost in his life as he was in mine. But they also struck me as manipulative and defensive, some blaming his own father for his addiction, none acknowledging much responsibility. He never said, "I wish I'd made sure you had a home and food. I wish I'd sent you to college or paid for school clothes." Mostly, the letters were about him.

Finally, I relented and established some contact. I spent a long afternoon with him. We exchanged odd letters and gifts. I wrote autobiographical pieces about visiting him in prison as a kid, about the time he brought me an electric racetrack for Christmas when I was eight, about the year and a half during my twenties when he reunited with my mother, moved in with her, and eventually started beating her again. I felt a complicated mix of guilt and satisfaction about using him as material. The writing became a big part of a relationship that had never been mutual. We were both having it, but not together.

It seemed likely that my father had OD'd. He'd had a seizure a couple of weeks prior. Since then he'd been drinking heavily, which everybody said was uncharacteristic. My mom's husband, who'd known him since high school, heard Charlie had been contacting old friends looking for drugs. On the Friday before he died, his sister's husband had driven nearly an hour to pick him up and take him to a court appearance. He'd been arrested for driving drunk. If drinking was uncharacteristic, why had all this happened? Maybe he wasn't drunk, but high. It was a question I never got around to asking.

I did learn that when my uncle arrived, he found my father so drunk he could hardly stand. He dragged Charlie to court anyway, but security wouldn't let him through the door. Back home, he stumbled off down the street, ignoring the pleas of both my uncle and grandmother. They hadn't been able to stop him. He never came home. Finally, on Sunday, they went searching for him. No luck. Then they got the call from the coroner. Cause of death was pending. All they had—we had—was the image of him lying in a parking lot for who knows how long.

My cousin's husband said he was sorry to break the news to me, but they needed my signature. That was the reason for the email. My grandmother had wanted to send me a letter with the news. She's old-fashioned in lots of ways. There'd be no funeral. Nobody wanted to honor or memorialize Charlie. To her mind, there was no hurry to be in touch. But state bureaucracy required my signature to authorize what the forms called the "final disposition" of my father's body. My mom was furious that his family asked this of me. But to my surprise, I was glad.

He'd be cremated. No need to embalm. This much was clear to everybody. The form was weirdly simple for such an emotionally complicated transaction. All I had to do was fill it out—in hurried, shaky ink—print it, sign it, scan it, and fax it to the mortuary. It was the first time I'd ever had any control over anything about our relationship. I was spooked. I was mourning more heavily than I'd expected, feeling a lifelong absence that had defined my life. Friends sent well-meaning condolences expressing vague understanding that I must be experiencing a complicated grief. The form gave me a ritual house for feelings that were hard to name.

The cultural narratives that shepherd people through grief mostly didn't apply to me and Charlie. As in life, the scripts and routines didn't fit. So many things normally taken for granted had to be made up—how to answer the question, "What does your father do?" for example. But the work had a payoff. It required me to be active in figuring out who I wanted to be. It was liberating in the sense that I wasn't constrained much by rules or expectations. As a kid, without realizing what I was doing, I started a lifelong practice of using books and music as a surrogate for the conventional stories and rituals my family had sidestepped.

In the weeks after my father's death, I let a song tell me how to feel. I listened to Death Cab for Cutie's "Styrofoam Plates" on continuous rotation. I played it on loop in the car. I listened to it on headphones at work. I blasted it when I was home alone. I'm grateful for a song that felt like the mourning I needed, a song about a guy who was "not quite a father, but a donor of seeds to a poor single mother." A single line—"a bastard in life, thus a bastard in death"—expressed the anger threaded through my of grief. When these gave way to the noise of furious drums and jangly guitars, I felt it in my internal organs. I mean this literally. It hurt in a physical and notably pleasurable way that must be what Aristotle meant by catharsis. That noise was a miraculous musical container, able to absorb the variety of feelings that fall outside standard-issue grief: shame, fury, pride, attraction, repulsion, reluctant understanding.

The sound turned my discomfort into pleasure. Isn't that what heroin does? I wonder if there's a sound that could help me understand what heroin felt like for my father. But that's one more question without an answer. My father specialized in sowing my life with these. Because my father was silent on the topic of heroin, I found myself returning to Burroughs, proud junky philosopher.

While the State of California's s conception of biology is simple, William Burroughs had a more expansive and fantastical notion of the addict's relationship to his body. The State focused on the stability of genes; heredity gave me authority over my father's dead body. Burroughs focuses on the mutability of our physical bodies, whose cells continuously die and are replaced by others. He argues the fluctuations of cellular life are attuned to the junk habit:

> *I have never regretted my experience with drugs. I think I am in better health now as a result of using junk at intervals than I would be if I had never been an addict. When you stop growing, you start dying. An addict never stops growing. Most users periodically kick the habit, which involves shrinking of the organism and replacement of the junk-dependent cells. A user is in a continual state of shrinking and growing in his daily cycle of shot-need for shot completed.*

It may have been the opiates that drove Burroughs's physiological fantasy. It's hard to imagine it'd be supported by hard data. If I had to guess, I'd say he probably based it on shreds of medical research, biological theory, and conversations he had when he was high.

The view of a contrarian—molded outside conventional stories or rituals—can be instructive. Burroughs accepts *junky* as an identity, but he rejects the stigma. We accept the daily use of some drugs: coffee, cigarettes, and alcohol, but not heroin. Junkies, as I learned from my father and many of his friends, can live for decades shooting up just about every day. They're not all dying young or wasting away. You can't necessarily tell. If they're poor, they'll lie, cheat, and steal their way through life. They'll disappoint you over and over again. But their bodies do sustain themselves, if they don't fuck up and OD.

Burroughs's isn't a life I'd hold up as an example for how to move through the world. He shot and killed his wife in a fit of romantic destruction. Even his descriptions of the daily life of a junky in books like *Junky* and *Naked Lunch* are mostly degrading. Still, he was a kind of teacher, one who has inspired and instructed an impressive number of people, and his theory of junky life does seem to speak for a group of people mostly derided and ignored. Many of his reflections on junky life speak to a burden of consciousness we all feel. It's not easy to find yourself in a body, knowing it belongs to you, aware that you only sort of know what makes you *you*, that you know very little about how the cells in the body you move through the world collaborate to make you distinct from everybody else.

> *Junk is a cellular equation that teaches the user facts of general validity. I have learned a great deal from using junk: I have seen life measured out in eyedroppers of morphine solution. I experienced the agonizing deprivation of junk sickness, and the pleasure of relief when junk-thirsty cells drank from the needle. Perhaps all pleasure is relief. I have learned the cellular stoicism that junk teaches the user. I have seen a cell full of sick junkies silent and immobile in separate misery. They knew the pointlessness of complaining or moving. They knew that basically no one can help anyone else. There is no key, no secret someone else has that he can give you.*

These junkies are basically struggling with the same fear and pain Adam and Eve discovered after they shared the apple. They find the key, eat it, and learn its secret: there's no key. In both cases, new input into the body delivers a new experience of the world. Writing accomplishes this too. If life without my father taught me anything, it was how to live without a key. Pleasure, to my mind, is relief from the strain of knowing how much we can't know about what it means to be alive. This means looking for the input that will help us experience more joy than fear, more engagement than retreat. For my father, heroin must have made retreat feel like joy, for a while.

Burroughs is certainly right that junk is a way of life. And death is part of life. For those still alive, death of a loved one is new input. It adjusts our relationship to the world in unpredictable ways.

When his cause of death was finally pronounced—through an amendment to the original coroner's report—it was listed as "acute alcohol and chlordiazepoxide" (a relative of Valium, with longer-lasting effects, used to treat anxiety and withdrawal, also known as Librium). Nobody knows where he got the Librium. But really, it was the heroin that killed him. The seizure, the alcohol, the Librium, and the parking lot were set pieces in junk as a way of life. So are the half-answered questions that have lingered since the final disposition of his body. So is the song I borrowed from somebody else's life, input that provided some relief, interrupted the degrading images of the last couple of days cycling through me on a loop.

17

IDAHO STREET

"I think she wasn't very nice to me," Paul will write by email two decades later.

"Polo," he says that day. My eyes are closed and I'm looking for Paul. The air is hot and so is the water. Leaves are sticking to my skin.

"Marco." Paul is yelling over the bleeping of "Funky Town." Mighty 690 provides the soundtrack. "There are so many leaves in this pool," he adds.

"Let's clean it out," I say. "Grab that pole with the net." We drag the pool for dead leaves, until we decide we'll never get them all and plunk back in.

"Marco."

"Polo."

"Boys. Lunchtime," Nanny calls.

I've been living with Nanny while my mom looks for a new house. I don't really know why we had to move out, but I'm glad. Craig's living here too, and we have a tenant, Doug Jr. He's Doug's son, and he moved in to help with the rent, even though Doug isn't Nanny's boyfriend anymore. Doug Jr. is twenty, a pre-med student and a surfer, with Doug's blond hair but longer.

The house on Idaho Street is two cool adobe rectangles stuck together, ranch style. JP and Sue Ellen were living here. They bought a house in Del Dios, so Nanny has taken over the lease. "I never thought I'd end up in Escondido," Nanny says. "That's for damn sure." But she's planted geraniums in big pots and she's found spaces for the apothecary chest, the painting of the dream girl, the loveseat, the birdcage.

My mom's staying with her new boyfriend Nick Yourgales. Nanny says my mom and Cheech are "running around" and that it's "facacta." They're too old to be acting like that.

Nanny's steady economic decline works to my benefit. The lower she sinks, the closer she gets to me. When I was born, Nanny still lived on Nineteenth Street in Del Mar. When it became increasingly clear that Ralph's alimony would not cover the taxes, she sold it for $250,000. (In 1980, it sold for $2.5 million.) She bought the smaller but equally elegant Bird Rock house, in La Jolla, where my mom and Stanley had their wedding. She lost that too.

I'm trying to act nonchalant with Paul about my new existence. Usually we are at Paul's house, where he's in charge. I grab the metal handle of the sliding-glass doors and tug. "Ouch." It's stuck. Paul grabs it and slides it open with no problem.

"Careful, boys. Try not to be little hellions." Nanny is grinning, but just barely.

There are two chicken salad sandwiches and two glasses of ginger ale sitting on sisal placemats at the round table in the dining room. Still wrapped in our towels, we sit and eat. Nanny has not looked at or addressed Paul. The girl from my dream stares at me from the wall behind him. Paul finishes his sandwich quickly, like it's a race. I'm trying to keep up. I gulp my ginger ale and say, "Nanny, can I have some more?"

"Get it yourself. You're big and ugly enough." Paul looks at me for a translation. He has never understood Nanny's humor.

Marco Polo on Idaho Street is Paul's memory, not mine. I asked him if he visited the house, because I couldn't conjure a memory of him there.

His response: "Yes, I did. I remember how many leaves there were in the pool and that we played Marco Polo. Your grandma made us lunch, and I think she wasn't very nice to me." I'm sure that if I was living in a house with a pool, I'd have invited him, if only to persuade him that I wasn't the poor hippie kid we both knew I was. Now that he reminds me, I know he's right. He was there.

Paul's Marco Polo memory is *associative*, triggered spontaneously in response to stimulus. Mine was effortful. I had to make a conscious attempt to find it. But then Paul's email seemed to transform my effortful memory into an associative. Ironically, it felt like mine after he fed it to me.

Associative memories are constant and outside conscious control. The frontal lobes, which process reasoned thought, activate the hippocampus. PET scans show increased blood flow through the hippocampus during moments of associative retrieval, and through both the hippocampus and the frontal lobes during moments of effortful retrieval. Daniel Schacter, one of the world's most renowned memory researchers, argues that retrieval cues, whether conscious or not, exert a powerful influence on the shape and quality of the memory produced. Memory is made in the cue's image. My Marco Polo memory was made in Paul's image.

Schacter might tell you my hippocampus was involved. Ensconced inside the lobes of the brain, along with the rest of the limbic system, the hippocampus is a peculiar object. Disentangled from its crevices and stretched out, it looks like two dangling penises, with soft beach rocks where the heads would be, each with three smooth rings directly beneath them, like the ridges of a vanilla soft serve. They dangle from the thalamus, which looks surprisingly like a scrotum, with slender mushrooms (called the hypothalamus) strung from its top. Evolutionarily speaking, the limbic system is the oldest piece of brain matter, originating with early mammals. Its work is primarily unconscious, much of it centered on emotions, appetites, and instincts. It's where Dr. Jekyll's Mr. Hyde lives.

The first three times I read Paul's email, it said, "I think she was very nice to me." I thought, "Yeah, obviously." On the fourth reading, when I realized my mistake, I thought, "Oh, God, I can imagine that." Nanny didn't like intruders walking all over her degradation. Plus, she was bemused by capable people. And Paul was a capable kid. With Ralph and Doug both gone, she had almost none of them in her life.

Paul *was* there. His memory is my cue. I know the Marco Polo game happened. But the memory is an implant, from Paul's hippocampus to mine. Paul's memory has reshaped mine.

Nichole and I officially hate each other at school, but today we are in the pool, choreographing a water ballet to "We Got the Beat." The adults are up on the party deck, a roofed platform with a kitchen and bar. They're digging into a box of pictures and reminiscing. We don't know it yet, but this will be the last gathering at Idaho Street. Things are about to change, and not for better.

"Look at this one of Jimmy," Ruth says. "Priceless." Nichole and I both know this means Jimmy Durante.

"He was always so nice to me," my mom says.

Ruth and Carl Fix, who were neighbors of Nanny and Ralph's when they lived in Del Mar, are over for a poolside barbecue to celebrate Nanny's new house. They've been divorced for years, but they are still a twosome for social events. They're both deeply tan with loud smokers' voices. Ruth's hair is the color of embers about to explode. Carl's huge hard belly is always on display. Their daughter Kim, a little younger than my mom, looks like a cross between the two of them, but the result is somehow pretty: gold skin, light freckles, and very straight and long blond hair. Kim is more reticent than her parents, but she parties with just as much gusto. They all smoke and laugh constantly. They always talk about Kim like she's a little girl they can't believe grew up. It makes me realize that Nichole and I will grow up too. Will we reminisce with them over cocktails and cigarettes?

"Oh, look at that little Cathy, isn't she the cutest thing?" Kim says, only half sarcastic.

"Mom made me put my hair in curlers for hours to get those ringlets."

"Oh, Jesus Christ, Cathy."

"Well, it's true. I hated those dresses."

"Well, you didn't hate them so much when Jimmy Durante was gaga over you."

They would die of irritation if they weren't too busy to notice that we have been rewinding the tape player to repeat twenty-second snippets of the Go-Gos for more than an hour. "Keep that thing away from the pool," my mom exclaims. "Do you want to electrocute yourselves?"

"Oh, Cathy, leave 'em alone," Carl says.

"It's not even close," I say. "It's three feet away." Nichole gets out of the pool and moves the tape player another three feet from the edge of the pool.

"Are you gonna fish them out when they electrocute themselves?" my mom asks Carl.

"Your mother is hysterical," Carl calls out to us.

"Are you gonna get out every time to fix the tape?" I ask Nichole.

"Can't we take turns?"

"Whatever."

Two incidents at school precipitated our hate. Nichole's boyfriend George Grejalva, the shortest guy in eighth grade, cornered me behind some lockers and beat me to the ground and stomped all over me with his feet. He did this because I was such a faggot twerp. The other incident involved Nichole's modeling career, which has been thriving for about six months now. I took the cards with her portfolio shots around and pointed out to people how her trademark long hair was dancing around on her trademark perky butt—which I called a balloon butt. Nichole was in a Jordache commercial on TV and in some magazine ads. Despite this success, Nanny kept hurting her feelings by telling her and Jennifer that she wanted to take Nichole to La Jolla for a makeover.

But we're not at school, and Nanny doesn't know about our hate. We haven't confessed it to each other, just everyone we know. For the purposes of today's party, we are collaborators.

"It's time," I call out, hoping to penetrate their laughter. Our choreography is ready.

"For what?" Carl asks.

"For the water ballet, Dad." Kim reprimands him with a slap on the shoulder.

"What the Goddamn is that?"

"Okay, ready," I say. "One, two, three."

I press play and scurry into the pool before the first frantic snare beat chimes in. We're in position, standing straight with our arms stretched up to the sun. The Go-Gos' instruments sound like toys, thin and high-pitched. The toy drums are joined by toy guitar, imitating the driving repetition of a punk riff. We lower our left hands to our sides and do a half twirl. *See the people walking down the street.* Belinda Carlisle's voice is every bit as tinny as the snare. *Fall in line just watching all their feet.* The choreography for the first verse involves the lowering of our right hands, another half turn, a descent underwater for an impressive synchronized summersault, and a shot back up, hands stretching to the sun.

We raise our right legs and spin toward each other on our left toes. We collide and join hands for a jitterbug routine, in honor of Nanny's days as a jitterbug champion. *They got the beat, they got the beat.* We're in a water ballet trance for two minutes and thirty-one seconds, concluding with a triumphant duo handstand as the Go-Gos climax above water, where we can't hear them, Belinda Carlisle and Jane Wiedlin duking it out over who's got the beat.

They adults clap. "Goddamn," Carl exclaims, displaying an ability to be exuberant no matter what the circumstances. "Shit," Ruth follows. "Watch your mouths, you two," Kim says.

"Very good," Nanny says. "Very graceful. You're like a couple of dolphins."

"What's that weird song?" my mom asks.

"It's the Go-Gos," I say.

"Remember when Paula was go-go dancing for The Lyrics? What was that, '68?" Kim asks my mom.

"What's The Lyrics?" I ask.

"Gary's band. They were really famous on the coast," Kim says.

"No, it couldn't have been '68. Paula had Justin by then, and Gary had both Bryan and Trever. It would have been more like '64 or '65. You're too young to remember, Kimmy," my mom says.

"I remember. I went to those Goddamn shows. I probbly shouldn't have, but I did."

They're all laughing. Nichole's watching me watch Nanny, who hits Carl with the dishtowel she's been wearing over her shoulder—I guess so she can clean up anything in an instant. She's subtle about it, but she's laughing at our routine. Nichole seems to recognize the betrayal and take satisfaction in it. I'm always lording my camaraderie with Nanny over her.

The sun is sinking now, but Nichole and I are still wet in our bathing suits. Up on the party deck, the pitch of the laughter is beginning to peak. "It Goddamn is too," Carl keeps saying. "It Goddamn is that Goddamn night in Ensenada. I remember you wearing that dress with the palm fronds on it, and Ralph in the red suit. That suit was red like a ruby."

"That's the last thing I want to relive," Nanny says.

"Remember it was in the paper the next day?" Ruth says. "Wife Midge Pours Martini over the Head of Portuguese Pepper Pot."

"I was so mad," Nanny says.

"He thought he was hot stuff dancing with that señorita," Carl says.

"He always thought he was hot stuff," my mom adds.

"Damn straight," Carl says.

I hear the slide of the door behind me and see Doug Jr. walk through.

"Honey, I'm home," Doug says.

"Shit, Doug Jr.," Carl says. "That kid look like his old man or what?" He doesn't look like his old man to me. More like Christopher Atkins. Which is a good thing. He's been really nice to me since he moved in, and I like it.

"Exactly," Ruth says.

"Vodka tonic?" Carl asks him.

"Got any beer?"

"Dos Equis," Craig says, handing him one.

The sun is just a pink-orange sliver over the roof now. I watch Doug as he takes a long gulp, puts it down, takes off his shirt, and dives into the pool with his pants on. The laughing crescendos as everybody soaked up the site of Doug's full-grown son. "He's as crazy as his dad," Carl says.

"Loves water as much," Ruth says. Doug swims the length of the pool, then surfaces, pushing his long wet hair over his head, and pulls himself out of the pool, water dripping from the tiny blond hairs all over his brown torso.

"Craig Harvey jacks off," Paul told me last night. "I think he's turning Japanese, I think he's turning Japanese, I really think so," he sang. Everybody knows that song is about jacking off.

Craig is popular, cute, shortish with longish sun-streaked hair and freckles, kind of like a junior Doug Jr.

I know Paul lies, but he's always been a wised-up kid, a few steps ahead of everybody else when it comes to sex. In fifth grade I was still earnestly chastising him for using the word *fuck*. Back then he said he had *fucked* his girl cousin in Nebraska. A lie. He also said he *fucked* his friend Theo. Another lie. But I want to believe Craig Harvey jacks off.

We're in Paul's room, playing Atari, Mille Bornes, and Dungeons & Dragons all night enclosed in fake wood paneling. My character is Roland, Pure Good, and Paul's is Cedric, Chaotic Evil. Paul made Cedric that way to force me to spend the night in the room with evil weekend after weekend. After a while, D&D for two gets old. You can only battle so many monsters and acquire so much power with only one rival traveler on your imaginary roads.

"Nicole Young told me about Craig. He told her he uses Vaseline."

"For what?"

"To make it slippery. I'll show you." Paul pounced off the bed toward his little private bathroom and produced a jar of Vaseline. "We'll lie on the floor where we can't see each other. We'll have a contest. See who finishes first."

We spread our bodies out in straight lines, rigid like canoes docked at the edge of a lake. I took my chunk of Vaseline and slid it around my penis.

"Ready, go," Paul said. Then, "Stop for a second. What percent hard would you say you are? I'm ninety."

"Eighty-nine?" I said, thinking I should sound less excited than Paul. Nonetheless, the game was a draw. We splurted at about the same time and there was no referee to weigh in.

Now I'm on the loveseat with the green and orange flowers, my trunks at my ankles, hard-on in hand. In my head I'm trying hard to sustain an image of Doug Jr. on the couch with his trunks at his ankles, holding his hard-on in two hands. "Mreow, Mrow, Mroooa." Bob, the stray cat Nanny feeds, is at the screen door, harassing me. Masturbation is the only time when animals are a nuisance.

I toss a throw pillow at the screen door and he starts back. Hoping he can't see me now, I look for the image of naked Doug, but it's not where I left it. I want to make myself walk into the living room and then to have Doug look at me and then back down at his dick. I want to make his eyes say, "Come over and touch it." I want to put myself on the couch with Doug, get our tongues in each other's mouths, going at it until we burst.

I'm close, very close, when I hear the Mercedes in the driveway. Quick and awkward, I'm grabbing for my trunks. They're sticking on my left leg and so it takes me several seconds to get them up around my waist. Nanny walks in before I can tie the laces at the waist.

"Hello, Uni. Your Nanny is now manager of the Rancho Santa Fe Grill."

"What?" I'm slouching in this weird position so that the top of my trunks will bend so she can't see that they aren't tied.

"I got a job."

"Really? Why?"

"To keep you in filet mignon, Unigagin. And Craig out of jail. I'm going to give Doug a job too. So he can pay the rent on time."

"Good idea."

"What's this pillow doing over here?"

"I don't know."

Adolescent sex is scary because it draws on the private worlds children create to exclude adults, but puts them to purposes we call *adult*. It feels good, but it's not allowed. It may not matter if the adults in question are about family values or free love. The kids will have sex either way, and it will scare them and their parents either way.

Adolescent sex was scarier for me than for Paul. He seemed curious in a clinical way, knew what he wanted and what he was doing. I was responding to physiological impulses that made me want to do stuff, but I wasn't sure what the stuff was. Together, we were a laboratory experiment in sex education.

Adult psychologists concocting theories about adolescents like us don't have the luxury of performing experiments like we did. It'd be creepy and unethical. So they observe instead. They've done a lot of both in the past one hundred years.

G. Stanley Hall published the first systematic theory of adolescence, around the turn of the twentieth century. His model was evolutionary, and his theory held that individual human development shared a series of phases with the evolution of the species. He described adolescence as a way station between the beast and the human, its turmoil a struggle between animal chaos and human civilization. In Hall's image, Paul and I were like two little beasts fucking our way up the evolutionary ladder.

Though subsequently ignored by most, the theory established a tradition of examining sexual behavior in adolescents. During the last century and a half, a vast number of adults like Smith with prestigious scientific credentials have devoted their lives to figuring out why adolescents behave the way they do. They have conducted extensive research and proposed numerous, complex, and battling theories to explain adolescent sex.

Of course, Sigmund Freud termed adolescence the *genital phase*, during which the libido, whose purpose is to motivate survival, emerges in the penis or vagina, after traveling through the mouth (oral stage, zero to one), anus (anal stage, one to two), the genitals (phallic stage, three to five), then everywhere and nowhere in the body (latency stage, five to twelve). If each of these stages is allowed to progress smoothly, without trauma or undue repression, the adolescent will become a "normal" sexual adult, with a battling id, ego, and superego maintaining a workable balance between bodily drives and social expectations. Freud imagined kids like Paul and me as little survivors, casting our pensises about in search of normalcy.

Anna Freud, her father's daughter, went further with her theory of adolescence, characterizing it as a developmental disruption. The emerging adult sex drive produces upheaval because none of the defense mechanisms of childhood keep it in check. Becoming an adult requires the testing of new mechanisms for restraining the all-powerful, sex-inflected libido. Paul and I had little restraint, but we were doing our best to manage the upheaval.

Boyd R. McCandless proposed his "drive theory" in 1970, suggesting that drives are the root of all human behavior and that adolescence is a period of learning to manage the newly emerging sex drive. The sex drive dominates adolescence, putting children in direct conflict with a social environment that inhibits sexual behavior. No question. When I had sex with Paul, I was in conflict with a world that didn't want us to stick our penises in each other's orifices to see how it made us feel. We'd have sex for two years before we met somebody who told us it was okay—a girl named Kim we met near the end of our freshman year in high school (more later).

University of Oklahoma psychologists David C. Rowe and Joseph Lee Rodgers have proposed the "d" theory—"d" standing for a latent genetic predisposition for adolescent deviance, including early sexual behavior, vandalism, drug use, and violence. They argue that the burgeoning sex drive is the underlying motivator in non-sexual acts of deviance, explaining why a deviant adolescent is predisposed to all categories of deviance, not just one or two particular antisocial behaviors. According to Rowe and Rodgers, sex is the root of all deviance. But Paul and I were thoughtful deviants. We'd been analyzing the norms of our schools for years, agreeing that they often seemed arbitrary and, frankly, stupid. But that didn't stop me, at least, from worrying endlessly that our sexual deviation was wrong. Everything in our world told me it was and so I believed it must be. It wasn't until a few years later, with another boy, when sex was combined with a giant crush, that I started to believe it must be good. The crush felt so good that it somehow trumped the stigma. And that was that. I never felt shame about gay sex again.

Temple University psychologist Laurence Steinberg has proposed that distance between adolescents and their parents both results from and provokes adolescent pubertal maturation. Drawing on observations of non-human primates, he concludes that parent-child distance during adolescence is atavistic—left over from an earlier phase of evolution, forcing children to seek sexual partners outside the family. I don't know about the atavism, but it seems true enough that adolescent sex helps kids create distance between themselves and their parents. All the kids in our middle school were busy building little sexual worlds invisible to adults. I'd be curious to know if these worlds felt as scary and secret even to the straight jock kids, whose sex was celebrated, as Paul's bedroom—the world of our experiments—did for me.

Adolescents are sexual children. One minute they're playing Marco Polo, and the next they're sliming themselves up with Vaseline and jerking off competitively, or clinically, or clumsily, or dreamily. We put them under the microscope because their behavior is supposedly incongruent. But adolescent sex is the norm, not the exception. This is the result I would like to report from the laboratory of Paul's bedroom.

I sleep right through the phone, five rings before Nanny answers.

"Cathy."

"For Godssake."

"Jesus Christ, Cathy."

"Okay."

"Craig, your sister's in jail. I have to go get her. She got a DWI."

In the morning, my mom is on the loveseat in the living room, which is too small and rigid for sleeping on. She looks like she's been stepped on. Her eyes droop and there is a bruised cast to her complexion. Her wiry Portuguese hair is mashed in some spots and standing on end in others. Her eyes are red and open only halfway. She's not looking at me or anybody.

"They're gonna take your license," Craig says. "They'll only let ya drive to work. That's what they did to me."

"Jesus Christ, Cathy." This has become Nanny's refrain. My refrain is to stiffen, cringe, and look away. "Was that Nick in the car?" Nick is twenty-two. Nanny says he's gross, and I agree. He's skinny and greasy, with a black shag and a long, bony nose crooked from fighting.

The episode is brief because Cheech shows up and puts a stop to it. "Hola, Midge. Where's your jailbird daughter?" Nanny is grinning at this. "Fuckin-A, Cat, you look like shit. It wasn't even a full moon last night."

Cheech takes my mom's misery in stride, like it's a movie she's watching. Liz Taylor is playing the heroine, a thirty-year-old woman whose fun-loving ways are wearing her down and whose histrionics are so exaggerated that pathos becomes jocular good fun. For Cheech, watching this movie is an occasion to party.

"Let's go to the beach. I'm driving," she says, and they're off. Nanny gives the couch a symbolic brush off as the door shuts behind them.

18

THE REAL IDAHO

Observer memory:

There's a kid looking out a window from a small white house. His mom, who is five feet tall and has short, thick, curly hair, is standing next to him, her hand on his shoulder. They're watching a 1970 beige Mercedes 280SL pull away from the curb. They watch until it pulls up to the corner and turns right out of sight and then keep watching. They don't say anything, and they don't cry.

Field memory:

"Boog, come here." There's something wrong, or she wouldn't call me that. She knows I'm too old for it. The DWI behind her, my mom finally found us a house to rent, a little bungalow in Escondido just a few blocks from Nanny. She's in the kitchen and I'm in the living room, facing the front window and the television, my back to her.

"Why?"

"I want to talk to you about something."

"What?"

"The Grill is going under. That lady who owns it is shutting it down."

"So Nanny won't work there?"

"No. She has to go to Idaho, to live with Lee." She means the real Idaho, the state. Lee is my mom's cousin, the one who lived with them as a teenager because his parents were murdered.

Lee lives in Sun Valley. He's a divorced alcoholic with two kids, Chris and Laura. Chris is my age and lives with Lee. Laura is fifteen and lives with her mom. Nanny will be taking care of Chris when Lee is flying. Lee flies drunk. It's a well-known family fact.

"She's going to Idaho to live with Lee." The sentence seizes me.

"She's moving from Idaho Street to Idaho?" It's all I can think to say.

I'm stuck in that sentence for weeks. I help Nanny pack. I help her move her antiques into storage, including the painting of the dream girl. I have a final dinner with her, my mom, and Craig. We eat filet mignon. I watch as the Mercedes pulls from the curb. I take phone calls and listen to stories about Chris sledding in the snow and what she is making him for dinner.

One day, a package arrives: stickers with a red filigree border and blue lettering on the inside that read JASON in an ornate typeface. There is a Polaroid in the envelope, of the Mercedes covered in mounds of snow. The windows are partially clear of the white stuff, and you can see a little of the dark brown interior. There's a house in the background. The Mercedes is saying, "Aren't you proud of me? I've been through so much since I saw you last. I'm worldly, and I'm surviving even though I'm frozen. Everybody in Sun Valley is rich."

I take one of the stickers and wrap it around the white border on the bottom of the Polaroid. There isn't enough space for the whole thing, so only the top half of my name shows.

Memory uses a variety of tricks to twist the past to the needs of the present. An *observer memory* is a view of the past from outside, as though the rememberer were watching the past with an objective point of view. A *field memory* is a view from inside the rememberer, walking through the action of the past. Freud distinguished between the two, noting that observer memories tend to be associated with fact and field memories with emotion. If we are attempting to recount facts—what happened—then we tend to look into the past from the outside and see ourselves as actors in the memory. If we are trying to capture the feeling of a memory, then we tend to see everything through our own eyes. According to Daniel Schacter, the latest laboratory studies have confirmed this correlation, with some exceptions.

Field memories are somewhat more common than observer memories. If you switch from a field to observer point of view, the degree of emotion you feel should diminish. But if you switch from an observer to a field point of view, your degree of emotion will apparently remain much the same. The implication is that once you've established yourself as an outsider to your own memory, you're insulated. But this is all rough statistical data. It doesn't hold true for every subject in a study—just the majority.

Observer memories distort the past by endowing it with a rich but false objectivity, field memories by limiting the rememberer to a personal account of what happened. Distortion has a negative connotation, but it's the way of the brain. There is no undistorted memory.

One lesson in all this is that we are stuck with the distortion, so we should learn to live with it, to understand it as one of life's fundamentals. I can play with my memories all I want, experimenting with field and observer positions, but the motive for remembering will shape the past I create.

Observer memory:

It's been twenty minutes since they finished dinner. The kid's in the bedroom, listening to the radio and writing a report on New York State.

Capital: Albany

Population: 15,690,538

Agriculture: Dairy and cattle, vegetables, apples

Industry: Publishing, tourism

Topography: Mountains, lakes, rivers, Atlantic Coast

Largest Cities: New York, Buffalo, Rochester, Yonkers, Syracuse, Albany, New Rochelle, Mount Vernon, Schenectady, Utica

Border States: Connecticut, New Jersey, Massachusetts, Pennsylvania, Vermont

Statehood: July 26, 1788

Flower: Rose

Tree: Sugar maple

He is mounting photographs of the Statue of Liberty and Niagara Falls, imagining cities with Indian names, drawing the leaf of a tree he's never seen.

There is a thirty-one–year-old woman arguing with a twenty-three-year-old man in the living room, which is separated from the kid's bedroom by a thin plaster wall. If you lift the roof of the house, you can look down at both rooms simultaneously. You can approximate this by standing out on the street or sidewalk in front of the house, because it's night and the lights are on inside and the curtains are half open in both rooms.

The man and woman are arguing because he was late for dinner and then didn't compliment the meal, which was taco salad and Dos Equis for the adults, Kool-Aid for the kid. The man says he liked the dinner but forgot to say anything. He was late because he was helping his brother move some shit into storage.

The argument escalates. The kid hears a muffled male voice say, "Fuck you, then" and a teary woman's reply, "Get out of my house." She sounds warbly, like a tape stuck in a machine. The kid flinches. The man says, "I'll get the fuck out," and kicks the coffee table. The kid hears a crash but still doesn't move. If you were to scan his body with a special lens that could see his cells, you would see they were very busy, swarming to create this outward stillness.

If you've got the roof off the house, you can see the still kid while the woman smacks the man in the face. You can see the man respond by pushing her to the ground. She falls easily. The kid only hears crashes. The man is punching the woman in the face. If you're watching from the sidewalk or street, you can see the kid lying on his bed with several sheets of paper and colored pens in his hand. In the living room, you can see a lot of movement. You can hear muffled voices.

After about forty minutes, the man says again, "I'll get the fuck out. And I won't fuckin' come back."

The woman replies, "Don't ever come back. Ever."

After about five minutes, she enters the kid's room and sits on the bed, streaked with tears, bruises on her arm, neck, and face. "He's never coming back," she says. "I promise."

Field Memory:

It's dark. The paper route took longer than usual tonight. I slid on some sand in the road on Ninth Street and wiped out on my bike and spilled all the papers. Then I saw these jerk stoners from school who knocked me down and stole my papers this other time.

"Hey, Fagaw," one of them said.

"Hey, Fagaw, what's the matter? You don't want to talk to us?" I kept pedaling. It was only about five minutes from being dark outside. I had nine papers left to throw. They didn't chase me. I heard one of their voices trailing behind me: "See ya next time, Fagaw."

It must be practically seven o'clock. *I have to get a front light for my bike,* I think as I ride home in the dark. *At least Nick won't be there.*

As soon as I make the turn onto Seventh Street, I see Nick's black truck, with its raised tires and shiny scratched and dented paint job. The truck looks like him. When I see it, I smell pot and hear Mick Jagger. I see the chewed-up food mushing around inside his huge dirty mouth. I think about the fact that Nanny's gone, no sign of returning. But life with my mom is all about the ups and downs. All I can really do is broadcast my displeasure by ignoring Nick and my mom as aggressively as I can.

I go in through the back door, into the kitchen. There's beef stroganoff in a skillet on the stove and dirty plates in the sink. The TV is on in the living room. I tighten the muscles in my torso. I shove my face into locked position. I only have to pass the living room for about two seconds to get to my room. I can get there.

"Jason, wanna watch *Hill Street Blues*?" my mom asks.

"Hey, Jason, get out here and watch some TV," Nick calls.

"No." I slide past them, but not before seeing their entangled limbs on the couch. I slam the door, too hard, and lie down on the bed. After about five minutes, I hear knocking. "Jas, come out," my mom says in a gentle voice. "Come out. What's wrong?"

"Nothing," I say. They know what's wrong. Asking is their way of trying to get me to collaborate, to be part of their relationship. I'm not doing it.

19

CHOSEN

And there appeared a great wonder in heaven; a woman clothed with the sun, and the moon under her feet, and upon her head a crown of twelve stars;

And she being with child cried, travailing in birth, and pained to be delivered.

And there appeared another wonder in heaven; and behold a great red dragon, having seven heads and ten horns, and seven crowns upon his heads.

And his tail drew the third part of the stars of heaven, and did cast them to the earth; and the dragon stood before the woman which was ready to be delivered, for to devour her child as soon as it was born.

And she brought forth a man child, who was to rule all nations with a rod of iron; and her child was caught up unto God, and to his throne.

—Revelation, 12, 1-5

The dream is different this time. Nanny's back from Idaho, but the painting's in a Bekins storage unit, wrapped in cardboard. Instead of the girl in the painting, I am this girl Maria Nelson from Spanish class, with a stick-straight, blond bowl cut and a dimple on either side of my mouth. The pink ribbon has become a ten-foot-long sidewalk. I walk its length, picking daisies. I wear jeans and a powder blue IZOD instead of the green smock.

I walk extra slow because there's nothing on either end. No running or skipping. No chaos, only terror. I only have those ten feet to walk, and I have to make it last forever, because there's nothing else. I'd be dead if I wasn't walking and picking daisies.

The guy with the bomb is in the sky, and I know he is Maria's dad. She's got one. For the moment, I've got Nick Yourgales. I can't picture him though. The guy with the bomb is always invisible. I know if I run, the chaos will drown the terror, but there is nowhere to run. This ten-foot sidewalk is the whole world. All I can do is walk and pick, slowly, forever.

We had to move again, out of the Seventh Street house and back to Del Dios. Nick has come with the move, with his bony body, shiny shag, and nose knotted from being broken so many times. Nanny keeps saying, "That man is gross. Just gross." The Seafood Market just went under, so all the Yourgales brothers are unemployed. My mom has a new job at the Fish House Vera Cruz, which just opened in San Marcos.

Nick and I are sitting in the living room of the new house on Del Dios Highway, each with our whole record collection at our feet. I've got about forty. He must have two hundred. "Start Me Up" is on the record player. Nick's smoking a joint. Every time Mick Jagger sings "You make a grown man cry," Nick sings along, all warbly, like the line expresses the depths of his being.

The house hangs over a slope on stilts, about ten feet downhill from the highway, looking out over the highest of the roads that traverse the valley. The neighbors down the hill have two horses, and Nichole earns money by washing, brushing, and walking them.

My bedroom is a tiny rectangle made from a temporary wall of wood paneling that rises only about three-quarters of the way to the ceiling, leaving about two feet of empty space at the top, open to the living room. My mom's room is downstairs, so at least she and Nick don't sleep within earshot.

I hear Nanny's Mercedes pull into the driveway, the hard soles of her shoes clicking on the stairs. She doesn't knock. "Jason, your Nanny's come to take you to dinner." We're going to the Fish House Vera Cruz.

"Hello, Nick."

"Hey, Midge, what's goin' on?" He blows some pot smoke. I know I can count on her never to invite him.

Nanny lets me put Mighty 690 on the radio. "Celebration" by Kool and the Gang is just starting. Along with "My Life" by Billy Joel, this is probably Nanny's favorite AM radio song. *So bring your good times, and your laughter too. We gonna celebrate and party with you.* I'm poking Nanny. "Do your dance. Do it."

"Okay, okay." She's doing a little jig with the steering wheel. Her silver hair is curled in perfect waves, the collar of her blue silk blouse up. "Okay, your part's coming up. You have to do it." When the chorus sings "Yahoo," Nanny sings "Ooo Hoo" in falsetto. Her notes are limp, but just as high as theirs. That's what's funny about it. "Jesus Christ, Jason. Are you trying to humiliate your Nanny?" We're both laughing.

By the time the song is replaced by a stream of commercials, we're on the highway. "What are you going to have?" I ask Nanny.

"I don't know. It depends on the specials, but maybe king crab."

"I'm going to have swordfish. Can we get the smoked albacore appetizer?"

"That might be nice." We get the smoked albacore every time.

We park and walk into the restaurant. It's decorated in nautical themes, with rough wood planks and walls covered in giant swordfish and fishing nets. "Hi, Midge, hey, Jason." The "gal" (as Nanny calls her) behind the counter waves. "That mahi-mahi looks beautiful today," Nanny comments. "Just came in," the gal replies.

"By the window?" the eighteen-year-old hostess asks. She's got perfectly blow-dried Brooke Shields hair draped over one shoulder.

"That would be nice," Nanny responds.

"She's pretty," I whisper to Nanny.

"If you like that type."

"Hello, welcome to the Fish House Vera Cruz." It's my mom. She's got a headband in her short curls and a corkscrew poking out of her apron. She's talking in a funny voice, imitating somebody's version of a traditional waitress. "Would you like to hear our specials, or start with an appetizer? Maybe some smoked albacore?"

"Yes, yes. Please, please." I'm begging, even though I get it every time. "And a Coke?"

"Chablis, Mom?"

"That would be lovely, Cathy. Not too busy tonight."

"Not yet. You're the early birds."

"Can we have some bread?"

"Jeez, Jas. Just hold your horses. The busboy will bring it in a sec."

"Can I have a cherry in my Coke?"

"Anything else, Prince Charles?"

"No, that's it."

Our bread comes, then our drinks, then the tuna. I love stabbing it gently with the tiny cocktail fork and dipping it into the tartar sauce, which is especially sweet. I eat three quarters of it, one piece after another. I also eat all the bread, except for the one piece Nanny selects, which she carefully butters and somehow makes last until the salads arrive. By now the place is filling up. "It's mostly old people," I point out.

"You better watch what you say. Your Nanny is an old person too."

"No, not like them. You have gray hair and wrinkles, but you're not old like them."

"If you say so, I'm not going to argue."

I decide to tell Nanny about my new plan. I've been thinking about it for two days. "I want to switch to A-Track."

Escondido schools are year-round, until ninth grade. Every student is assigned a track, A through D, which determines the cycle of their vacations, nine weeks on, three weeks off. The tracks are staggered, so one track is always off, which is how they make room for us all.

"I'd be with Nichole," I say, even though she's a year behind me and we'd have no classes together. "My mom and Jennifer could carpool." If I were on A-track with Nichole, we'd have the same vacations, but that's not the real reason I want to switch. I don't want to be a faggot twerp who gets beat up at school. Switching tracks is a chance for a new start.

"That sounds like a pretty good idea."

I knew none of the adults had thought of this. They would assume I would never make such a big change to make their lives easier. If they had thought of it, I certainly would have refused.

"One swordfish and one giant pair of Alaskan king crab legs," my mom says, delivering our plates. "Don't those look good, Mom?"

"I'll save you some," Nanny tells her. "I'll never eat all this. Jesus, Mary, and Joseph."

"Nanny and I have a plan." Nanny doesn't object to my distortion.

"What kind of plan?"

"For me to switch to A-Track. With Nichole. You and Jennifer could carpool."

"Why? What's got into *him*?"

"Nothing," I say, annoyed. "It just makes sense. I can finish seventh and eighth grade on A-track. So what?"

"We'll think about it."

New Paul is a weird towheaded kid with tons of freckles. His white hair is just like Maria Nelson's. They even have the same haircut, the kind that falls in such a straight line that you can see the jagged edges where their moms cut it on the ends. His house sits on a cul-de-sac. His stepfather, also named Paul, sells insurance or something.

New Paul is on A-Track, like Nichole. His house is on the route Old Paul and I take from his house to the frozen yogurt store. "It's a five-mile walk" is one of Old Paul's mantras, "a good distance for cardiovascular exercise." He gets chocolate and peanut butter with Almond Roca topping, and I get vanilla and raspberry with fresh blackberries, both extra large. They come in deep styrofoam cups with long-handled spoons. I always eat slow, doing my best to outlast Paul so I'll have some left when his is just melty residue scraping on styrofoam.

New Paul's house has become a pit stop. Today, nobody is home but him and his sister Jenny. "Come to my room," he says, then stops at the end of the hall and slides a framed print of a flowery landscape off the wall, revealing a jagged hole about a foot in diameter. "That's where my stepdad punched through the wall. He was aiming for me." He puts the picture back, careful to straighten it.

I've been trying to figure out how to tell someone about the dream. The new version is making me feel like it's really important to talk about. When I do, it's easy. I just start telling, and they just keep listening. The pink ribbon, the painting, the guy with the bomb, the terror of skipping, the chaos of running, the sidewalk, the daisies, Maria Nelson. I tell them about stuff I never even noticed before, like the stars that twinkle all around the ribbon. I tell them about the weight of the bomb, about how I can feel it crushing me.

"It's in the Bible," New Paul says.

"What?" I read the Bible obsessively for a few months in fifth grade. It's been a couple of years, but I don't remember any ribbon roads in outer space.

"The bomb symbolizes the end of the world."

"The apocalypse. Freaky born-agains say 'the Rapture,'" Old Paul says.

"Maybe it's in space because the world is gone," I suggest.

"That's it, that's it." New Paul is getting excited. I look at him, then at Old Paul. If it's true, maybe the stuff he and I have been doing at night is all a test. Maybe I'm supposed to prove my strength by resisting.

I just read Stephen King's *The Stand*, and I have been having a lot of secret apocalyptic fantasies anyway. I envision myself an eight-hundred-page hero, leading a group of post-apocalypse stragglers on a journey to the ruins of some distant city where we will congregate to realize my vision for a new world. This world will be utopian, of course, but my fantasy doesn't get this far. I am more focused on myself as magnetic leader, attracting the most capable survivors, who, one by one, will find me and offer their undying allegiance.

"You could be Jesus, the Second Coming." New Paul has gotten Old Paul excited too. "And don't you think it's weird that we're both named Paul, like the apostle?"

It does seem weird. When Jesus returns, he'd have a dream like this. And it explains the way the dream feeling haunts me. It's so scary and all-encompassing because the message is so important. I always knew it was a message, but I couldn't interpret it. And here the two Pauls are telling me I am the Second Coming. I am already amassing followers and the apocalypse hasn't even come yet. The only problem with this conversation is that it stirs up the dream feeling, just when I'd been doing such a good job keeping it still. Now I'm awake, but living the dream.

The part I can't say out loud is that I know if I want to save the world, I have to stop the stuff with Old Paul. If we start hanging around New Paul more, maybe we won't have the chance. I have to switch to A-Track.

"Mine is sort of hard," one of us says. So far changing tracks hasn't stopped the experiments Old Paul and I are conducting.

"How much?"

"Like fifty-five percent."

"Mine's getting hard, but it's only like forty percent."

"Are you sure? Let me see. Let's compare."

We unzip and pull them out. They are of course getting harder by the second, but we ignore that for the sake of the rules. "You're right, mine's harder, but I think it's like sixty-five now. Touch it, see if it gets harder."

"It jumped. It jumps when I brush my finger on the head. Look. Look at it jump."

"Now I'm one hundred." I've succumbed again.

"Me too." Paul jumps up, his boner pointing the way to the Vaseline, and returns with the jar open, ready for scooping.

We lay side by side, fists sliding the lengths of our slippery dicks. "Does it feel better slower or faster?"

"Slower, I think."

"I know what you mean, but I like it faster. Try it."

"It's good faster."

"Now slower."

"I can't decide." We both speed up.

"I'm close."

"Me too."

It's a contest to see who shoots farther. My first spurt lands in my belly button and Paul's two inches above, but my second one is just below my left nipple. Paul's lands next to his right nipple. He wins.

Toe to toe, dancing very close, barely breathing, almost comatose.

"I hate Blondie," New Paul says. It's official. I've changed to A-Track.

"Why?"

"I think she sounds creepy."

"It's a band, not a she."

"Whatever. Her voice gives me the creeps."

"Well," I say. "This song spent twenty weeks on the Top 100 last year, two weeks at number one."

"People like Satanic music," he replies.

New Paul is staying over for the first time. We have to get up at four and walk to Old Paul's house. When we moved to Del Dios, the closest paper route I could get was over by his house. We have to get there in time to fold and deliver the papers by seven. The walk will take at least an hour. We decide it's best not to go to sleep. We're reading "The Revelation of St. John the Divine" with Mighty 690 on in the background. Even though I defended it, "Rapture" is spooking me a little too. When she sings, Debbie Harry sounds like she could be a demon, and when she raps she sounds too casual about apocalypse. The song is on the radio all the time, but it still feels like a coincidence to hear it in the background as we read out loud about flying angels dressed in bloody garments bathed in fire battling dragons and storming the sky in search of the banished Satan and his legions of damned followers. Debbie Harry sounds like the voice of the harlots and abominations and idolaters and murderers and fornicators of the Earth.

Wall to wall, people hypnotized, and they're stepping lightly, hang each night in Rapture.

"You know, the rest of us might not even be alive," Paul says. "If there is a nuclear bomb, almost everybody will die. San Diego will be a main target, 'cause of the Navy base and Camp Pendleton."

"I wonder how I'll know where to go."

"You'll just know."

"The first thing I want to do is save Nanny."

"Okay, here it is, right here at the beginning. This is what I was telling you about. 'Jesus Christ, who is the faithful witness, and the first begotten of the dead.' This is it, don't you see?" Paul says. "And down here, 'He cometh with clouds; and every eye shall see him, and they *also* which pierced him: and all kindreds of the earth shall wail because of him.' The thing is, I can't tell from your dream if you are the Second Coming of Jesus, or just a leader. I mean, you are in space, and that's Heaven, right? But you might just be getting a prophecy."

I'm reading, skimming really. It's confusing. I can't tell half the time what's happening. But here, here's something. "'And the fifth angel sounded, and I saw a star fall from heaven unto the earth.' That stirs up the dream feeling. I felt it again when I read it to you."

"A star falling from heaven. It could be the bomb."

We're sure we're on the brink. It'll be a year or even less. "Okay, here's one: 'And I saw another mighty angel come down from heaven, clothed with a cloud; and a rainbow was upon his head, and his face was as it were the sun, and his feet as pillars of fire.'" I felt it again.

"It's the beginning of Chapter Ten," Paul notices. "Don't you see?"

"What?"

"The other one was the beginning of Chapter Nine."

But I keep the truth to myself. I never mention the beginning of Chapter Twelve, when the woman clothed with the sun, standing on the moon and crowned with twelve stars, must fight with the dragon to protect her unborn child. The dragon is eager to devour him, and so to protect him she flees to the wilderness. When the dragon finally tracks her down, the earth opens its mouth and swallows the flood of bile he unleashes upon her. By this time, the woman's seed has grown to fruition and left her womb. He has important things to do, so he leaves her behind. The dragon follows, determined to devour him after all. I don't mention the travails she went through to have him, but I can't stop thinking about what my mom went through to have me, thirty-six hours of labor.

"It's almost 3:45. Should we just go? It's okay if we get there early. Old Paul will be folding papers. Plus, his sister is supposed to get there at like 4:30 or something, from Phoenix."

"She's a lesbian."

"Really?"

"Yeah."

"That's an abomination," he says. I nod.

We tiptoe out of the house, shut the door so Nick and my mom won't hear, even though they know we are going. When we get up to the highway, we realize what we're doing. We haven't thought about the quiet or the black, but here they are. And here we are in them. It's cold for San Diego, in the forties, and we can see our breath. Coyotes are yowling. First one, in falsetto: "Yip-yip-yoo-ooo, yip-yip-yoo-ooo."

"It's just a coyote," I say.

"They sound almost like people crying," he says.

Soon, dozens of coyotes are yipyooing their heads off. I'm used to coyotes, but this is creepy. "When I was little, they ate my baby duck, and some of our chickens too. Cats are always getting eaten by them. But they don't do anything to people." Except spook them. As the yowling gets louder, we walk faster, but this starts to remind me of the dream, speeding up to drown out fear, so I grab Paul's shirt-sleeve and make him slow down.

"What's that?" Paul asks, pointing to a dome-shaped something, about the size of a house.

"I don't know. It looks like a nuclear power plant, like the one in San Onofre."

"Was it there before?"

"No."

"Oh, God, it could be tonight. That could be why the feeling was so strong when you were reading the Bible."

Then, in the sky, I see a precise stream of chartreuse light, like lightning, but horizontal, moving in a quick, silent path. It's greener and more orderly in shape than lightning. It vanishes, but with decision, like I saw it while it was on its way somewhere and then it got there. "Did you see that?" I ask.

"What?" I'm pointing, and there's another one. "Shit. What is that?"

"That one was a little smaller." Then another. Each of these appears as though it's slicing through the galaxy into our dimension and then through the other side and onto another. They are silent, purposeful, and as bright as bright gets. But the night stays just as dark. The coyotes yowl. We walk, looking for more UFOs. But none come.

"Do you notice it's getting light?" Paul asks after twenty minutes or so.

"You're right." We round a corner and see that our nuclear plant is an overgrown pepper tree. "That's it?" I ask. "Is that what we saw?"

"That's where it was, but it's not what it looked like." The coyotes have stopped yowling.

We're fast-walking now. When we finally get to Old Paul's house, we're out of breath. Our fear settles into exhilaration as we walk down the driveway. We're safe, ready to tell. His sister's Jeep is in the driveway. Mary's in her thirties. She's got short dark hair and she's wearing a flannel and jeans. You'd call her sturdy. Her girlfriend's got curly hair and is wearing flannel too.

"We saw a UFO," New Paul says. Old Paul is in the garage, sitting in a heap of newspapers, his and mine to roll.

"What did it look like?" he asks.

We tell him and his sisters. And we tell them again. The lesbians are humoring us.

Then Old Paul offers, "Tonight is planetary convergence. It's a rare event. All the planets are lined up. That's why the sky is so bright. Look."

"Yeah," Mary adds. "They call it the Jupiter Effect. Some people think the world's going to end or the Second Coming or something. People are paranoid about earthquakes. In Arizona, they kept telling us not to go to California." The Pauls and I exchange a collective glance. The evidence adds up.

We can see what must be planets, brighter than usual, ranging from yellow-white to chartreuse, forming a line across the sky, which glows violet. "That one's Venus," Old Paul says, pointing to a planet with flares of yellow light shooting out on four sides. We stand in the driveway, the five of us, watching the sky fade to lavender, and then pink—the same shade as the ribbon road from my dream. As the pink becomes blue, the planets dissolve into it. We stare so long that our papers will be at least an hour late, no matter how much we rush our folding. It doesn't matter, though. The Apocalypse is nigh.

"Did you hear?" Old Paul asks. "Paul and Jenny are moving. *This* weekend."

"What? How do you know?"

"Becky told me," he says. "They're moving in a hurry. Something to do with their dad."

"Why didn't they tell me? What happened?"

"He probably just got a new job," Paul says. "It's pretty ridiculous," he adds, "that he thought you were the Second Coming." *He thought it? They both thought it. We all did.* But Paul's moved passed it, and he's giving me the cue to come along with him.

"Roll," he adds, handing me the many-sided lavender die. Each week is a little more, a contest or an experiment with greater risks and stakes. Dungeons and Dragons is a world you create, and once you enter, you want to keep going back until it replaces the real world.

My Roland is Pure Good, like Christ. As a psionist, he has mental powers that other characters can only gain by defeating enemies and acquiring their possessions. Paul's Creon is Chaotic Good, a cleric. Clerics are never pure good nor pure evil. They are spiritual knights, holy men who ride horses and slaughter enemies. They're realists.

We're after an elf who stole an anti-demonic spell. Roland can't kill the elf because he's just a petty thief. Pure Good doesn't kill Petty. But Creon needs a shield worth twenty points to buy the time it will take to duel him. Roland is using his psionic talent to impress the Wizard who doles out the shields. The lavender die sputters and jumps before it lands on twelve. "Yes," Paul says. "Exactly what you needed. The shield is ours."

"But would Roland give it to Creon, if he knows he's going to kill?" I'm trying to figure out how Paul can live with Chaotic Good, a clumsy footfall away from evil.

"If Roland has doubts, Creon has his sword to persuade him."

"What time do we have to get up for church?" I ask.

"Nine thirty service. So at least by eight forty-five."

"Should we go to bed?"

Under the covers, lights out, neither of us assumes a sleeping position. Backs straight, heads facing the ceiling, covers stretched to our chins, eyes closed, it's a standoff.

I crack first. "Was that a coyote?" I made a deal with myself that if I let myself do this tonight, I would never spend the night again. Roland is Pure Good. He keeps every promise.

"I don't think so," Paul says. "But I can't fall asleep." Either because he doesn't want to make me feel bad or because he's horny too, he accepts my defeat. "I'm like forty percent," he says.

There's no going back. Old Paul is just Paul again with New Paul out of the picture.

"I'm thirty," I say. Then I feel a palm cup my penis, outside the cotton of my boxers.

"You're at least sixty," he says. In other words, *You're hornier than I am.*

In retaliation, I reach down and cup his penis, already poking through the peehole in his boxers. "So are you," I say. "Maybe seventy."

"That feels good," he says. "I'm like ninety now."

"Yeah, me too." Paul slides the covers down to reveal our two hard penises. We both have full-grown crowns of pubes framing them by now.

Each week is a little more, a contest or an experiment with greater risks and stakes. Rules make it clinical. We reach for each other's swords, each savoring the rush of prickly warm lust glowing through our nervous systems. "You're a hundred now," I mutter, not able to speak in full voice.

"You too." Paul starts to adjust his body, maneuvering his head in the direction of my penis. We swallow each other's swords.

"Oh man," I hear Paul say, coming up for air. During sixty-nine, we've been discovering, time becomes as meaningless as it does in D&D. "It's three forty-five. We have to get up in five hours. We should finish."

"Okay," I say.

"Should we swallow?" he asks.

"Okay," I repeat, a little breathless.

"But be quiet. The vents," he says, pointing to the air vents that travel through the roof, all over the house, including his parents' bedroom.

"Tell me when," I whisper.

"Okay." We're riding the waterbed's little waves. It doesn't take long. Only a few more slurpy humps. "Now," Paul says. A thick injection coats my mouth. If I'm Pure Good, I'll never return.

20

COCAINE

I'm sleeping at home, even though it's Friday night. New Paul is gone for good, and the enduring Paul has family in town. I'm an expert sleeper. I go under like quicksand. It's one of the joys of my life. I float beneath my skin, where being thirteen means nothing and nobody ever heard of heroin. Since Stanley, the only intrusions on my sleep are fights between other people. Tonight this never happens.

My eyes squint open. The red numbers on the digital clock radio say 11:17. I've slept ten hours. I hear an orchestra of loud whispers spilling over my three-quarter wall: Cheech, my mom, and a male relative I won't name. They're trying to keep it down so they don't wake the kid. *Where'd he come from? Where's Nick?* I haven't seen this relative in at least a year, and Nick hasn't been here in over a week.

"He just up and went?" Cheech says.

"Apparently," my mom says. "It sure looks that way."

"Heroin," our visitor says, sniffling like he has a cold.

Nick got in a motorcyle accident. He broke his nose (again) and just about everything else. He was in the hospital for a couple of weeks, on morphine. When he got out, he started doing heroin. "For the pain," he'd say, when he and my mom fought about it. Now's he's gone, thank God.

I wish I weren't awake. I can taste the smoke from Cheech's cigarette. My mouth is dry and cracked and smells like a fart. I have to pee pretty bad.

I want to wrap myself in quicksand and walk to the bathroom. Instead, I squeeze into my Pat Benatar T-shirt and walk, one foot in front of the other, seven steps to the bathroom door.

"Speak of the devil," Cheech says, sniffing too. "We thought you'd never get out of that Goddamn bed."

The three of them are sitting around the dining room table, a green trash bag on the floor next to them. There's a scale on the table. I've seen scales like this, but only on TV, in old-fashioned butcher shops. It's got a stainless-steel platform and one of those bars like a ruler with numbers on it. Cheech has a little spoon in her hand, measuring little piles of white powder onto the scales. She's got a mirror in front of her, with a mountain of the stuff on one half and some hills on the other. My mom and our visitor are scraping the piles into tiny plastic baggies. *Scoop, separate, measure, scrape, seal.* Where do you even get bags that tiny?

I walk into the bathroom and shut the door. I pull my penis over the elastic of my pajamas and let the liquid rise. At first it stings, but just a little. Once the pee starts to really pour, all I feel is warm. It doesn't matter what's stirring in the living room. To prove this to myself, I back all the way to the closed door. I'm at least two feet from the toilet. My aim is perfect, and my stream is smooth, no jagged edges. The stream lands dead center in the bowl and makes a constant gurgle sound. I wish I could pee forever. Would it start to sting again? Would I pee my whole body out until I was invisible or dead? Would the bowl overflow and flood the house? Would I drown and take the adults with me? I never find out because the pee starts to dwindle. I inch closer to the bowl as the stream becomes a dribble. I'm impatient about finishing up and don't shake it all off, so when I put my penis back it makes a quarter-sized stain on my pajamas.

"Hey," Cheech says to our visitor, as I walk back into my room. "You should get some business advice from the kid. He's full of it."

"God, Cheech." My mom, sniffing too.

I sit on the bed for a minute, then put some shorts on and walk into the living room, never pausing in my beeline for the front door. "I'm going to Nichole's."

"Hey, Jason." It's our visitor. "Come here."

I do.

"Don't tell anybody about this. Nobody. Okay?"

"Don't worry," Cheech adds. "He never talks unless he wants to tell you what to do."

"Okay."

"It's important." He's serious.

"Okay."

"Nice Ops," he says, looking at my shorts. "I know the guys that started that company. They're millionaires now. I used to hang out with them when I had the surf shop."

"Go ahead, Boog," my mom says.

For three or four days, they are very focused on the bags and the powder. *Scoop, separate, measure, scrape, seal.* Like a factory. They seem excited.

I don't tell anybody. Even now, I'm squeamish about telling the story.

Cocaine is the least hippie drug imaginable. The fact that it replaced pot, acid, and heroin in my world meant the revolution was over. We were fallout, riding somebody else's cultural wave.

In the brain, cocaine is strong and fast, like a bully—but only if it's snorted, injected, or smoked. People have chewed coca leaves for centuries without getting addicted, becoming paranoid, committing suicide, or neglecting families. The powder is a salt: cocaine hydrochloride. It's made through a process of crushing the leaves, soaking by turns in solvents like alcohol and kerosene until crystals form. Crush these, and you've got the powder that filled up our house.

Of course, cocaine is a ubiquitous symbol of the quick-paced, hungry eighties. Even its cellular properties fit. Cocaine inhibits the reuptake of dopamine. It bullies dopamine to keep it from entering cells, leaving a lot of "extra-cellular" dopamine roaming the body, making you feel good. It alters consciousness more quickly than most drugs, but it has a very short half-life, so it dissipates quickly too, within about thirty minutes. So once you start snorting, you want to snort more, to keep that dopamine roaming. Alcohol increases the intensity of a cocaine high and lengthens the chemical's half-life. Scientific studies have demonstrated this, but users figured it out first. My mom and her friends sure knew it. Unfortunately, if you keep this up for any duration, you're almost certain to get depressed. It wouldn't be surprising if you started to have suicidal thoughts. You might get paranoid or delusional.

I hated those long nights. It was bad enough that my mom kept dating junkies, but it got worse when she started snorting cocaine. Just when Nick disappeared and I thought things might get better, the cocaine arrived. The parties, fueled by the dopamine wandering through their bodies, were loud and long. The aftermath of the parties was lingering and bruised. This period, the settling in of my adolescence, took place in three settings—at home, where you never knew when the adults would pull out the cocaine; at Paul's house, where sex experiments consumed everything; and at school, where I landed in the target position, taunted and bullied. Sleep, the one thing cocaine prevented, was the only break I got.

They're dirty. They're stupid. I can practically hear jaws clenching and razor blades scraping mirrors, just under the surface of the voices and anxious laughing. The nights have been getting later and later, and our living room is getting fuller and fuller since we moved into Sue Ellen's guesthouse, my fourth house in two years.

The guesthouse is a tiny ramshackle box just a couple of minutes from the lake. It's painted white with a thick gloss of red trim over hundreds of layers of clumpy paint. Our toilet is in a converted closet, something you would only see in New York City or Del Dios. The shower is an enclosed plastic rectangle in the backyard. My room has a view of Sue Ellen's house out back. She bought this place when she divorced JP. Our red doors match the Volunteer Fire Department across the street.

The sound moves from the living room, through the hallway (which is also the kitchen), and squeezes under the gap at the bottom of my bedroom door. No single voice finishes a phrase or a string of laughs without the interruption of another. My mom's is a bell slightly out of tune; Craig's is a lawn mower running out of gas; Cheech's is the biggest bass horn; Sue Ellen's is the hybrid offspring of a goose and a lovebird; Casey's, because he's twenty-two and the cutest cook at the Fish House Vera Cruz, because he drives a motorcycle and is always tan, because he drinks beer but has a perfectly flat stomach, is a relaxed male lion who knows he will inherit the pack. I don't know who else is out there, but I hear hyenas, skidding tires, light thunder, and a crying baby.

They're idiotic. They're morons.

"Uncle Craig is going to live with us until he gets the money to buy his boat," my mom told me right after we got here. His presence makes the whole thing seedier. He and my mom have to sleep in the same bed or take turns using the couch. Craig drinks Gallo Chablis in the morning and sends in rebates from packs of Camels and leaves black razor stubble in the kitchen sink and dirty ashtrays all over the house.

The sound wave swells, my mom's bell riding the crest. "It's true, Craig. It is too. Be quiet." My mom's telling that same old story about evil Mrs. Bowman trying to drown her.

"Don't contradict a lady," Cheech booms. "You'll be sorry."

"Tell them about the uniform, Cathy," Sue Ellen coo-honks.

"It was always starched, the creases ironed just so." She says *just so* in her exasperated five-year-old voice. "And she would march around like this." I can see her putting her hands on her hips and doing her stern Mrs. Bowman walk, her face squeezed into a grimace of authority.

"What a hard life," Cheech sounds. "Famous daddy. Pool. Perfect ringlets. Poor Cathy."

"So what happened to all that money?" Casey is surveying his pack.

"Her famous daddy ran off with it. And another woman."

"That part's true," Craig says.

"Money does not buy happiness," Sue Ellen says. "Who said that?"

"John Lennon," my mom says.

"That was 'love.' Besides, John Lennon got it from some philosopher."

"Sweet Jesus, now we're talking philosophy?" Cheech bellows.

"Maybe it was Jesus, the greatest philosopher of all time," Casey growls.

The scraping on mirrors, sniffing noses, and gulping of wine are like musical accompaniment. All I can think about is how gross it is to put straws in noses full of snot and suck in lines of powder, which must mix with the snot and get crusty in your nose hairs. I know it's even grosser to pass the straw and the mirror to your bloodshot neighbor, who then snorts up traces of your snot and maybe a nose hair along with his portion.

They'll stop soon. They'll go to bed. My room is at the other end of the house from the living room, but they might as well be sitting on my bed, staring me down, blowing smoke up my nose, and sprinkling white powder in my hair.

"Me and Cat are sisters." Cheech blows her hardest and deepest. "Big Port-a-ghee and little Port-a-ghee." If they were really sisters, Cheech would be my aunt. But Cheech is different from anybody I'm related to. Cheech is capable of discussing her own shortcomings, and she wants to talk about mine too. She doesn't discriminate between strengths and weaknesses. To her, it's all just the shit that makes people tick.

"I'll take Little Port-a-ghee," Casey says. Then I hear slurpy kissing sounds.

"At your own risk, man," Cheech says. I can see her shaking her head in warning.

I'm trying to wipe these people off the face of the earth with my thoughts. *They're dirty. They're stupid. They're idiotic.* I pull the pillow over my head. Writhe a little. Turn over. Take the pillow off. Breathe. *They'll stop soon. They'll go home.*

When I work myself up into enough fury, I stiffen my body, rise, open my door as noisily as possible, march into the living room, and ask in a taut rubber-band voice, "Can you please be quiet?" My superiority complex entertains them. The sight of me, a diminutive thirteen with feathered brown hair, angry almond eyes, and skinny limbs, is hilarious. They try to act serious, suppressing their smirks, and I go back to bed and listen to their muffled spurts and squeaks.

"Hey," my mom whispers as loud as she can. "Hey, Casey, let's go for a ride." My mom loves the back of a motorcycle. I hear her say this all the time, like it's a slightly naughty secret she wants the world to understand.

"I know," cousin Bryan says to Dave and me. "You can't fool me. I want some."

"You know *what*?" I ask, remembering my sixteenth birthday, when he told everybody he knew it was his fault that I "am the way that I am."

"You're on coke."

"What?" Maybe he got the idea because we didn't really eat.

"I want some."

I look at Dave, who's grinning a little. We are not on coke.

"Bryan, we're not on coke," I say.

"You are, aren't you?" he asks Dave.

"No," Dave replies, grinning. He seems to get Bryan and doesn't have to say much.

We're sitting in the dark, in a little cove by Lake Hodges. I've been living in New York for a couple of years. This is the first time Dave has met my family. My mom's living in Del Dios again. She's living in a house with a pool, with her brother Gary and her boyfriend Billy, just up the street from the house where she and Cheech helped Gary weigh and sort all that coke into little baggies. Billy is a guy they've all known since high school, a friend of Charlie's, also a junkie. But tonight the drugs are all in Bryan's head.

"You sure?" Bryan asks.

"We're sure," Dave says.

"Well, whatever," Bryan responds. "See that star up there." He points to a bright one.

"I think it's a planet," Dave says.

"Exactly. That's where my friend lives."

"What friend?" I ask. I've learned not to correct Bryan when he shares a delusion.

"This guy I met. He's a vampire."

"Where'd you meet him?"

"The beach in Carlsbad. I know some people on a couple of these other stars too."

Bryan is weirdly comforting. It's been a long day and a bad night. Dave met Nanny and Ralph. They came over and sat by the pool while we swam. Ralph is a little stooped now, so he's even tinier than he's always been, and he seemed to follow Nanny like a duckling with its mother. His voice even sounds like a quack, the words *fuck* and *Goddamn* still punctuating all his sentences. Ralph is reliably entertaining, and Dave likes an eccentric, so it was a promising start.

Then Dave and I went to get groceries for dinner. We bought eight giant and expensive fresh tuna steaks. When we got back to the house, my mom was pulling out of the driveway in her white Karmann Ghia. Billy in the passenger seat and Nanny squished in the back, looking out the window like a scared but resigned hostage. Ralph must have gone home. He always knew how to dodge the worst of it. "It took you long enough," my mom snapped at us. "We're going to happy hour." She had that bloodshot look.

"But we've got stuff for dinner," I said. She peeled out of the driveway, stirring up dust.

They got back two hours later, around seven. Billy said he'd cook the tuna like they do in Hawaii. Bryan showed up with his girlfriend. When we finally sat down, it was well after dark and the tuna steaks were overcooked hunks of brick caked in some kind of sweet barbecue sauce. My mom seemed too drunk to notice. Bryan devoured his. Dave and I picked at ours. When she thought nobody was looking, Nanny quickly picked her steak up with a fork and returned it to the platter. I was glad Dave got to see that, because it was a gesture that summed her up. She might be living out her old age in poverty, but she would preserve her dignity by refusing to eat bad food. As soon as dinner was over, my mom passed out on the couch, noisily. Nanny said she had to get home. That's when we decided to walk to the lake.

I've been on the brink of panic since the happy hour incident, but Bryan is calming me down a little. With Dave as witness, my family seemed a little too real, the history a little too present. But Bryan's friends on the stars dwarf the rest of it somehow. My mom will lose the house in a couple of months. Billy will start doing heroin again. Ralph won't live much longer. Bryan will continue to believe we're on coke and just don't want to share. But Bryan's friends on the stars are vampires and will live forever, hopping universes like it's nothing.

21

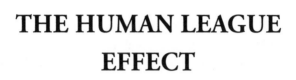

THE HUMAN LEAGUE EFFECT

The Mozart effect became a household term in 1993, after *Nature* published an article by a University of California–Irvine team of neuroscientists entitled "Music and Spatial Task Performance." It was one of those scientific articles whose influence well exceeds the tentative conclusions it draws. Music makes kids smarter, it was reported. It makes them better at math. It will get them into college. Pregnant women held speakers up to their bellies. Parents demanded more and better music education in schools. Never mind the modesty of the Irvine team's conclusion: that students performed better on a paper-folding task designed to test spatial reasoning for a ten-minute period after exposure to a Mozart composition.

The results were not duplicated with other, less "structured" forms of music. Kids were not going to get smarter listening to the Ramones or New Kids on the Block. The study had widespread emotional appeal because its promises were rooted in two cherished concepts: tradition and competition. Your children can be better than others if they are immersed in music, but only music that represents what Victorian cultural critic Matthew Arnold called "the best which has been thought and said." This is not hip-hop, not bubblegum, not folk, not punk, not synth-pop, not grunge, not screamo, not disco. Maybe it's jazz. Mainly it's Mozart.

None of this would seem to bode well for me. Parents-to-be on acid hallucinating Jim Morrison did not promise to make my fetus smarter. Klutziness with "special task performance" was one of the primary symptoms of my dyslexia. The scientists were not conducting experiments to measure the effect of The Human League on gay adolescent hippie kids growing up in the hippie-free zone of the early eighties.

Dozens of follow-up studies were conducted: mapping connections between music and memory, music and mood, music and political affiliations, music and delinquency, music listening versus music playing, music and the unconscious, musical motor skills. Most of these studies stuck to classical music as the touchstone, while a few extended the range to jazz, to test the idea that different types of music had different effects. For example, one study found that background music enhanced memory during studying *if* the same music was replayed during recall. Students who listened to Benny Goodman's "Sing Sing Sing" recalled what they had learned more effectively when it was replayed than they did when Mozart's Clarinet Concerto in A was played and vice versa. But there's a wrinkle. It also turned out that recall was stronger when different genres of music with similar tempos ("Sing Sing Sing" and Tartini's "Devil's Trill") were replayed. The brain seemed to be responding specifically to tempo, not to a researcher's idea of what is aesthetically sophisticated.

A few studies have focused on popular music, usually heavy metal and rap, mainly to look for correlations between violent music and adolescent deviance. One study suggested that exposure to hip-hop increased the racial sensitivity of white high school students. As with any area of brain research, it became clear that the central finding of the study—that music is related to other brain functions—led to a cascade of more complex (though pretty vague) conclusions. After all, listening to music involves multiple auditory perceptions (pitch, tone, rhythm), memory, emotions, cultural literacy, imagination, and countless other cognitive and perceptual functions.

The scientific literature on music and the brain is vast, and many questions will probably remain unanswered indefinitely. But I'd still like to know: if Mozart can help a child fold paper with more dexterity and there is a correlation between listening to Tupac and the development of empathy, what might happen in the brains of thirteen-year-old gay boys when they listen to Phil Oakley sing about the coming of the mirror man over an ocean of synthesizers?

Eric Seavey and I are sitting under the monkey bars, our lunches eaten. Eric, a Mormon kid, is practically Albino and was preppy before *The Official Preppy Handbook* came out six months ago and transformed the fashion habits of the entire white population of the school. But he's not cool preppy. His oxfords are grey pinstripe and his sweaters from the Men and Boys store, with initials where alligators should be. Neither of us has friends, so we've made an alliance, hanging out together at lunch to create the illusion of companionship. Eric is known for his intelligence, and he appreciates the fact that I can keep up with his conversation. I appreciate that he appreciates this. He overlooks my attempts to ape his upper-middle-classness. For some reason, he is willing to hang out with me despite the fact that I'm a magnet for crazed bullies.

"What do you think of 'Crocodile Rock' so far?" he asks. We're both in People Movers, the "advanced" chorus, the one you have to audition for.

"It's pretty good. I don't get the choreography."

"Fagaw," we hear. Steve Cunningham, the latest crazed bully. Our conversation has been a hiding place, a bad one. "Fagaw, there you are. What the fuck? Yo, Eric, why do you hang out with this fag?" He's wearing black cords and a black Blue Oyster Cult T-shirt. The stoners are the only white kids who resist the Preppy Revolution.

Steve grabs me by the collar and pulls me to my feet and then punches me in the stomach, hard. "Heh-heh-heh," he laughs, just like a cartoon villain. "Why don't you do some pull-ups? I saw you in PE. You can't even do one. I'll teach you." Another punch.

I'm paralyzed, the wind knocked out of me. He raises my arms and molds my hands to the metal bars. "Pull, Fagaw, pull." I won't do it. Another punch.

"Pull! Fuckin' pull!" No. Punch. He pushes me, and I swing. I can feel the blisters forming on my palms. "Swing like a monkey, faggot. Swing." I'm swimming in nausea.

My blistery hands give out. I'm a breathless crumble in the sand. "Faggot monkey." He grins and walks off toward the empty football field.

School used to be a relief. Not anymore—and not just because of Steve. The whole school seems to have acquired faggot radar. I feel like a pinball, banging around, dodging punches, drowning in dingdong jeers.

"I want to let you help choose our new songs," says Mrs. Jarvis, her big oval glasses swinging against her breasts. Mr. Jenkins, the music teacher, isn't a singer, so Eric Jarvis's mom comes in to coach us. She has a salt-and-pepper perm with the tightest curls you can get and wears draping faux-silk shirts.

Twenty of us—ten girls, ten boys—are seated on risers that form a half circle around the piano. Dena Prestininzi, the People Movers star, who once sang "New York, New York" and "Cabaret" on *Good Morning San Diego*, darts up her hand. "What about something classy, like Streisand's 'People'?"

"That's a difficult song," Mrs. Jarvis says. Dena gives her a sarcastic smile. *She* could sing it, we are to understand, if only the rest of us could. "But I'll write it on the board."

Six more hands go up, including Jeff Herbert's. He's a surfer way too cool and cute for People Movers.

"The theme from *Ice Castles*. 'Through the Eyes of Love,'" Edie Flaiz suggests.

"'Celebration,'" Rick Schirmer suggests.

"'Goodbye to Love,'" Kelly Decker offers.

"'The Piano Man,'" Stan Clark says.

"'Don't Go Breakin' My Heart,'" Maria Nelson proposes.

Mrs. Jarvis has called on everybody with a raised hand, except for Jeff Herbert, whom she considers a troublemaker because he surfs and hangs out with high school kids. Jeff's chest has a distinct shape, even though he's pretty skinny. Even when he wears an IZOD, it's tight, with the buttons undone all the way, hairs sprouting at the V-neck that make him seem like a man. Nicole Young told me once that she went all the way with him.

Pausing to see if his hand will go down, Mrs. Jarvis finally concedes and nods in Jeff's direction. "'Save It for Later' by the English Beat. Well, they're really called the Beat, but in America they're the English Beat." Heads turn in his direction, some in disdain, some, like mine, in awe. "It's ska," he says. "The new British Invasion. It's about to hit. Hard. Great harmonies." Mrs. Jarvis doesn't even write it in on the board. She doesn't like his tone, like he knows something she doesn't.

Ska? British Invasion?

"Well, let's vote," she says, like Jeff never said anything. "But before we do, I'd like to make a case for 'Through the Eyes of Love,' because it's a risk. It's bold. And for 'Don't Go Breakin' My Heart' because it has good parts for girls *and* boys."

Hands go up. We choose "Through the Eyes of Love" and "Don't Go Breakin' My Heart." Stan pounds his fist on his thigh when "The Piano Man" gets only two votes.

Ska? I haven't ever imagined that there could be a *new* kind of music. The idea replaces Steve Cunningham and Cheech and Craig in my thoughts. I enjoy the frustrating fact that I am totally unable to imagine what it might sound like. I think about ska for days. I ask Paul, but he doesn't know. I ask Sue Ellen, but she doesn't know either. "Why don't you ask that kid Jeff?" she suggests. I wish I could.

My mom's late picking me up. I'm waiting for the the VW Bug on the lawn in front of school. The crowd is dwindling. Jeff Herbert is one of the few who remain. He's hanging out in a car with his sister Julie and her friend, who are fifteen and go to San Pasqual High.

Queen is blasting from inside the car, "Don't try Suicide." The girls are snapping along with Freddie Mercury. *Don't do that. You got a good thing goin' now*. The song is two years old, the B-Side to "Another One Bites the Dust," which hit number one on *Billboard* in 1980, but for some reason everybody at school is into it right now. Julie's friend, blond and feathered like her, is singing out loud, *Don't try suicide. Nobody's worth it. Don't try suicide. Nobody cares.* She's more heavy metal wail than Mercury's rockabilly groove. *So you think it's the easy way out. Think you're gonna slash your wrists this time. Baby when you do all you do is get on my tits*. She sings "tits" at twice the volume, straight at Jeff. *You need help, you need help, you need help*, she continues. As soon as the song ends, Julie takes the tape out and throws it to Jeff like a football. He runs for a touchdown, slow enough to let the friend tackle him. As they roll on the grass, in this way that makes me think maybe they're not just friends, a new sound comes out of the car. It doesn't sound like anything I've ever heard. I love it immediately. The singer sounds British, and he sings in this way that is so relaxed he's almost slurring: *Save it for later, don't run away and let me down, you let me down*. It's the song, the one Jeff talked about in People Movers. "Save It for Later." The English Beat. Ska. About to hit. Hard.

The Bug's engine sucks up the sound like a vacuum. You'd think I would be glad to have only a small audience when my mom and Cheech finally show up, twenty-five minutes late. But Cheech is in the car, smoking. Her smoke rings sharpen my anger before I even notice it's a joint in her hand. *God*, I say to myself, *aaauuuggghhh*, not for a moment imagining Jeff might think this is cool. As we pull off the curb, I see Julie's friend raise her pinched fingers to her lips and pantomime sucking a joint. Then, I swear, I think I see her and Jeff kiss, with tongues, in a whir behind us.

"That's illegal," I say to Cheech.

"No fuckin' way?" she replies, as though I have taught her a valuable lesson, and we spurt off toward home.

Three weeks later, at noon on a Saturday, Paul and I are in his room, playing D&D with the radio on in the background, tuned to 91X, the hard rock station. Robert Plant is whimpering about the price of a stairway when, abruptly, the needle scratches right through his falsetto. Then silence.

"They screwed up," Paul says, savoring their fallibility.

Then a male whisper, "Sex," over the sound of synthesized drums, a cynical mechanized melody, and the sound of a breathy orgasmic woman singing over the man: *Feel the fire, feel my love inside you, it's so right. There's the sound and the smell of love in my mind.* "What the?" Paul asks. I have no answer.

We can't do anything but listen and hope. *I'm a toy come and play with me say the word now. Wrap your legs around mine and ride me tonight.* We stare at each other, at the speakers, back at each other. *I'm a man. I'm a goddess. I'm a man. Well, I'm a virgin.* We don't list percents, but it's safe to assume we're each at least forty.

The song fades, and a male DJ with a British accents, says "That was Berlin, 'Sex (I'm A),' and you're listening to the new 91X." We have just witnessed the birth of San Diego's first new wave station. The weekend is a revelation. We hear the English Beat—and not just "Save It For Later," but also "I Confess," "Tears of a Clown," and "Mirror in the Bathroom." We're introduced to Modern English, Adam and the Ants, Elvis Costello, Japan, Bauhaus, Blancmange, Joy Division, Madness, the Cure. We hear the full spectrum of punk: the Clash, Generation X, Dead Kennedys, Social Distortion. I hear ska, not just the English Beat, but Bad Manners and the Specials. We already know Duran Duran, the Eurythmics, ABC, and Culture Club. They're here too. The station doesn't seem to have that many records, so we hear most of these bands six or seven times over the course of the weekend, enough to learn the names and memorize the choruses. We leave the radio on constantly, even while we sleep, which isn't much. It becomes a good way to cover the sound of our experiments.

"What's that song from 91X, the one that goes 'La la la love plus one'?"

"Haircut 100. 'Love Plus One.'"

"I like that one," Nichole says.

"Queer name. They sound preppy to me, but sad preppy, like *Catcher in the Rye*," says Sue Ellen.

"They're cute," Nichole says. She likes nerdy, preppy guys.

Sue Ellen is the first adult who has ever talked seriously to me about books. Nanny reads Book of the Month Club selections, but she doesn't talk about them, except for sometimes their plots.

"I don't get it," I say. "He's crazy in that book."

"He's a crazy preppy. He's the kind I would have gone for. It would have turned out that he had no money and the MG he drove was his friend's dad's."

I'm still wearing khakis, a navy oxford, a navy IZOD belt, and of course my navy topsiders. But these clothes don't feel right anymore. They're not Haircut 100 preppy. They're not new wave.

"Then I started going for the John Steinbeck types, the ones with stubble and a big plan. It was less confusing."

"I read *The Pearl* in Mr. Sullivan's class," I say, trying to figure out what Sue Ellen's talking about.

"Oh, the one about how money is the root of all evil. That's bullshit. I mean, it's true, but it's still bullshit."

Mr. Sullivan never mentioned any of this.

"Mom, I'm hungry," Jimmy Freddy says. The baby born at our house on Lake Drive, the one Mona bit after she fried her brain on acid, has grown into a four-year-old version of JP, a round balloon of a kid with too much energy and a dangerous imagination. Jimmy Freddy is what Nanny calls a *holy terror*. A few days ago, Nanny was over and she found him swinging a huge stick like a sword. When she told him to put it down, he looked at her and said "fucking cunt." Nanny screeched with shock.

Last week, Nichole was babysitting Jimmy Freddy, along with her sisters. They were all playing in a plastic, kid-sized pool. Jimmy Freddy pulled his peewee out of his trunks and aimed it at the girls, screaming, "Ready, aim, fire." He doused them all, chasing them in and around the pool, his excess splashing off them and mingling with dead bees and oak leaves in the water. This confirmed our suspicion that he was a demon. Sue Ellen's response was a philosophical, "Jimmy, do you really think that was a good idea?"

"I'm hungry," Jimmy Freddy repeats.

"You just ate, Jimmy. And you're too fat anyway," she replies.

"But I'm bored," he says.

"Sing that song for Jason and Nichole."

"Here comes the mirr-o man," Jimmy sings. "Here comes the mirr-o man."

"Says he's a people fan," I say, not singing.

"Here comes the mirr-o man," Jimmy finishes, with a stomp.

"He's been practicing," Sue Ellen said. "Who sings that one?"

"The Human League."

"Trippy Name."

"Knock, knock, knock." Nanny announces herself as she comes out the back door. "Here you are, Uni. I've been looking all over the house." Since she got back from Idaho, Nanny is living in an apartment rented by her sister Mary in Alpine, a mountain town in southeastern San Diego. It's an hour away, so we don't see her much.

"Searched every nook and cranny, Nanny?" Sue Ellen cracks herself up.

"Very funny, Sue Ellen. Very funny." Nanny is patiently condescending. "Come inside, Jason. I have some paint chips to show you."

"For my stripes?"

"Yes, Uni, for your stripes."

Nichole and I follow Nanny through the back door and into my bedroom. She hands me three slim cards with paint samples on them, a range of teals, violets, and dark purples. I climb onto one of the twin beds Nanny gave me and hold the chips to the wall. I've been begging my mom and Nanny to let me paint three new wave stripes across the wall. "Let him express," Sue Ellen weighs in when I bring it up. My mom and Nanny agree in principle, but they roll their eyes at the flamboyance of her phrasing.

"Those colors clash with the bedcovers," Nanny mentions.

"It's true, but they're pretty," Nichole says.

"I don't care," I say.

"Okay. It's your room."

"I like this one, this one, and this one," pointing to the lightest teal, the brightest violet, and the darkest purple. "Where's my mom? Let's ask her if she'll paint it."

"Oh no," Nichole says, pointing out the window. "Look."

"Jesus, Mary, and Joseph," Nanny blurts.

Through the glass, we see Jimmy Freddy in the driveway holding a kitten over a rusty barrel full of water. The kitten, a black puffball with orange and white spots, dangles and struggles. It's drenched. Jimmy Freddy is grinning. Up and down, he dunks the kitten. "Get that Goddamn kid," Nanny says.

By the time we get outside, the kitten has been dunked six or seven times. Jimmy gives it up easily. "Jesus Christ. Sue Ellen. Sue Ellen!" Nanny is yelling. She never yells. She cannot comprehend Sue Ellen—one of the few subjects on which we disagree—and she can't stand Jimmy Freddy. Sue Ellen seems flummoxed but mostly annoyed at Nanny. *Are you* yelling *at me?* her eyes ask. *The nerve.* Nanny stares back with disgust.

The kitten is limp on the concrete. It's pathetic but alive, taking tentative steps to flee its persecutor, its wet fur blacker, oranger, whiter.

I remember the angry looks exchanged between Nanny and Sue Ellen as though seeing them through a crystal ball, magnified, clarified. The standoff signals a wrinkle in my worldview. It has a big afterlife in my psyche. Since I can't bear the conflict between the two adults who seem to offer me salvation, I escort that part of the memory to consciousness several times daily in the coming weeks, months, and years. I rehearse the dead end. I want to tear it down, take a jackhammer to it, find a resolution, get these two women to understand each other. Nanny clings to a life and aesthetic more difficult to sustain every single day, with each dollar spent, each painting or antique desk she sells. Sue Ellen refuses to acknowledge that the world outside doesn't conform to the spacey trip she's on. They are my role models, and I want them to cohere.

Dream of better lives, the kind which never hate, trapped in a state of imaginary grace. I'm sitting in the concrete driveway, my radio next to me, listening to Modern English's not-yet-classic "I Melt with You." Sue Ellen is in her studio, the windows open. "This sounds just like sixties psychedelia. I used to listen to music that sounded a lot like this." Sixties? I spend a couple of seconds entertaining the idea that she is right. Impossible. I tolerate her ignorance, but I remember that statement for the rest of my life.

The chorus fades out, and Translator's "Everywhere that I'm Not" begins, drums and jangly guitar, desperate male voice. The guy singing sounds like sex to me, like that's really what he's asking for.

"She's in New York. She's in Tokyo. She's in Nova Scotia," Sue Ellen says. "But he's not. He's sort of like Mick Jagger." She has gone too far now. Mick Jagger? I don't even bother with a response. Sue Ellen is threatening to interfere with the cellular transformation that listening to 91X has initiated in me. The music reorganizes brain cells first, but the chain of chemical exchange spreads through the entire nervous system, setting off a cascade effect through the metabolism, respiratory and digestive systems, even bone structure. The notes in the songs are arranged to topple rock 'n' roll, whose macho dominance has made it the stuff of oppression, but they are also shepherding my personal transformation.

New wave is not a single kind of music or people. It's a revolution gaining momentum, a loose band of genres and devotees committed to rejecting rock dominance and mainstream mediocrity. Punks have stolen the guitars, Goths have turned to the dark history of humanity to rescue poetry from trite and tacky love songs, New Romantics have painted their faces, programmed their synthesizers, and plundered Byron and Shelley for inspiration. And Ska Boys have turned to their dark-skinned brothers and sisters for collaboration in the musical struggle for liberty. They have instigated the metabolic reconfiguration of my adolescent viscera.

The songs, even the ones overplayed, are cogs in the factory of my alteration. I begin to imagine the revolution at home: Del Dios liberated from the post-hippie losers and rebuilt under the direction of my new wave heroes. Annie Lennox will be king; David Sylvian will oversee the bulldozing of houses and rebuild them as little Japanese palaces of beauty; Peter Murphy will run the Del Dios store, selling ripped fishnets and red wine distilled from the blood of corrupt politicians; Boy George will be the local priest, presiding over art-directed funerals; Robert Smith will revamp the Volunteer Fire Department into a new wave dance club, where cool people in their teens and twenties from all over San Diego will gather with their hair dyed blue and red and black and burgundy, waving their arms like snake charmers to the beat of mechanized drums. I am swirling in synth sounds, urbane irony, sexual innuendo, and futuristic melodies. The sounds diminish everything that has come before—my whole life, the history of music, the history of the entire world—to mere nostalgia.

New wave is about the future. A coalition of musicians in Europe and America have gone to work assembling the new me, crafting a milieu in which I would find my shape.

I'm a citizen in this new world, walking Del Dios roads arm and arm with Anabella from Bow Wow Wow, singing along to Haysi

Fantayzee's "Shiny Shiny," which plays over the town's loudspeakers. Adam Ant is leading a makeup tutorial in the park.

For some reason, David Sylvian is standing out in front of the house, platinum bangs hanging over fire-red hair, just a little gold eye-shadow, a pale powder, brown (not black) mascara, and lipstick to match the hair, our door, and the fire truck across the street. I wonder if Sue Ellen can see him, directing a crew composed of members of Bow Wow Wow, Adam and the Ants (minus Adam, who is, as we know, preparing his make-up tutorial in the park), The Pretenders, and The Clash. Skinny as they are, these are the muscles of the Revolution. Anabella holds a pick-axe. Chrissie Hynde is wearing a yellow helmet and a red plaid flannel cut off at the sleeves. Sylvian is giving quiet orders, half-distracted, as he pores over architectural plans, spread out on a platinum drafting table, glancing every few minutes at the house, white paint flaking, then the driveway, cracked concrete, me sitting on it with my radio, fiddling with the antenna to improve reception. I wonder if Sue Ellen is anxious or excited about the demolition and reconstruction of her guest house.

"Let's keep the door intact," Sylvian says. "I want to incorporate it into the new design."

22

RED DOOR

Two weeks ago, Nanny made a decision, something she does rarely and reluctantly. Home is too volatile: Cheech and Craig with their white powder, Jimmy with his kitten murdering, Sue Ellen with her *laissez-faire*, and my mom with her motorcycle boyfriend. Eighth grade is over, and I'm living with Nanny again.

I've never lived with air conditioning. It's hot in Alpine, in the nineties every day in the summer. I love feeling sealed up in a cool box, like the apartment is its own world with its own climate. This apartment, though far from upscale, is the closest I've come to the tract house of my dreams. The sheetrock and carpet are brand new. So are the kitchen appliances. Everything is white and beige, the blankness filled out tastefully with Nanny's art and antiques. I settle into days of *The Price Is Right* and filet mignon sandwiches on white bread. The way Nanny makes them, the soft bread sticks to the meat, the mustard or horseradish a spicy glue.

We hardly get any channels, but for some reason we get this LA TV station that airs a show called *MV3* on Wednesdays at four, an hour-long new wave American Bandstand. It's the highlight of my week. Besides the usual Missing Persons, Berlin, and Siouxsie, it plays stuff you don't hear much on 91X: Cee Farrow, Fashion, Bauhaus.

Nanny and I read out loud to each other, first *The Hotel New Hampshire*, and now *The Right Stuff*, about astronauts in Florida, where Mary lives.

The doorbell rings. Gary is late. My mom is already here. We're having a turkey dinner even though it's not Thanksgiving. We're all staying over, Gary and Kate in what's usually my room, my mom with Nanny, me on the living room floor. Nanny and I have been ensconced here for a couple of months. This is the first time we've had visitors. They feel a little like intruders.

Nanny says Gary's new girlfriend Kate is a witch. She belongs to a coven. When I open the door, Gary and Kate are standing there with a big red, shorthaired dog between them. "Hi, Jason," Gary says. "How's it goin'?"

"Hello," Kate says. The dog's tongue is hanging out, its floppy ears drooping, tail whipping Kate's shiny purple polyester wraparound skirt, wrapped around a teal blue leotard. Her skin is very pale, her hair henna red, wavy and feathered, way out of style. She has a blunt, slightly off-center nose, wears purple lipstick on her scrunchy lips, and looks over me suspiciously to see what's going on inside the apartment. Even the dog smells like pot. I can tell Nanny notices by the way she's holding her head as far back as it will go, turned slightly up so her nose can breathe air from above.

"Well, can we come in or what?" Gary says.

"Hello, brother," my mom says from the couch, where she sits with her glass of White Zinfandel.

"Hello, sister," he says. "You remember Kate?" The dog runs over to my mom.

"Well, who is this?" she says. "Hello, big red boy."

"That's Zack," Kate says.

"Hello, Zack," my mom giggles.

"Hello, son," Nanny walks out of the kitchen, dishtowel draped over her shoulder. "Hello, Kate. A glass of wine?"

"Sure," Gary says.

"Okay," Kate says.

"Jesus Christ," Nanny says, noticing Zack. "Where is that giant thing going to sleep?"

"He sleeps with us," Kate says, righteously. Nanny raises her eyebrows, surveys the room, lands on me, and turns on her heels to head for the wine in the refrigerator.

"No school today?" Gary says.

"I'm on vacation. I go to SP when I go back."

"SP?" Gary asks.

"San-Pa-squal-High-School," my mom says, pronouncing "high" and "school" in a fake voice, her imitation of a hoity-toity person, to show how big for my britches I am.

"Oh, man, high school," Kate says. "I feel for you."

"Why?" my mom asks.

"He is obviously too smart and creative for high school," Kate says, even though she's known me less than five minutes.

Nanny's back with two crystal glasses filled with clear pink wine.

"He's been staying out here," my mom says.

"Oh really," Gary says. "What do you do out here?"

"He watches MTV on the neighbors' television, mostly."

"MTV's okay," I say. "But I like MV3."

"What's that?" Kate asks.

"It's a video show, from LA. They play new wave, New Romantics, punk, post-punk."

"I see you know your music." I know Gary plays bass. He made a record with his old girlfriend Sarah. He used to play with Huey Lewis. But I see little connection between that and the music I like.

"I guess so," I say.

"What's for dinner?" Gary asks, sniffing the air. Zack, lying at Kate's feet, sniffs along with him.

"Turkey dinner," Nanny says.

"All the fixins," my mom says.

"Any hors d'oeurves?" Gary asks.

"I'm hypoglycemic," Kate says. "You don't want to see me have an episode."

"Some nuts?" Nanny asks.

"I need something more substantial," Kate says. My mom and Nanny lock eyes.

"Deviled eggs?" Nanny asks.

"That will be fine," Kate says.

She was going to save the eggs for later, since dinner is still a few hours away. We had it all planned out. "No onions. Just the way Unigagin over there likes them," Nanny says.

"Uni who?" Kate asks.

"Uni-gagin," Gary says. "It's what our gramma used to call everybody."

"I hear your cousin is a punk," Kate says to me.

"Bryan?"

"What?" my mom asks, defending her nephew.

"Punk rock," Kate says. "You know, the Sex Pistols, mohawks."

"Bryan has a mohawk. He paints his whole body green," I say.

"I hear Trever got all A's and B's," my mom says, mainly to Gary. "Jeannie said he loves it there." Bryan and Trever moved to Wisconsin with their mom and her new husband.

"He's always been smart," Gary says. "Madison is a cool town."

"It's supposed to be very cosmopolitan," Kate says.

"What do you mean?" I ask.

"You know, cool people, art, music."

"So guess what, Mom?" Gary says.

"What now?" she asks. "Do I want to know?"

"Kate and I are going to move down here, back to San Diego."

"What brought this on?" Nanny asks.

"Tired of Sonoma," Gary says. "Kate likes it here." There were floods. Gary's recording studio and greenhouse full of giant pot plants were swept away.

"I've been up there so long. The writers' scene is okay, but I'm ready for something new."

"You're a writer?" my mom asks.

"Science fiction," she says. "I write short stories. I wrote a novel. Trying to publish it."

"That's rad," I say.

"I've got to go baste the bird," Nanny says, disappearing around the corner into the little kitchen. "Want to help me, Cathy?"

Kate and Gary and I talk while they cook, about the music I like, the books I'm reading, San Francisco. Kate tells me that if I ever want her to critique my writing she'd be happy to. Gary says Bryan and Trever are coming for a visit. I can hear about the punk scene from Bryan.

"I heard that," my mom says from the kitchen. "I don't think he needs to be learning all about the punk scene."

Gary and my mom have always had a different way of raising children. My mom smokes pot, but she pretends not to. Gary smokes it with his kids.

Perception shapes reality. Neuroscientists and philosophers agree on that. Or, as Douglas Hofstadter puts it, more dramatically, consciousness is "a kind of mirage." Antonio Damasio calls it a "movie-in-the-brain." We're all living our mirages or movies alone, unable to crawl inside each other's and know what it feels like to be anybody else. Nanny can't feel my fear of my mom's boyfriends or my love of new wave; I can't feel her nostalgia for lost luxury or confusion about the near future; neither of us can know what's in my mom's head while I'm gone or anticipate how she'll get our attention.

Philosophers call the basic units, or tracks, of the movie mirages *qualia*, and neuroscientists have adopted the term. Qualia are the subjective qualities of any given perception: what it feels like. The wetness of wet. The painness of pain. The redness of a red door. Philosophers use a sadistic thought experiment to explain the concept.

Imagine Mary the Color Scientist. She is raised from birth in a colorless room, with gloves on, no mirrors, nothing that would allow her to see the color of her own body or the color in anything around her. Then, a team of scientists teach her everything there is to know about color—about light and waves, the rods and cones of the eyes, the neural pathways that produce sight. Once she knows everything there is to know about color, Mary is released. Will she be surprised by the sight of a red scarf? Philosophers line up on one side or the other. Some try to reconcile the two. Some argue the thought experiment misses the point. Nobody seems to care much about poor Mary.

Neuroscientists can't explain how the brain produces the subjective feeling of red. They use the term "explanatory gap" to describe the fact that they can explain how the brain perceives red, but not how it endows the perceiver with the conscious sense of redness. What they do know is that the eyes and brain manufacture redness, as they do everything we perceive. Our eyes see only a partial picture of the environments we fix our gazes on. Our brains fill that picture in, largely through expectations built on past experience, mood, temperament, and physical state.

Humans can compare notes and agree that though they can't share each other's qualia, what they are sensing seems similar, if not identical. But with a different set of eyes and a different type of brain, it's anybody's guess what a dolphin or a cricket or a being from another galaxy might see when shown Mary's red scarf. Some evolutionary biologists call the perceptual world of any given species an *umwelt,* meaning a species-specific sense of the world. Humans like to think of the human brain as the apotheosis of perceptual organs, but other species can sense information lost to us. Certain butterflies can detect each other's ultraviolet patterns and certain birds can navigate based on a sense of the earth's electromagnetism.

If what we see, hear, smell, taste, and feel depends on mood, personality, experience, intelligence, and a host of other subjective qualities unique to each individual, then it's no leap to say that every human possesses a distinct umwelt. I think about my mom's umwelt. I think about Nanny's. We are forever looking for ways to test and match each other's umwelts, to sense in unison. This is what love feels like. It's what art sometimes feels like. It's what spiritual transcendence feels like. Ever-present but hardly noticed rituals help groups of people to climb over the explanatory gap and match up the shape of each other's realities.

I guess writing this book is my attempt to give other people an approximate experience of my evolving childhood umwelt, the sum of my ongoing stream of qualia, to compare mine with the qualia streams I imagine for the people around me. I'll never experience the qualia of my mom's despair, or Nanny's anxiety, or Sue Ellen's bemusement, or Paul's precociousness. Writing about it is as close as I can get.

"We've got to go see your mother," Nanny says.

"Okay," I say. I start high school soon, and I'll have to move back in with my mom.

We leave our Alpine sanctuary and wind our way to Del Dios in Nanny's Mercedes. When we arrive, we walk into a time warp on the front steps, in front of the red door, all our attention on the glossy fire engine red, thick and uneven because it covers layers of chipped paint. The current layer must be pretty new, because it hasn't chipped yet. We stand on the doorstep, looking at the door. We hesitate. Nanny is tense, but she is so often tense.

I study the glass doorknob. It's a little imperfect mirror, reflecting the red but also the green of the shrub beside the doorstep. I don't want to go in. Nobody ever talks about it, but Nanny and I know that my mom is furious that I've been living in Alpine. The knowledge burdens our every moment—our reading aloud, our filet mignon, even my masturbation. My mom's anger is powerful. People go out of their way to avoid it.

We don't have the luxury of knocking. You don't knock at your own house, no matter what's inside. Nanny opens the door. "Cathy," she warns. "Cathy."

It's dark in the middle of the day. All the curtains are drawn. My eyes take a minute to adjust, so I smell it first, a stale salt smell. It smells like red to me. My mom is on the couch with clumps of white bandages stained brown wrapped around her wrists. Her dark hair is a matted frizz. We don't know it, but she called Jennifer after she slit her wrists. Jennifer got help, stayed with her, then left her to sleep.

"Jesus Christ, Cathy. Jesus Christ! What the hell is wrong with you? Are you stupid?"

I melt. I feel my body fade and shrink until I am a transparent doll-sized kid crouching in the corner of the room, receding into the wall.

"Jesus Christ, Cathy, what have you done?"

My mom isn't talking. Her eyes open only slightly. Her lids are skewed, off-kilter, scrunched. It isn't like her to sit still while somebody accuses her of anything.

"What the hell do you think you are doing? Cathy. Ca-thy. Goddammit, Ca-thy. Cathy!" Nanny sounds like she's shaking my mom with her voice. "You have a son. Goddammit!"

"He doesn't need me."

No, I don't. Right, I don't.

"He lives with you now." *Recede.*

"Cathy, goddammit, he *loves* you. *We all* love you."

My mom looks straight at me. She opens her eyes all the way. I can see her in them now, awake and ready to fight. "No, he doesn't. Look at him."

Stay still. Look down.

"Goddammit, Cathy, just stop it. Stop it."

"It doesn't matter. He doesn't give a shit about me. Just ask him. He doesn't need me. He doesn't even love me. I'm not fucking good enough for that little shit."

"Stop it, Cathy. Don't be stupid."

"He doesn't care if I die. He'd be better off. Right, Jason? Right?"

I love you, Mommy. I can't say anything. I am too guilty. Without me, my mom has no reason to live. She hasn't ever been an adult without me. I am her life, and I've left, and I'm only fourteen. I've made it clear that she shames me and I am better off without her.

I love you. I stay silent, receding.

The silence lasts maybe twenty minutes. We turn around and head back to Alpine. Nanny keeps muttering "Jesus Christ" to herself.

23

NEW LIFE, NEW SONG, NEW RELIGION

It's a perfect day for a barbecue. It's eighty-seven degrees now, not too bad, but by six thirty, when people start to come, it will be cooling off.

My mom and Sue Ellen had a fight after the suicide attempt, so we moved into a tiny, awkward house about five minutes up the hill from the lake. My mom sleeps in the living room. I'm in the bedroom. Gary and Kate are staying with us until they find their own place. They're in the garage.

This is the first family event since my mom tried, or supposedly tried, to kill herself. I've been pretty good at not thinking about it, but today it's playing in my head like a movie. Jennifer is the one who found my mom, and she's the only one who has mentioned it since. She asked me if I was okay. I said *yes*. One syllable was all it took to escape the question.

Nanny is the first to arrive and the only one who has to drive, which means the Mercedes is parked right in front of the house for all to see. It's almost like the house doesn't exist. For this barbecue, at least in my mind, we are all Mercedes.

The lawn fills up, everybody planting their feet to get a good grip so they won't topple down the hill. Plates get piled with burgers and dogs and potato salad. Cups get filled with Coke or wine. Beer cans get popped. Plates get licked clean and cups and cans drained. The sun sets red over the mountains between us and the coast.

"Did you see that guy Ryan?" my mom asks Jennifer.

"Oh, yeah, with the salt-and-pepper hair," she says. "I know him. He's on the fire department. You like him?"

"We're going on a date," my mom says.

"You mean the hippie guy?" I ask, disgusted.

"He's not a hippie," my mom says. Jennifer laughs as I stare in horror at the gray curls drooping off the head of the wiry guy on the lawn, with his long, skinny sunburned nose, bony knees peeking out of cutoffs, tank top showing off a surprisingly muscular, if thin, torso.

"He looks like one to me," I say.

"Well, I'm going out with him."

At this, Nichole comes over. "I heard that, Cat," she says. "Cat likes Ryan," she says, like she's talking to one of her girlfriends from school.

"I'm going inside," I say.

In our box of a living room, Gary and Kate are sitting on the couch with our new neighbor Carrie Jo, on our single chair, all holding plastic cups of wine. "What do you write?" I hear Kate asking Carrie Jo. "What genre?"

"Short stories, mostly. And essays. I wrote a romance novel, but I haven't published it. That's where the money is."

"You may be right," Kate says. "But I can't write like that."

"What's your genre?"

"Science fiction. I've published a few stories. I'm working on a novel now."

"I'd love to read something," Carrie Jo says.

"I don't show my unpublished work," Kate says. "But I can give you one of the published stories." I sit on the floor between Bryan and Carrie, taking this in.

"Kate's stories are trippy," Gary says.

"I've never really read science fiction," Carrie Jo says.

"Oh, you should read Ursula Le Guin," Kate says. "She's a goddess. A genius. Science fiction is the literature of our time."

Have I walked into someone else's party by accident? I've heard the word *novel* twice. I've heard *short stories*. I've heard *essays*. I've heard *literature of our time*. How did this happen? I feel as drunk as they are.

"Jason's a writer," Kate says. "Aren't you?"

"I don't know," I say.

"I've seen you writing in your composition book," she says, like she's been watching me.

"That's just song lyrics," I say. I've kept up my practice of writing imitations of my favorite lyrics. Right now Depeche Mode's "New Life," Howard Jones's "New Song," and Duran Duran's "New Religion" are on deck.

"Poetry," she corrects me. "Lyrics are poetry. Aren't they, Gary?"

"Sure," he says. "Good ones."

"Give us a reading," Kate says. Carrie Jo's raising her eyebrows. She doesn't approve of drawing children out like this.

"Really?" I ask. I'm proud of a couple of my songs.

"Sure. We'll workshop it."

I scramble through the hallway-bathroom to get my journal from my room, my feet wavy from the adults' drunkenness.

When I get back, I sit back down on the floor, legs crossed, and say, "Okay, I wrote this one for Duran Duran. It's called 'Mixed-Up People.'" Carrie Jo raises her eyebrows higher to indicate that Duran Duran, her daughter's favorite band, is not poetry.

"I've lost my place again," I read. "I'm running with the faces of a hundred thousand men. The road was clear. But now we're near, there seems to be no end."

As I'm reading, my mom walks in. "What's that?" she asks.

"Jason's lyrics," Kate says.

"Not bad." Gary says. "Those are pretty good."

"Jason, I'm telling you, those are better than anything I wrote at your age. You are a writer," Kate says.

Paul and I are sitting on the lawn on the side of the house, letting the Sun In take. We've got the bottle between us and periodically one of us picks it up and sprays his bangs with the sticky, salty-smelling stuff. "You're turning," Paul says. "It's twenty percent lighter." I pull my bangs down and strain my eyeballs upward to get a look. The strand I'm pulling is glittering orange as the sun shines through it.

"Yours is working too." His bangs are a burnt orange now, getting lighter. Ryan pulls up in his truck, his big head of curls smiling out the side window as he comes to a stop.

"Nice hair," he says, walking right up to me and patting my bangs.

"Ha ha," I say. "Be careful. It's got Sun In in it still."

"Gross," he says, looking at his sticky palm. "Your mom here? I'm just stopping by."

"She's inside."

After only about seven minutes, Ryan comes out, my mom behind him. "We're going down to Hernandez Hideaway for Happy Hour," my mom says. "There's stroganoff you can heat up if you're hungry."

"Okay," I say, pretending for the moment Paul's not here. I'm embarrassed that he's seeing my mom being wooed, but glad that she's going out.

We play records. Howard Jones, Tears for Fears, Echo and the Bunnymen, the Human League. We read the lyrics carefully as we listen. We debate Howard Jones's sexuality. "Sometimes I'd like to go to bed with a hundred women or men," he sings.

"He's bi," Paul says, getting comfortable with the word. "I think I'm bi," he says. "You are too."

I'm not so sure about this, and not ready to say the word out loud, not about myself. "You think he is?"

"It's obvious." And so the conversation turns, until the sun goes down. It's time for bed.

Nanny's twin beds are kitty-corner with each other. I'm in one, Paul in the other, our feet facing each other. From my bed, I have a view of Jon Bon Jovi's thick chest hair. Paul's head is next to Tom Cruise's hairless chest. "I'm forty percent," I say, my hand secretly caressing my dick, which is more like eighty-five percent.

There's a pause. "Do we have to do this every time?" Paul says, off the script. Another pause. This one stretches into unsleeping silence, very loud inside my head, pulsing in my dick, which doesn't get any less hard even though I'm exploding with frustration and hurt. *Do we have to do this every time? No, we don't. I never want to. I always plan not to.* Yet every time, I do, and that's because of Paul. It's because he supplies the opportunity. He has been very eager to supply it *every time*, up to now. I lie here with my forty percent penis and think this same set of thoughts, one on top of the other, until my mind is worn out.

It's 9:30 p.m. on New Year's Eve. Bryan and Trever are finally here. Gary and Kate found a place in Del Dios, and the boys are going to stay with them for a few weeks. The adults are all at a party at my mom's friend Brian Tucker's house. Bryan and Trever are planning their own party. They have pot.

Bryan's mohawk isn't very long, maybe three inches high. He doesn't spray or spike it. But everybody at the store is staring at us anyway. They know me but not my cousins, one too punk and one too manlike to be friends from school. Bryan is about to turn eighteen. Trever's fifteen, but he's taller and thicker than his brother. Trever is dressed normally, jeans, blue T-shirt, light brown wavy crew cut, vans. He's the only cousin with blue eyes like Nanny's. Bryan is in jeans and a T-shirt too, but the jeans are ripped at the knees and the T-shirt says DEAD KENNEDYS across the chest. He's skinny and tan, and his mohawk is darker than my hair.

"Take me to an airport and put me on a plane," Trever keeps singing. It's Bryan's favorite song. "Hurry hurry hurry, before I go insane." Bryan carries a six-pack to the counter and pulls out his wallet.

"You got ID?" Fran asks.

"Nah," Bryan says. "It's for my dad."

"No dice," she says. "Tell your dad he's gotta come in himself."

"Worth a shot," Bryan says, grinning at her.

"Happy New Year anyway," Fran says.

"I have an idea," Bryan says. He whispers to Trever. "Follow us, cuz."

Walking Lake Drive at night is spooky, because even though there are no streetlights, the oaks seem to make shadows over the darkness. There's no shoulder on the road, so it feels like you could be struck by a car at any moment. Most houses are dark, but a few of them boom with light, voices, and music. We pass a field with two rusted-out cars and a house with llamas, which seem to be kneeling in the dirt, asleep, before we reach Brian Tucker's house.

"I'll be right back," Bryan says.

"No," Trever says, "I'll go. I won't be as noticeable."

"Whatever," Bryan says. "Jason, you come with me." He leads me down a path through the brush and pulls up a piece of blue tarp. "Bingo," he says. "Our ride to paradise."

We are going to hijack Brian Tucker's kayak.

Trever skids down behind us. "Ready, here I come," he says, holding up two bottles of Champagne. "Let's get this show on the road." He tosses the bottles into the kayak and grabs the front end. Bryan grabs the back. I hold onto one side, barely able to get a grip, not bearing any weight at all. We walk about five steps before Trever says, "We gotta turn this thing over. It'll be a fuck of a lot easier to carry."

"What about the Champagne, bro?" Bryan says.

"You carry it, Jason."

"And the oars, genius?"

"We'll each take one," he says. I grab the bottles, one in each hand, and follow them to Lake Drive, under barbed wire, and down a dirt path to the lake, where we jump in and launch. The lake is shiny and black, an archetypal ripple of moonlight extending from the island, our destination, to the shore. It isn't actually an island, but a lump of land that juts out from the town of Rancho Bernardo on the other side. To us, though, it is an island, uninhabited except by a few deer and maybe some mountain lions. When we get about halfway, Trever takes the oars out of the water. "Bry," he says. "You got the pot?"

"Right here," Bryan says, patting the pocket of his jeans. "You got the pipe?"

"Right here," Trever says, patting the pocket of his T-shirt. "And the lighter." He hands them both to Bryan, who pulls out the baggy and packs the pipe, lights it, sucks, holds his breath, and releases with, "Aaahhh, this is the life."

He hands the pipe and the lighter to me. I look at him, pause, and hand it to Trever.

"You don't want any, cuz?" Trever asks.

"No, thanks," I say.

"It's okay. You're old enough," Bryan says.

"Shit," Trever says. "I'd been smoking for a few years at your age."

"That's okay," I say.

"Whatever floats your boat," he says, lighting and sucking while Bryan giggles, quick and high-pitched. Trever laughs the smoke out of his lungs, choking on it but seeming to like it.

"Okay, let's get this show back on the road," he says, rowing us out of the pot cloud we're in. When we get to the shore, Bryan and Trever debate the most secure position for the kayak, worried it will float out and we'll be stranded. Once it's safely on the shore, a couple of rocks propping it in place, we head uphill and settle on a spot where two big rocks in the ground form a clearing in the brush.

"We can keep a lookout for mountain lions from here," Bryan says, even though we're in a perfect spot for mountain lions to see us without us seeing them. Trever pops both bottles of Champagne, one after another, putting his mouth around the first to stop the bubbles from spilling out and handing me the other. I hesitate before copying him, losing some froth to my shirt, but getting a big gulp anyway. I must make a funny face, because Bryan is cracking up.

"I love you, cuz," he says.

"What's not to love?" Trever adds. I take another gulp of Champagne while they pass the second bottle between them. Trever takes a hit off the pipe, offering it to me again. "Now that you have a little of the bubbly in your gut, maybe you'll change your mind."

"No, thanks," I say. The stars are gliding in tiny circles, barely perceptible.

"You'll like it, cuz," Bryan says, not goading, just trying to give me a good time.

"I don't think I will," I say. I have to hold out on this point. It's one of the important things differentiating me from everyone else.

They drop it. We guzzle Champagne until we fall asleep, floating in a sky full of gliding stars.

It's raining, hard. I'm in bed but not sleeping. I'm thinking about changing things at school. Bryan and Trever have gone back to their mom's, but Bryan's mohawk made an impression. I want to turn mod. I don't want to be like the real mods you see at school or in videos by the Jam, with army-green parka and thrift-store polyester, riding Vespas. But at school people call all forms of punk and new wave *mod*. I want to be newro, but I call it *mod* so my mom and others will understand what I'm talking about.

What I really want to be is Shane Carlin. Shane is a junior. He's tall and skinny, wears black eyeliner, tight jeans, big boots, ripped T-shirts, and a bone choker like Adam Ant's. Two days ago, Shane was on the same bus with me, not the school bus but the city bus, which I sometimes take home from school. I swear he looked me up and down. I can't figure out why.

The front door bangs open, and with it the sound of the rain gets louder. "Shit," I hear my mom say in a loud slur. "Shit." Then stumbling. "Shit." The door doesn't bang shut.

"That's it," I hear. "That's it." I hear what sounds like the coffee table thrown against the wall. "Shit."

I'm thinking that if I just ignore it, she'll stop. But the banging and slurry shouts keep coming. I decide I'd better go out there. When I get to the living room, my mom is standing in the center staring at the furniture like it's been plotting against her.

"That's it," she says again.

"That's what?" I say more than ask.

"I'm done," she says. "I'm done," barely glancing at me.

"With what? What are you done with?" I ask, assuming the tone of a firm, rational parent unfazed by the hysterics of a toddler.

"Why would you care?" she says.

It's only been a few months since the suicide attempt. We've changed our house, my mom's changed boyfriends, I've changed my bangs. But she can't change her brain, and I can't change my mom.

"You wouldn't understand," she screams. "That's it," she repeats, turning and trotting, literally, out the open door into the rain.

I follow her, watching as she trots past the garage and disappears toward the hill in back. I follow, slower, my hair and pajamas soaked instantly. When I get to the other side, I see her crawling on the grass, peeling it to get to the mud underneath, dark curls pasted to her face.

"Come inside," I say. "What are you doing?" I should say *Mom*, but I haven't used the word in more than six years.

"No," she screams. "Leave me," she says. "Leave."

Finally, I do what she says. I go inside, sit on the couch in my muddy wet pajamas, and dial the phone. "Nanny," I say.

"For Godssake, Jason. What time is it?"

"My mom is freaking out."

"What now?" I tell her what's going on. "I'm going to call Gary," she says.

When Gary gets here, I'm still on the couch, which is soaked now too. "What's going on?" he asks, beads of rain in his short Afro. I tell him and he goes outside. I hear yelling.

"Leave."

"What the fuck are you doing, Cathy?"

"Leave."

"You're coming with me."

A car door slams. Gary comes in. "I've got her. Go back to bed. I'll take her to my house to sleep it off."

24

MANIC AND DEPRESSED

My mom is not the only mother on our street whose episodes are cycling out of control.

The Carrie Jo screech is louder and more throaty than usual. These are the sounds that earned her the title "Crazy Lady of Del Dios," which is saying something, given the population here. Nichole's little sister Angela and I are crouched under a pepper tree across the narrow dirt road from the house, listening. Summer, Carrie Jo's daughter, is Angela's best friend. Since I moved next door to Summer, the three of us have become a unit.

We can picture her red face, pug nose, and coarse blond hair flying. We can picture Summer backing up into a wall until there's nowhere to go. "Suu-mmmm-eerrr. Do? You? Think? It's. Easy? Raising? A child? Like. You?"

Summer's answering, it's not loud enough to hear. She could never scream like Carrie Jo.

"I didn't have to do it." You can hear the pain in her throat in every screechy syllable. "I never had to do it. I didn't need a baby."

"I think we should knock on the door," Angela says.

"And then what?"

"Say we're here to see Summer. Play innocent. 'Hi Carrie Jo, can Summer come out and play?'" She says this last part in a deep voice, like the exorcist.

Without thinking about it, we walk to the door and knock simultaneously. No answer. "Suu-mmmm-eerrr. Come here now. Don't you ignore me." We knock again. The screaming stops, but still no answer. We wait a full minute and raise our two fists again. This time, the door swings open, Carrie Jo greets us, red face, flying hair, pug nose. "Yes?" she says, clipped but pretending not to be hysterical.

"Is Summer home?" Angela says.

"She's busy. She's got homework." We can see Summer slouched against the hall above the stairs to her room, a skillet and rolling pin on the floor next to her.

"Hi, Summer," Angela calls, ready for trouble.

Summer looks up. Carrie Jo looks back. "Can I go out?" Summer says.

"Do what you want. It's not going to change anything." Carrie Jo disappears into the part of the room we can't see, and Summer runs, full sprint, through her house and out to us.

In the full sun, we see that Summer has red marks in the shape of fingers on both sides of her neck. Her eyelids are puffy, eyes pink. "She said I looked like a whore. I was wearing the makeup Nick Rhodes wears in the 'Girls on Film' video. She asked me if I wanted to be like the sluts in the video. She told me to take down all my posters if I didn't want to be a whore."

"She's a witch," Angela says.

Chippie, Summer's pet chicken, follows us to my front door. Summer has lots of chickens, for the eggs, but Chippie is the only pet. He comes in the house. He comes when you call him. He's a hen, but we call him *he*. "Chippie, go home," Summer says, wiping her eyes.

"He can stay," I say. "Why not?"

"We don't want the witch to boil him into stew," Angela says.

Angela and Summer examine my posters. Summer says, "Tom Cruise is a babe."

"He's cool," I say, even though he's not, even though I've never seen a movie with him in it. Angela and Summer know this, but they don't object.

"I'm hungry," Angela says.

"Want to go to the Store?"

"Carrie Jo won't give me any money," Summer says.

"Carrie Jo," Angela says, scrunching her nose in imitation of Summer's mom's pug nose and doing her best impression of her screech. "Suuu-mmmm-eerrr. No junk food. Here," she screeches, holding out her two palms, "eat these delicious alfalfa sprouts."

We all screech it: "Suu-mmmm-errr."

"Come with me," I say, leading them to the kitchen. I open the freezer and pull out a frosty jar of quarters, dimes, nickels, and pennies. "My mom's tip change," I say. "This is where she hides it."

"From who?" Angela asks.

"Robbers," I say, digging out seven quarters, nine dimes, eleven nickels, and about twenty pennies. It's harder to tell what I've taken if I spread it out over various denominations. We have enough for a cherry pie, Honey Bun, Twinkies and Zingers, a Snowball, three sodas, and probably some candy.

From: Summer Bello
Subject: re: writing a book
Date: September 4, 2002
To: Jason Tougaw

hey—no fair!!
I want to write a book of my life as well. I'm way more fucked up, and had a way more fucked up childhood. If you do include me in your book, I want to be like, a WHOLE chapter! You can write about how Angela came running to

> your house fearing for my life, and how my mom was THE Del Dios "crazy Lady".

I haven't heard from Summer in at least three years. To be fair, she hasn't heard from me either. Summer moved up near Santa Barbara during my junior year of high school, with Carrie Jo and her new husband. While she was there, she found out Carrie Jo had lied to her all her life about who her father was. It wasn't Jim, the guy who molested her. Life was hell with Carrie Jo, so my mom and Ryan agreed to let her move in with us, into my room. We had to share a bed for my entire senior year of high school.

But then Summer started doing crystal. After high school, we saw less and less of each other. I moved away, and she had a series of relationships with women and men. When she's with a man, she wants a woman. When she's with a woman, she wants a man. She became a dental assistant to support herself. Now she's married to an architect named Andy. She's taken his last name. They've settled in Oakland. Whenever I see her, she teases me. "Look at you, Mr. New York hipster."

Summer has tracked me down to tell me she finally knows what's wrong with her: bipolar disorder. It took three suicide attempts and two hospitalizations to figure it out. She's relieved, in a good place, she says, going back to school.

> *From: Summer Bello*
> *Date: September 5, 2002*
> *To: Jason Tougaw*
> *Re: re: Writing a book*

> My major is going to be English, minor in journalism. I wasted a bunch of time taking all those chemistry and biology classes in preperation for hygiene school (which I DO NOT want to persue now!!).

I want completely out of the health field! I actually am setting my sights on editing. I don't like to say too much, in case I fail. school is harder for me—being crazy and everything.

I am actually quite inspired by Elizabeth Wurtzel. She reminds me of myself. I'm sure many women say that. She does ramble on in her writing, but hey, she got to be a music critic for The New Yorker and New York Magazine. talk about dream jobs!!

Right now I am reading *Bitch*, as well as Hunter Thompson, (ok, I'm only reading *Fear and Loathing in Los Vegas*, which an eighth grader could read—but were you impressed for at least a second?).

I was hoping you could give me some tips on some interesting classes, or books. I guess I have to take Shakespeare. I want to take classes that study the bible. Wurtzel makes it sound so scandalous!

I don't know if I can work at another dental office as long as I live.

Hello Starbucks 8$ an hour!

No more shopping sprees at Banana or 50$ manicure/pedicure every two weeks, but thats ok. I have been reading a lot of Buddhist writings, and even gone to the Zen center a few times. My materialistic way of thinking has been changed quite a bit.

ok—now I have had way too much coffee, and I am rambling.

Talk to you soon,

I am going to attempt to call Angela again, and maybe go visit her since I have two weeks off.

xoxoxo,

summer

In her memoir about manic depression, *An Unquiet Mind: A Memoir of Moods and Madness*, Kay Redfield-Jamison writes, "I have become fundamentally and deeply skeptical that anyone who does not have this illness can truly understand it." I'm sure she's right.

Aside from Bryan, nobody in my family has submitted to diagnosis. But diagnosis of mental illness is always a guess, if an educated one. The symptoms of bipolar disorder fall into two categories, *mania* and *depression*. Mania may involve increased energy, restlessness, euphoric moods, extreme irritability, racing thoughts, fast talking, distractibility, lack of concentration, little sleep, unrealistic beliefs in one's power, poor judgment, spending money, increased sex drive, and drug abuse (especially cocaine and alcohol). Depression may involve ongoing sadness or anxiety, a feeling of emptiness, guilt, worthlessness, or helplessness, loss of interest in pleasure, decreased energy, fatigue, restlessness, irritability, too much or too little sleep, erratic weight loss or gain, chronic pain, persistent illness, a penchant for physical injury, and thoughts of death or suicide. The symptoms sound like my mom—sometimes. My father's behavior seems to fit the profile too, though decades of heroin complicate things. They sound like Carrie Jo—and later, like Summer. But of course there are variations on the diagnosis and the experiences it tries to describe, which range through psychosis, mild depression, hypomania, rapid cycling, mixed states. And of course, many of these symptoms overlap with those that belong to other diagnoses. And of course, the names for all these diagnoses and symptoms change with the decades.

Currently, psychologists call both the mania and depression *episodes*. If enough stress ensues, any given episode may tip over into psychosis. Episodes typically recur periodically for the duration of a life. As with so many mental illnesses, it is becoming apparent that bipolar disorder cannot be traced to a single cause. Rather, a combination of genetic markers creates a predisposition toward bipolar disorder. Little is understood about the physiology of bipolar disorder, and while preliminary studies suggest that the bipolar brain may possess enlarged basal ganglia or grey matter deficits in some places and excesses in others, nobody is ready to explain what this might mean. The studies, hypotheses, and theories cycle through labs and psychiatric clinics. In the meantime, the bipolar brain can be stabilized with lithium or anticonvulsants. Sometimes antipsychotics are prescribed. As with my parents, people often treat themselves with whatever mood-altering drugs they can find: alcohol, pot, cocaine, heroin, valium.

Bipolar disorder has traditionally gone undiagnosed because the line between personality and illness is impossible to draw. *She's moody*, people will say of a woman who screams threats at her daughter. Or *she's erratic*, of a woman who insists on crawling in the mud during a torrential downpour. Or *suicidal*. Or *irresponsible*. Or *delusional*. Or *mean*. Or *self-obsessed*. *She's the Crazy Lady of Del Dios. She's the daughter of the Portuguese Pepper Pot.*

I'm not qualified to diagnose anybody with anything. I know better. But I wonder nonetheless.

The phone rings. I just got in from Princeton. It's the fall of 2003, and I've just begun my third year teaching there.

"Hello," I say.

"Is Jason there?" an unfamiliar male voice asks, deep and hesitant.

"This is Jason," I say.

"Jason," the voice says, trying to sound upbeat. "This is Trysten Robinson. Do you remember me?"

It sounds familiar, but I'm not sure.

"Summer's friend," he adds.

"Oh, Trys," I say. That's what we called him, what Summer called him. Trysten was Summer's age, a sweet blond kid who became Summer's conscience, an anchor for her. He wore freshly washed knit shirts and pressed khaki pants. His joviality was the smart kind, not the deluded kind. Summer loved him more than anybody.

"How are you?" I ask. I haven't heard from Summer in over a year. Last time I did, she'd had a breakdown and ended up skipping out on Andy and spending a week doing heroin with a prostitute in the Mission. She was doing better, but planning to leave Andy.

"I have some sad news," he says.

"Summer?" I ask.

"She OD'd." He heard it from a friend who heard it from a friend.

"On what?"

"I don't know," he says. "But she died."

"Oh, God," I say, in a hot fog.

"It's weird, though, because it's all secondhand, and I can't find any real proof. I Googled her and all I got was this creepy article from a San Diego paper about medical marijuana. They interviewed Summer, who said she was bipolar and that medical marijuana keeps her from killing herself."

We talk for a while about Summer's hard life, her going back to school, her suicide attempts, what he's doing, what I'm doing.

"Is there a way to search death records in San Diego County?" I ask before hanging up.

"I'm going to try," he says.

25

RYAN AND CATHY, I PRONOUNCE YOU

We are plastic, according to neuroscience. If there is a single idea in brain research that has become doctrine in the last few decades, it's *plasticity*. Like plastic, your brain is malleable. It changes constantly. (Other connotations of the term—cheap, artificial, dehumanized, crowding the Earth with non-biodegradable molecules—are unfortunate side effects.)

Brains are plastic in part because synapses, the *connections* between neurons, are at least as important as the neurons themselves. A synapse exists for the duration of an exchange between cells. Their comings and goings mean the structure of a brain is constantly shifting, if only slightly. Brain structures don't just reshape themselves wholesale from moment to moment. They're largely stable, but gradual shifts can amount to significant change. These changes are most evident in stages of development common to the species, like the shift from childhood to adolescence, or when an individual undergoes a major psychological change, like becoming a drug addict, experiencing a psychotic break, attempting suicide, finding enlightenment, getting married or divorced, "going mod." But most of the changes we experience are less high profile.

Plasticity is the latest in a very long tradition of metaphors devised to explain brain function. For centuries, philosophers envisioned a homunculus—a tiny creature at the controls—inhabiting the dark place in the brain, pulling levers and making consciousness happen. Descartes characterized the mind both as a bell pull used to communicate between servants in disparate sections in a great house and as a microscopic system of hydraulics. Early twentieth-century neuroscientists conceptualized the brain in terms of the steam engine, the camera obscura, the telephone switchboard.

William James famously called consciousness a stream, and a generation of novelists got busy illustrating the power of his metaphor: Virginia Woolf sought an elusive lighthouse located deep in the streamy labyrinths of her character's minds; James Joyce revived Homer's Ulysses and turned twenty-four hours into a thousand pages of meandering epiphanic lewdness; William Faulkner conjured the sound and the fury of flashing color interior worlds dense with tangled thoughts and sensations. James, less influentially, also compared consciousness to a bird's flight, whereby periods of free flight are punctuated by perchings, or moments of attention.

The computer was the dominant metaphor for several decades: the brain being the hardware, the mind the software, and sensation the external input. Recently, metaphors of plasticity—network, web, ecosystem—have displaced the computational model. The brain, according to the network, web, and ecosystem metaphors, is a dynamic system of systems and subsystems whose interrelationships are vast, asymmetrical, and fluctuating. And somehow this ecology becomes self: we are this ecology.

We choose these metaphors because of what they reveal—in this case, the vast interconnectedness and malleability of brain function. But metaphors also conceal. The problem is that we tend not to see what is concealed until a given metaphor has begun to outlive its usefulness. We probably won't begin to see what plasticity conceals for decades, but it foregrounds the possibility of change. It suggests reinvention.

My guess is that three decades from now, we'll have a metaphor that suggests qualities about the brain we don't yet see or understand. But for now: we are plastic.

The change is definitive.

My bangs are light yellow straw now, long enough that a few strands of scorched hair cover my eyes while most of it spikes above my forehead in the cockatoo style Howard Jones sports. I've got on loose, light gray pants with pockets on the sides of the leg. Black cotton boots with a big tongue sticking out the top and a long-sleeved grey shirt with black specks on it, collar up. I'm wearing brown eyeliner, which my mom approved begrudgingly, and brown mascara, which she didn't notice. It's the first day of sophomore year. I'm braced, because Paul already got taunted and shoved at registration.

This is my debut walk across campus. "No big deal," I told my mom. "Lots of kids are mod," using the term for her sake. The lies don't ease my nerves now. I can feel eyes on me. As soon as I climb the stairs from the drop-off area, I hear the first jeer: "Dude, check it out. Fagaw went mod."

I walk, one foot then the next, until I reach my locker. I open the door to make a shield and lean against it. I breathe, a deliberate breath, deep, strained. Before I finish, Shane Carlin rounds the corner in floppy leather boots, ripped and bleach-stained jeans, studded belt hanging around his waist—outside the loops—Adam Ant bone choker, blue eyeliner that wings off the corners of his lids, white streak in his brown bangs. His walk is casually lanky, like he's in a Bow Wow Wow video. He glances at me, looks away, glances back, smiles just barely at the corners of his mouth, locks eyes with me for a slow-motion second. I feel him take his arms and wrap them around me. I feel him whisper in my ear, "You look great."

One foot in front of the next, he disappears around a corner, just like that. *Was that smile good or bad? Did he like how I look? Was he making fun of me?*

"Hey, Toug," I hear Nichole say. "Nice eyeliner." It's her first day of freshman year. I can tell she's nervous for me, and it's annoying.

"Shut up."

"I'm only kidding. Jeez."

Nichole has short hair now, with a Sun In streak in the bangs, and she wears a big plastic pink jewel of a brooch. She's in the category I was in until today: mod supporter but not mod. There are lots like her, most of them girls. At San Pasqual, at this point, there are seven or eight full-fledged mods, none of them actually mod. In fact, hardly anybody fits a category, even though the categories are well defined: punk, newro, mod, ska, goth. Most of us are a mix, stylistic mutts.

Although *mod* is a misnomer, we don't reject it entirely because it demonstrates our accomplishment: complete removal from the social fabric of high school, which also means nearly instant immersion in a new social milieu comprised of a network of others like us from high schools all over the county. Eight or ten at each of dozens of high schools means there are enough of us to gather and become a force—at malls, concerts, coffee shops, thrift stores. We spot each other right away in the Adam Ant collars, Robert Smith bangs, Siouxsie eyeliner, Thompson Twins clam diggers, Jam polyester turtlenecks, Chrissie Hynde leather.

"Has anybody said anything?" Nichole asks.

"Not to my face."

"Oh my god," she says.

"What?" I say, annoyed on the verge of getting mad. She's not helping the way I want. I want her to tell me I look cool, that everybody else is stupid.

"No, Mr. Sensitive," she says. "It's Paul. Oh my god."

Paul is walking toward us, hair dyed blue-black, eyeliner to match, black T-shirt way too big, black slim-cut pants, his mom's rosary around his neck. "Oh my god," Nichole says again. Paul's transformation is more iconic than mine. He is Robert Smith, though a little darker, with some Jesus and Mary Chain and Bauhaus thrown in. I'm Howard Jones, who has top ten hits, wishing I was David Sylvian or Fun Boy Three, who aren't famous in America.

"Some fucking stoners threw paper airplanes at me," Paul says, like it's a badge of honor.

"Jason Meyer has been going around saying 'Fagaw went mod,'" Nichole says.

"He's jealous," Paul says, "because he's so ugly." He's laughing like a maniacal Satan. It's part of his look. "Here comes Amy," he coughs through the laugh.

"Hi, boys," Amy says, looking us up and down. "Who's this?" she says to Paul.

Paul knows Amy Buzick from his history class last year. They talked about music all year. I've never met her, but I've been studying her for months, like I've been studying Shane and his girlfriend Gabby, looking for the combination of signifiers I could adopt to let people know who I really am—no, who I might become.

"This is my friend Jason," Paul says.

"Cute," Amy says. "The mascara works. But you could use some lipstick."

Relief. I've done it. "And this is Nichole," Paul says.

"Hi there," Amy says. "What do you think of these boys?"

"They're just Jason and Paul to me," Nichole replies.

"Jason, Nichole," my mom says, "you remember your Grandpa Ralph?"

"Yes," Nichole says, half lying so she won't hurt his feelings.

"Of course they Goddamn remember me," says the tiny man in a candy-apple-red tracksuit with silver grass sprouting from his scalp. "Who could forget?"

"Ralph!" Nanny says. "For Godssake."

"Whatsamatter, Midge? The kids got a sense of humor. Don't you, kids?"

"Yeah," I try to say out loud but manage only to mutter.

"Well, this is it," he says, pointing to the doublewide he just moved into. "See these?" he asks, pointing to a row of tall blooming rosebushes. "These are my pride and joy. Well, these and my needlepoint."

"Who ever thought the Portuguese Pepper Pot would do needlepoint?" my mom says.

"Gotta do somethin'," Ralph says. "What the fuck else am I gonna do? Huh, Jason? Huh, Nichole?"

Our tiny grandfather, the one who died three times, the one who has been married six times now, the one who wooed Nanny by breaking his back in the cavalry, climbs Astroturf stairs up into his new mobile home. He just showed up two weeks ago, with a wife in her twenties named Cherie, ready to reunite with the one real family he ever had. He and Nanny, we know, were married twenty-three years, by far his longest. He was never around, always on the road, always riding, always partying. He was rich. He doesn't seem rich now, which may be why Cherie skipped out after less than a week.

The four of us file in behind him. The two main things you notice are photographs and oil portraits of Ralph, mainly in his jockey silks, hung everywhere, and needlepoint strewn on the floors and tables: placemats, floor mats, Kleenex holders, toilet seats. They're all in different themes: autumn leaves, Santa Claus, roses, thoroughbreds. "Let me show you Midge's new bedroom," he says.

"Ralph!" she says. "I never said—"

"You will," he says. He's right. She'll move in. But she'll stay only for a couple of months before he drives her crazy and she moves into a separate mobile home in the same park.

It's taken twenty years for them to move from their beachfront mansion to an inland mobile home park. They navigated the phases between there and here separately, but they are back together for this last one.

"This is the closet," he says, opening a door to a room the size of my bedroom. Clothes hang in two tiers on every wall. Shoes and slippers line the sides of the floor. Belts, ties, necklaces, medallions, and scarves hang along the back.

"Wow," I say. "It's like a store in here."

"No shoplifting," Ralph says, cracking himself up.

"And where do you imagine I'd put my clothes?" Nanny asks.

"I'd make room for you, beautiful."

"Oh brother," my mom says.

"'Oh brother' is right," Nanny says.

"Hey, these are totally newro," Nichole says, scrolling through a row of frilly silk blouses in bright colors, many of them with inlaid floral patterns on them.

"All custom-made," Ralph says.

"Is this what Kay dressed you in?" my mom says.

"I dress my Goddamn self," he replies. "Nichole likes 'em. Don't ya, princess? What'd you call 'em?"

"Newro," she says. "It means New Romantic. It's what Jason is." They all glance my way, eyeing my pegged black pants, army-green ruffled tuxedo shirt, black slippers, rhinestone necklace, blond bangs.

"See that?" Ralph says. "Got his grandpa's taste."

He's back. Things are changing. Nichole and I agree it's weird. Our family has a patriarch. And he's a maniac.

It begins with the faintest synthesizer, like all music video weddings. Our family has a patriarch, even if he is a kook, and now my mom is marrying a pretty regular guy. My dreams of normalcy are sort of coming true, just as I've begun to pursue my own brand of abnormal.

"Almost Paradise" is my mom's favorite song. Mike Reno from Loverboy and Ann Wilson from Heart admit their fears of love unrealized and cherish the love they find. He thought dreams belonged to other men. Her heart used to beat in secrecy. But now they're knocking on Heaven's door. Does that mean they're dying? Sweep: the hill of weeds and wildflowers behind our new house in Elfin Forest, a crowd sipping Champagne with buffet tables in the background, an arched trellis strung with bougainvillea.

Cut to interior of our new house, ranch style, low ceilings, sunken living room, my mom in the bedroom: a makeshift wedding dress she bought at Charlotte Russe, sheer white stretch lace dress over a fuchsia leotard and slip. She's pulling on a garter, with Cheech's help, half-full Champagne glasses in their hands. Bathroom: Ryan shaving, in grey slacks and grey shirt. He's cut his hair short, curls castrated, mustache trimmed. He doesn't look like a hippie anymore. He owns a landscaping business. He's not an addict. He's nothing like any guy my mom's been with.

Cut: the band setting up. Gary rounded up some of the guys from the Lyrics. The wedding is a reunion. Everybody's here to see what becomes of your friends after they drop out of high school, get pregnant, marry, unmarry, and marry again. The band didn't get famous, but most of its members still surf.

Sweep the crowd again, this time lingering on groups in conversation.

Cousins: I'm wearing a tuxedo jacket I got at the thrift shop. I've left my bangs down, because my mom wanted me to, and I'm not wearing eyeliner. Nichole's bangs are teased up. She's all ruffles and poofy sleeves. Bryan's mohawk, clipped for the wedding, makes it a lot easier for me to introduce my new look to the extended family. Trever's crew cut makes his head look square, like a grown man's head. He's taller and more muscular than we are.

Elders: Nanny is talking to Doug and his new girlfriend Barbara while her older sister Florence, who still has money, nods along, a witness, however supportive, who confirms Nanny's shame.

Friends and neighbors: Jennifer in a turquoise cotton dress with her big-bellied, long-bearded husband Bobby. He was Craig's best friend in the old days. Something happened in Hawaii, and Jennifer eneded up with Bobby. Now they're here with their daughters, Angela and Alicia. Bobby and Jennifer will be divorced within the year. Carrie Jo is smiling with her big teeth at JP and Sue Ellen while Summer sits among them with dazed eyes like a drugged prisoner.

Siblings: Close-up on Craig's face, forlorn, sunburned, eyes wide, afro just beginning to grey, not listening to Kate, who's talking to him about the oaks in Elfin Forest, wondering who the elves are. Gary's behind them tuning his bass, intent, enjoying the one-sided conversation between him and the rest of the crowd.

In-laws: One of these things is not like the others. Ryan's parents are distinctly suburban, possibly Republican, both smoking, with big gold rings on their fingers, bodies like battleships. Keith, my new nine-year-old stepbrother, stands between them, chocolate mop hanging over his forehead, black almond eyes squinting in the sun. Ryan's brother Phil is six four, only twenty-eight, with a thinning dark brown faux hawk, dresssed in black and studs. "Poser," Bryan whispers to Trever.

The bride and groom carve two paths through the crowd, grinning hard. A friend of Ryan's with a mail-order license performs the ceremony. The synthesizers hush. The wind blows some oak leaves around on the grass. Bride and groom lock eyes and listen to wisdom, repeat vows, exchange rings. "Cat and Ryan, I pronounce you man and wife." People cry.

Each journey through the assembly line ends with Champagne in a plastic flute, lined in neat rows like sparkling soldiers. Bryan hands me some Champagne, hands Trever some, hands Nichole some. Spoons scoop wild rice. Forks jab hunks of chicken Kiev.

Wide view: Elfin Forest, a stretch of oaks between Del Dios and San Marcos. Wider: From high in the sky you can see it dotted with houses and dominated by a smelly dairy farm. Rumor has it a cabal of Satanists live here, and you can see why. The oaks are thick, the caverns they form so deep they turn day into night—good places for secret rituals.

Cut back to the teenagers' table. Nichole is sipping her Champagne. Bryan and Trever are gulping. I follow their lead. Bryan returns every few minutes with our flutes refilled.

The dance of the bride and groom. *Almost paradise. We're knocking on Heaven's door.* The sparse clouds speed up. Wind softens the heat. Men and women cut in and dance with the bride, some pinning green bills on her stretch lace, a Greek tradition adapted for Elfin Forest. The people twirl. Bryan hands me and Trever two flutes full of sweet bubbles. I sip to cool my mouth down. I look away from the dancers, at the clouds, but they're starting to spin too.

Cut to bathtub. I'm lying in it, my clothes, vomit-caked, in a pile next to it. Shower streaming cool water on me, a look somewhere between agony and relief on my face, yellow straw hair wet and plastered on my forehead.

Bryan's standing over me. "Hey, cuz," he says. "You came to." He's been there. He understands. My stomach gulps, rises, convulses. I hurl my upper body erect and let the frothy scallop and chicken slop pour between my legs, only landing a few stray bits on my skin. Bryan aims the shower head at the slop, washing it toward the drain. Bryan's mohawk, his smile, and the cool water ease the spins. I press my cheek against the white porcelain.

Zoom on the shower stream, close enough to feel like we're in a waterfall. Cut to bedroom. Posters spin. Robert Smith with smeared lipstick. Morrissey, alienated fade bobbing. David Sylvian, red glasses falling off his nose and floating down the river. Tears for Fears, black bangs swinging slowly, depressed. They spin like the inside of a children's top. The walls expand and contract, rise and crescendo.

"Knock knock," I hear Ryan's voice. The door, swept up in the spin, creaks open. Three heads lean in: Ryan, my mom, little Keith. "How you feeling, kiddo?" Ryan asks, amused. They all smile. This would never have happened with Stanley or Nick, or any of the others. Whatever else is going on, we have become a unit—something like a family.

Spinning posters blur, then fade.

26

ANTI-HIPPIE

The Aztec Room at San Diego State is smaller than the gym at school. Eowyn, her sister Kirsten (a senior), Paul, and I got here at noon. We were second in line. This is our first big gathering of the people we want to be: dyed hair, much of it spiked; ripped shirts; safety pins; makeup outside the lines of features; big boots; loose pants, belts hanging on hips; thrift shop prom dresses torn up and re-sewn; striped tights and studded belts.

Kirsten finds us amusing. She drove us here as a favor. She's a good sport. She's got her hair sprayed in a fake asymmetrical shape and she's wearing a brooch, but she is not one of us. Eowyn has an actual asymmetrical cut, which she trimmed herself for the concert, with spikes up the side and lightest blond (that's what the package called it) bangs teased and hanging over her left eye. Paul has his crucifix on, his black mushroom hair, smeared red lips and black eyes. I'm dressed in homage to Howard Jones, whose concert we're here to see: blond bangs cockatoo-spiked, the rest of my hair dyed copper, black leggings, cloth boots, white T-shirt with the collar torn out, and my tuxedo jacket over that.

We file inside, a mob of hair dye, Aqua Net, big makeup, and striped tights, and storm our way to the stage: front row center. The mob files in behind us until our waists are pressed firmly against edge of the stage.

"Hey," I say, hitting Eowyn on the shoulder. "It's the list of songs." I can see a sheet of paper with the set list under the hugest synthesizer.

"I can see it, but I can't read it," Eowyn says.

"Me either," Kirsten says. "How can you read that?"

"Jason's got better than twenty-twenty vision," Paul says. "He always has."

"'Don't Always Look at the Rain' isn't on there," I say. "I can't believe it."

A synthesized tribal beat shoots through the room. The mob screams. The stage begins to rotate and the bouncy melody washes over the beat, screams escalating. We see a flash of cockatoo hair, then—leap—Howard Jones is standing right in front of us, a portable synthesizer strapped onto him, headset mic on his head.

"I touched his leg," Eowyn says.

"Oh my God," I say. "I think I did too." Kirsten is smiling. Paul is dancing with his eyes closed, bangs swaying. The mob on our back piles up, pushes harder.

The crowd is suspending the people on our backs off the ground. "Can you see the guy on my back?" I ask Paul. He's maybe nineteen, with white hair spiked in the back but hanging over his forehead, shaved on one side.

"Yeah," he replies. "He's cute."

"He's got a hard-on and it's rubbing on my back."

"I bet he goes to SDSU," Paul says.

I've never been so close to a guy this cute, this cool, or this old. For an hour, as we scream and jump, the cute guy's crotch chafes my back. I'm pretty sure he's doing it on purpose. Now and then I feel his fingers brush my hair or my neck. During "Pearl in the Shell," the last song before the encore, I feel his hard penis slam deep into my shoulder blade and slide down and rub against my butt. "On and on and on," Howard Jones sings. "On and on and"—slam, rub, slide—"on." The show is over.

"More," the scream sounds. "More." We pound the stage. People stomp.

Finally, the intro to "What Is Love," a sparse, suspenseful riff: a bass, a bell, a single horn. Then, a beat. Howard Jones is back in front of us, strapped into his synthesizer. The college guy's hard penis rubs in the crevice between my shoulder blades. I catch a glimpse of his huge smile, one hundred percent absorbed in the song. Howard Jones finishes and bows. Last song on the list. The scream climbs and swarms. He stands still. "More. More. More." He nods, smiles, shakes his head. Bows again.

"'Don't Always Look at the Rain,'" I shriek, loud, nearly hysterical. Howard Jones looks straight into my eyes, then looks at his piano, the real one, then back at me.

He walks over to the piano, sits down, plays a few notes, stops, looks out over the scream, plays the notes again. The scream subsides. He sings quietly, feels his way through the song, lingers on the last few sparse notes, opens his eyes, and points at me. He offers another bow. The scream soars. He leaves the stage. The scream subsides and the mob loosens, shaking the blond guy and his hard penis off my back. He's laughing, filing out ahead of us with two girls with nose rings. I keep my eye on them as we walk. They drift toward campus until the dark absorbs his white hair.

Kirsten smokes a clove cigarette on the drive home. "Did you see him sing that song I asked for? Did you see it? Did you see him point at me?" They did.

"It was such an inspiring show," Eowyn says.

"He's a great performer," Kirsten says.

"True," Paul says. "But he's a little bouncy. 'Don't want to be laden down by the doom crew,'" Paul imitates, bouncing his hands in the air, offended by the lyric.

"He's positive," I say.

"Yeah, well. There's a lot to be doomful about. What about apartheid in South Africa? Or all the orphans with American fathers in Vietnam?"

"Or the fact that girl babies are murdered in China?" Kirsten says, blowing sticky clove smoke out the window.

"Or homeless people right here in America?" Eowyn adds. "Or Ronald Reagan?"

"Robert Smith is God," Paul says, a non sequitur.

"Here we go," Eowyn says.

Kirsten drops me and Paul at his house. We slide through the glass doors to his room, strip off our gear, down to T-shirts and underwear, and lie on the waterbed.

"Was that guy really hard?" he asks.

"I swear," I say.

"College boy," he says.

"He was cute, wasn't he?"

"Don't get too excited. The friction would make anybody hard."

"Would it make you hard if it was Weird Al in front of you?"

"Gross."

"Or how about Robert Smith?"

"Definitely," he says, rubbing his underwear, stretched over a penis at least sixty percent hard. He pulls the band down over the head and tickles it. His dick bounces, harder now, at least eighty percent. "Let's do sixty-nine," he says. We rotate, pulling off each other's underwear. Paul puts his hand on my head, which he doesn't usually do. After a few minutes, we come up for air. I stretch out, rotate, face Paul, our dicks touching, our heads close together. He takes his hand and wraps it around both dicks. I can feel the pulse in his beating warm against mine. He rubs. I dart my mouth toward his and kiss his lips. He opens his mouth a little. Our tongues touch for a few seconds. He pulls away. "No," he says, backing away and lying on his side, looking at the ceiling. "We can't do that." He grabs my dick and rubs hard. "No kissing."

We finish, then lie on our backs, not sleeping. "No," I keep hearing in my head. Paul and I have never been boyfriends, but now he's becoming a reminder of what he's not, what he'll never be. I try to drown the thought with the image of Howard Jones pointing at me or the feeling of the white-haired guy's penis along my spine.

At school, with our new mod friends, Paul and I pretend our sex life is history. We've moved on. It's easy, because we've always sort of pretended it wasn't happening. When we walk up to our group at lunch—grown now into a loose oval of eighteen or twenty kids who look like us—the concert is all there is to tell. Nothing about sixty-nine, nothing about no kissing.

"It was so beautiful," Eowyn is bragging for me. "He sat down at the piano and just played it, nothing programmed. He even pointed at Jason."

Over the course of four or five months, every week or two, someone new shows up to school having *gone mod.* They show up with their hair dyed, their clothes ripped or velvet or army green. We circle them. They eye us. If we decide they're serious and successful, we send an envoy, usually Kim or Gabby, always a girl.

Nichole walks up with Paul and Buffy, who's living with Nichole now and just started SP. We've known her since we were babies. Her mom, Paula, is Jennifer's best friend and used to go-go dance for Gary's band. Buffy's the first girl I ever tongue-kissed, during a game of truth or dare when we were barely twelve, before Paul and I ever jacked off together. They've joined our oval even though they aren't newro, mod, punk, or goth. Buffy's brashness and Nichole's spiritedness buy them entry.

"Jason," Lisa, the most hardcore goth girl at school, calls to me. "Everybody's going to Club Zu this weekend."

"Really?" I say. Club Zu is in Solana Beach, the only one-hundred-percent new wave club in town. It's all-ages and owned by this nineteen-year-old named Kelsey, a first-generation newro. He and his friends are royalty.

"How are you gonna get there?"

"On the bus. You're coming."

"I want to. How are we getting home?"

"We'll get a ride," she says.

"Or sleep on the beach," Paul says.

Out of nowhere, a precisely cut quarter of an orange pelts me in the forehead and lands in my lap. I feel a sting of juice in my eye. I feel my mascara smearing. By the time I focus, our oval is drenched in a downpour of thuds: bananas, pears, tomato slices, bread crust, anything found in a jock's packed lunch. Seven or eight football players are hurling unwanted food from a distance of thirty feet, showing off their strong arms for a group of girls who look on, laughing in admiration.

Mr. Cavanagh, the chemistry teacher, walks by. "Okay, you've had your fun," he says to them. "Settle down."

Lisa and Gabby rise. They walk straight up to Mr. Cavanagh, Lisa flipping the jocks off on the way. "Hey, none of that," Mr. Cavanagh says to her. "I'm warning you."

"Those guys just pelted us with food," Gabby says. Gabby's got long, naturally blond hair and wears mostly denim and leather. She's undeniably beautiful, so she confuses everybody's categories. She could probably be a cheerleader if she wanted, but she'd rather listen to The Clash. Billy Idol kissed her from the stage once. All this gives her the balls to talk to a teacher this way.

"I'll tell them to settle down," Mr. Cavanagh replies.

"That's it?" Lisa asks. "They get told to settle down? I'd get expelled for that shit."

"You'd better settle down yourself," he pauses, looking her up and down, "young lady," saying this last part like he's not sure it's true.

"Disperse. Disperse," the mall security guards command in limp imitation of military authority. "Limit yourselves to groups of four."

We're a group of five: Paul, me, and some girls I find kind of scary. Tiffany, a new girl from school, brought us here. The scene at the Carlsbad Mall is a new league, and Paul and I are trying out for it. All the most hardcore kids from miles around gather here. If they accept us, our transformation will be complete.

Two of these girls, hair long and spiked high and wearing layers of old lingerie, just announced proudly that two Marines paid them $20 to eat each other out back by the dumpsters. Another one just told me all about the abortions her friend has had. Then the four of them dispersed, which meant prancing toward the escalator, giving the guards the finger, one flaring her pierced tongue. "You can tell they scare the shit out of the guards," Tiffany tells us.

I've been coming to this mall since I was a toddler. My grandmother used to take me here to shop for school clothes. I can't stop picturing her walking through here with some crew of goths taunting her.

"The rest of you, move," one of the guards says. "No loitering."

I've never been on the wrong side of the law like this. A pregnant woman pushing a stroller veers away from us. Tiffany grabs both our hands. "Come on, boys," she says, skipping.

When we've traveled almost the entire length of the mall, Tiffany yells, "Warren! It's my Warren! Warren is the cutest newro boy in Southern California," she says to us. A guy with hair colored just like mine, red along the sides and back with light blond bangs hanging over his pink-shadowed eyes, gives Tiffany the hang ten sign, thumb and pinky raised. I've only ever seen surfers and metalheads do this. I feel like a poser version of him.

"My darling," Warren yells to Tiffany.

"Warren loves me." She giggles and runs at him. They give each other a huge kiss, with tongue. Warren's masculine under his makeup, and as cute as any famous newro: wide green eyes, plucked eyebrows, full lips painted the color of bougainvillea.

"Who are these adorables?" Warren asks Tiffany. Paul and I look at each other. We've arrived, and we're a little scared.

"This is Jason," she says.

Warren grabs my hand and rubs my palm with his thumb. "Charmed," he says, giving me a deep taste of what it feels like to have his eyes look into you.

"And this is Paul," she says. He grabs Paul's palm, rubs it, with the same attention to the eyes.

"Warren's bi," Tiffany says, right in front of him.

"But Tiffany is my one and only," he says, giving her another kiss. "Come meet my friends," he says to all of us. My eyes dart from him to this guy with huge matted curly black hair, black lips, tons of smeared white grease and black cobwebs on his face. A six-inch yellow-white skeleton hangs from his ear, connected by a chain to his skull nose ring. He's all in black except for his red cape.

"Disperse. Disperse. Limit yourselves to groups of four." The limp command of the guards is a relief this time. Tiffany walks off with her fingers entwined with Warren's. Paul and I are flanked by two tall, large-boned girls, one white and one black. We're in.

"Jason, don't be a wuss," Buffy says, handing me the joint. The smell of the burning joint reminds me of Stanley, and JP, and Cheech, and Nick. Ex-hippies and newly minted newros have one thing in common.

We're in Nichole's dining room. Bobby and Jennifer are out to dinner. Buffy, Nichole, and Paul have already had two hits each.

"Yeah, Toug. Just try it," Nichole says, looking at Paul, smirking, then snorting out a laugh at nothing. "You'll like it."

"I'll hold the joint for you," Buffy says. "It's already lit."

"Maybe," I say.

"Okay," she says, "here." She sucks on the joint, eyes closed, lips pursed. The end glows redder the longer she sucks. Buffy opens her eyes, puts her hands on my head and her lips to my mouth. I open. She blows the smoke inside. When she pulls away, I cough, and the smoke pours out of me, like it was always pouring out of Nick. I can almost hear Mick Jagger's falsetto.

"No," Buffy says. "You have to breathe it in. That's the whole point."

"Okay, listen," Paul says. "You have to just take a breath and hold it," grabbing the joint from Buffy to demonstrate. He sucks it in, points to his rising chest, and then says in that squeaky sucked-in voice Nick always talked in, "Holding, holding, holding...breathe out. Just like that." He puts the joint to my lips. I suck.

"Harder," Buffy says. I suck harder. The end of the joint glows redder. I suck again.

"Okay, now breathe," Paul says. I do. It feels like a cheese grater shredding my throat. I cough uncontrollably, then heave. I have a mouth full of puke. I run to the bathroom and spit it in the sink. I feel another heave, and the burrito I ate after school rises through me into the sink, full of refried beans. Buffy, Paul, and Nichole are all at the door, smirky with bursting giggles.

"Poor Toug," Nichole says.

Hips wave and duck. Arms move in unison, right to left, fists gently closed like they're pulling a big lever. When the chorus comes, *You spin me right round, baby, right round, like a record baby*, several dancers interrupt the lever pulling for a brief miming of a record turning, palm down, on cue, *right round round round.* Kelsey, the nineteen-year-old owner of Club Zu, is on stage next to Warren's friend with the capes and skeletons. I don't want to be, but I'm afraid of this goth guy waving his arms like a snake charmer, legs together, swaying. Kelsey wears red plaid pants, a black sweater, and black boots. His hair is black and stands up straight off his head. He seems to be looking at nothing, like he's too inside the music to notice all these people who've come to his club from all over San Diego County in their newest outfits, hair freshly dyed.

I'm eyeing Kelsey's two friends, who round out the trio of what I consider the coolest people on earth. Tara is tall, pale, lush, the biggest and most gorgeous goth girl here. Her hair is black with royal blue roots, eyes pale blue, black eyebrows, lips in black liner, diamond in her nose. Brian is tiny next to her, with a crimped copper bob, black eyeliner, no lipstick, brocade vest, pegged black wool pants. They're friends with the Thompson Twins, who hang out here whenever they're in town for a show.

As "Dead or Alive" smoothes into the intro to Visage's "Fade to Grey," I hear Paul tell somebody, "This is the twelve-inch." *One man on a lonely platform. One case sitting by his side.* I can't help staring at Kelsey and his friends.

"You want to be introduced?" Shannon asks. "You think Kelsey's cute?"

I do, but that's not it. I want to *be* them. I adjust the dangling rhinestones in my ear and feel sticky wet behind my lobe. Paul pierced my ear before we caught the bus, with a needle and rubbing alcohol. He told me to wear the stainless-steel stud he had from when he got his pierced at the mall, but I was dying to wear my new rhinestones.

"We're going outside," Paul whispers, "as soon as the song ends." *Wishing life wouldn't be so dull.* Pull, wave, duck, charm, bend, sway.

"Okay, come on," Paul says, hooking arms with a girl I've never seen.

"I heard Steve Strange has AIDS," she says as we squeeze through the waving ducking swaying bending crowd. She's talking about Visage's singer.

"Really?" I ask.

"It's the rumor in London," she says.

Warren and Tiffany flank us, with two short girls with shaved heads. "Let's go."

"Where are we going?" I ask.

"Just come on," Warren says, patting his back pocket.

We follow him down the alley behind the club. There are some concrete steps leading to a path along the cliff, where you can climb down to the beach. We can hear waves crashing.

Warren sits on the steps, surrounded by girls. Tiffany climbs to the top. She and Warren haven't held hands or kissed all night. The rest of us fill in around them. Warren takes a lighter and pipe out of his pocket, digs around some more and pulls out his pot. "Yum," he says, holding the baggy up to the light from the street lamp, flicking the pot with his index finger and watching it bounce and settle. "Sticky bud. Hawaiian."

Every now and then Warren starts talking like this, flaunting the collision of his full lips painted red and the surfer words coming out of them.

Warren fills the pipe gently, careful to rub the sticky bud into dust without losing any. He lights, sucks, breathes in, hands the pipe to a tiny girl with raccoon eyes, who lights, sucks, breathes, hands the pipe to a dyke named Scratch. "Oh yeah," Warren says, breathing out a cloud of smoke. Somehow, filtered through Warren's lungs and clinging to the salt in the air, the dense sweet smell seems to have lost all traces of my mom and her boyfriends and brothers.

Paul takes a hit. He lights, sucks, breathes, hands the pipe to me. I hold it to my mouth and flick the lighter. The flame burns my thumb. I have trouble keeping it lit long enough to burn the pot, but I'm determined. I suck in a cloud of smoke as Paul spurts one out, coughing, laughing. "I can't stop," he laughs. "I can't stop."

"You get a hit?" Warren asks, hopping off the steps and reaching for the pipe.

"Yeah," I say. My ear throbs. There's a scab growing around the fastener at the back of my lobe, gluing the heavy rhinestones in place. I got a hit. I'm high, like Warren, with Warren.

"Let's dance," he says. "Put on your red shoes," putting his arm around me, lighting the pipe, sucking, and then blowing the smoke into my mouth, grazing my lips.

"I'm so stoned," Paul says as we walk. "Oh my god, I feel like I'm floating." I'm not sure if I feel anything or not, but Warren's lips just touched mine.

"Floating on a cloud of love," Warren says.

"Oh my god, could you be any more of a cliché?" Paul says.

When we show our stamps and re-enter, Kelsey and his friends are dancing to "Collapsing New People" by Fad Gadget. We duck and wave to blend in, sway and bend with the crowd.

At the stroke of 2 a.m., the lights come up and the dancers shield their eyes in imitation of vampires stranded under a rising sun. "I hate to say goodbye," Kelsey announces over the sound system, "but you creepy ghoulies have to go out into the night. Before the lights melt your foundation." People pretend not to smile as they circle each other out the door, onto the sidewalk, into cars. Warren's friends have a car, but it's full.

"Let's hit the beach," Warren says. "Watch the sun rise. First bus is five forty-one."

We follow him up the concrete stairs, seven ride-less, beach-bound stragglers in melting foundation. We have to navigate wobbly stairs with rope for banisters. We feel around in the dark with our feet for a spot without rocks or seaweed. We sit, stars above us just enough bright to see the sand particles creeping into our velvet, spandex, lace, and wool. We can hear the waves and just see their froth. Warren lights the pipe, making his face glow. His lips are puffy, sucking, his eyes almost transparent.

"It's so fuckin' cold," Paul says. We all have our arms wrapped around our torsos.

"Let's cozy up for body warmth," Warren says, shaking out a shiver. We huddle, a line of beached newros. "Pot will help." I close my eyes and pretend to sleep while the rest of them light, suck, and breathe, until I really am sleeping inside a dewy sweet cloud.

I wake warmer, sun on my face, one of the girls shaking me. "You have to see this," she says, pointing to the glowing pink sun over the cliff behind us, ascending the lavender sky. "Look at the sun," she says. The pink grows oranger by the second. It's almost striped: bubblegum pink, red orange, pure orange. There's an L-shaped speck of black toward the bottom, like dust on a camera lens. I touch the scab on my ear and feel fresh blood.

"It's a sun spot," Paul says, sounding encyclopedic, as usual. "It's probably fucking up satellite communications. The fog's making it so we can look with the naked eye." Periwinkle waves lap tan sand at our backs, their white froth invisible now, canceled out by the white dawn bleaching the sky and sand.

27

HOW DOES IT FEEL?

"I like this one," I say, holding up a rhinestone choker.

"Get it," Lisa says. I'm at JC Penney in the Carlsbad Mall with Lisa and Nick, a goth girl and newro boy from school.

"It's $19."

She's all in black, including her lips, eyes, and cheeks, holding a string of imitation black pearls. She looks at me, then at Nick, and stuffs it into the pocket of her black pea coat.

The jewelry is displayed on swirling racks, which makes it look like a fake jewelry farm. From behind my carousel, all rhinestones—earrings, bracelets, necklaces, brooches—I can see the fawn-haired elderly saleswoman behind the counter minding the cubic zirconia, her attention fixed on her notepad.

Nick's at the rack next to me, looking at fake rubies to match his hair. We're watching Lisa harvest black jewels—fake onyx pendants, fake hematite earrings, black rhinestones. When the outer pockets on her pea coat are full, she starts stuffing the jewels into inner ones.

Inspired, I slide the rhinestone necklace into a pocket in my black stretch pants. They snag on the way down. Nick plops ruby earrings into the front pocket of his blouse. It's easy.

Fawn barely glances at me as I walk past her. It feels right to move away from the scene of the crime, to prove to myself that I've committed the act without any dreaded consequence. I choose another carousel and pluck a rhinestone bracelet to match the necklace. I see Nick drop something into his pocket. Lisa brushes past me. "Let's get out of here," she says. Nick and I file in behind her.

"That hag didn't see us coming," Lisa says as we walk out.

"Excuse me," a guy with a brown mustache says to Lisa. "May I see what's in your pockets?"

A guy with an identical mustache approaches me and Nick. "Empty your pockets, please," he says. I take out my matching rhinestones. Nick takes out his rubies. We hold them in our palms. "This is store property," he says. "You're under arrest." Lisa is dumping black jewels into the palms of mustache number one.

"Turn around, please," one of them says. Two pairs of handcuffs click in succession, one for Lisa and one tying me and Nick together. They're tight and pinch even my skinny wrists. They escort us back through the arches into the fluorescent glare of J.C. Penney. Heads turn, look us over top to bottom, and shake. Fawn stands outside her counter, arms folded over her blue vest, staring without expression. The mustaches lead us up two escalators, through a door marked NO ENTRY, and into a security office.

They sit us down in a white office with grey vinyl chairs. Number one hands us each a pad of paper. "Write down your names, birthdays, parents' names, addresses, and phone numbers." We hand the pads back, scribbled on.

The mustaches disappear into an inner office, leaving us handcuffed on grey vinyl chairs. "Fuckin' assholes," Lisa says when they shut the door.

"My parents are gonna freak," Nick says.

For the next two hours, we wait. Finally, real police arrive, two of them, in real blue uniforms, with sunglasses, badges, boots, and guns in holsters.

"You have the right to an attorney," one of them says to us. "Anything you say can be held against you in a court of law. Now come with us."

"Where are we going?" Lisa asks.

"The Carlsbad Police Station. We'll contact your parents from there."

I feel like JP, I feel like my father. Now I have something in common with them.

The uniforms stand us up and lead us out into Appliances. We glide back down the two flights of escalators, passing Hardware, Menswear, Toys, and Electronics. Heads turn like dominoes as we pass. We are proof that dyed hair is the first step toward juvenile delinquency.

The uniforms squeeze the three of us into the back of the police car and snap the doors shut. "Seven-minute ride to the station," one of them says. "Hold tight." As we leave the mall, a pair of teenaged boys on BMX bikes give us the thumbs up. A pair of Marines grab their crotches. A goth girl sitting on a sidewalk looks at Lisa and crosses herself like a Catholic priest.

The station is buried in eucalyptus trees. The uniforms lead the three of us into a cell with orange bars and a padded bench. The other leads Lisa to a cell within the cell. "Sit tight," one of the uniforms says. "We'll track down your parents." He pulls our three sheets of truth out of his shirt pocket, locking the orange bars behind him.

"These things hurt," I say to Nick.

"I know. They suck. But I wish I could steal a pair for Gabby," he says.

I can't laugh. I don't want to picture these cuffs hanging from Gabby's belt. I don't want to imagine the conversation she'd have with the principal for wearing them.

Finally, we hear a uniform say, "The beauties are on the bench, and the beast is in the back cell."

"Did you hear that?" Nick says. "We could sue for that."

"Which one of you is Jason?" a uniform interrupts.

"Me," I say.

He slides back the orange bars, uncuffs me, snaps the cuffs to Nick's other wrist, and leads me out into the waiting room. "Bye," I mouth to Nick.

"Bye," he mouths back.

Ryan and my mom are sitting in orange plastic chairs, the only people waiting. Ryan raises his eyebrows. My mom brushes me with her eyes, then looks at the ground, like she never looked at me at all. "Nice work," Ryan says.

"You'll receive some paperwork," the cop says. "If you plead guilty, you'll probably get community service, here in Carlsbad."

"Okay," I mouth. I can't get my throat to make noise. If I do, we'll have to start talking.

The seat of Ryan's truck is dusty. There's a pair of hedge clippers on the floor. The back is full of lawn mowers and tools. My wrist is still red from the cuff. "You definitely ruined dinner," Ryan says as we get in. After that, we're quiet.

"Sit down," my mom says when we get home. "We are going to talk."

We sit. "Where's Keith?" I ask, deflecting.

"Never mind," my mom says. "I am sickened. I never thought I'd see the day—" Ryan interrupts with a hand on hers, squeezing it.

"It was pretty fuckin' stupid," Ryan says.

"I didn't raise you this way," my mom says. "How could you steal like that?"

"I don't know," I say.

"I didn't raise you to steal. We let you put the posters up. We give you money for the records. We buy you the clothes."

"My clothes are from thrift stores. They hardly cost anything."

"This is no time for lip," Ryan says.

"Well, it's true."

"Shut it."

"We even put up with the makeup and the hair dye."

"It shouldn't be *putting up with.*"

"What?" my mom asks, disgusted. She's hung out with criminals all her life, dated them, and now she's disappointed in me for being one.

"I thought you were so open-minded. You were hippies, remember? What's the difference?"

"That was about positive things. We were for peace. We were talking about love."

"Whatever."

"Black clothes, makeup, acid music," she says. "This is about negative things."

"Shut up." I raise my voice. "You don't know what you're talking about."

"Stop," Ryan says, grabbing my wrist across the table. I yank, but he holds on. My wrist burns where the cuff was. I push the chair out from under me and yank again, thudding on the floor.

"Get up," my mom says. "You're going to listen to this."

"You can't tell me what to do," I scream. "You. Can't." My mom starts to cry. Ryan is red like an eight-hour sunburn.

I walk to my room and shut the door, carefully, without slamming it. As soon as it's closed, the dream feeling takes over. Not the slow panic but the fast chaos. I walk across my bedroom, to the wall, and beat it with my fists. I swing at the window and my left hand goes through it. The sound of glass shatters the chaos. I'm on the floor, a shard jutting out of my wrist, blood all over my arm. Ryan and my mom enter, tentatively.

"You can't tell me what to do," I repeat, using my bloody arm as a shield as I squeeze past them. I go to the bathroom, unroll a big wad of toilet paper, pull out the shard of glass, and walk out the front door, holding the toilet paper to my wrist. The blood streaks to the elbow.

Walk. One foot, the next foot. I head for Escondido Boulevard, because it's big, with lights and an occasional person. It feels more like going somewhere than the side streets. Maybe I'll get a coffee mixed with hot chocolate at the twenty-four-hour donut stand. I realize I don't have any money. How would I order anyway, with a bloody arm? One foot, the next foot.

Cars drive by, most above the thirty-five-mile-per-hour speed limit. I pass a teenage Mexican couple, in full uniform: black slip-ons with brown soles, white undershirts and gold crosses, long hair lightened red and ratted in the front for her, slicked black fade for him. They're holding hands, kissing. They barely glance at me. The toilet paper is drenched now, sticking to my arm. There's a white van parked parallel to the sidewalk. I decide to walk around it. Its door slides open. A guy, at least thirty, grungy brown hair and beard, in flip-flops and a T-shirt too big for him. "Hey," he says, smiling.

"Hi."

"What's going on?"

"Nothing," I say, eyes darting involuntarily to my arm.

"You party?"

"What?"

"You party?"

"I don't know," I say.

"You want to party?"

"No, thanks," I say.

"Ah, come on. You look like you need to party."

"No thanks." He creeps me out, but he doesn't scare me. When I say no, I'm walking the right side of the line that seems to keep people in my family from diving over cliffs that will kill them. We survive, just barely. That's our thing.

"That's too bad, man," he calls. I walk on. One foot, the next. The chaos is wearing off, replaced by a bubble of slow panic. Every step is the same endless pace over pink ribbon, the same short infinity sidewalk lined with daisies. The same shapeless guy with the nuclear bomb hovers in the inky sky, stars twinkling like the rhinestones I stole today.

I turn back to the side streets, even though I know they will be quieter, slower, a better Petri dish for panic. I have a plan. My friend Melissa lives at the top of the hill. I run the whole way but stop to catch my breath before knocking. "Who is it?" I hear Melissa's mom calling. I don't know what to say. I can hear Melissa and her mom talking. "Jesus," her mom says, opening the door. Her hair is foamy with auburn dye, twisted into a knot on top of her head. It seems like somebody gets her hair dyed every night in Melissa's house.

"What happened?" she says, not really meaning it as a question. I've met Melissa's mom twice. Melissa says they moved from Minneapolis. But she lies a lot, and loves Prince, so none of us can be sure it's true. I'm pretty sure her mom's boyfriend is a heroin addict.

"Oh my God, Jason," Melissa says, hands in surgical gloves covered with brick-colored dye. "You're bleeding."

"Sit down," her mom says. "Let's take care of that. Melissa, see if we have any big bandages. And peroxide and rubbing alcohol." She takes a cloth to my arm. "This is just water," she says. "It won't hurt much." Melissa, de-gloved, hands her gauze, bottles, bandages. "This is just peroxide. It won't hurt. There's still some glass in there," she says, pinching it out with the cloth. "It's not that big. It's just deep."

I don't realize it until it's gone, but the panic has subsided. "There," Melissa's mom says. "You're all fixed up. You can sleep here, but I need to call your parents."

How does it feel? To treat me like you do? When you've laid your hands upon me? And told me who you are? Six slow crisp beats interrupted by six quick ones crowded in upon each other, a sound like knives chopping. This beat may be the most widely recognized sign in our world. New Order's "Blue Monday" is our anthem. But I have a secret. The song that defines us, makes me feel the slow terror from my dream.

"If you were gay right now, you'd have to be crazy to have sex, with what's happening with AIDS," Mr. Bryant, our English teacher, said. They showed a movie about AIDS in all the social studies classes on campus and everybody's talking about it. We were in the library when he said it, to me, Gabby, Amanda, and this girl Tania, a rocker girl who wears cat's-eye liquid eyeliner and prefers mods to stoners. My research project is on Boy George. I wanted to do the connection between New Romantic music and the Romantic poets, but Mr. Bryant said I wouldn't find information on New Romantics in the *Reader's Guide*. He smiled when he said I could do it on Boy George.

When he said it, "You'd have to be crazy to have sex," I got hot on my face and neck. My hands shook, like Nanny's do. I looked at the table for a second and turned around and walked toward the stacks, in the middle of the conversation, without any explanation. After I left, he asked the rest of them, "Is Jason gay?"

I dream about Mr. Bryant almost weekly. Sometimes I'm at his house and we're having sex in his bed, under white sheets. He has black hair, receding pretty far back on his scalp, a matching mustache and chest hair that shows through his open collars. He's shorter than me, but he's muscular and stocky. He wears chinos tight across his butt and always has a bulge in his crotch. In the dreams, he loves to kiss for hours. He loves to hold me, his muscular forearms reaching around my back, his hard stomach rubbing on my skinny one. How would it feel?

Now I have to go to class. I could never skip Mr. Bryant's class. He's by far my favorite teacher, and Creative Writing is by far my favorite subject. His first name is Lane, so he shares a name with a plus-size clothing store, but that doesn't make him any less charismatic. He has a Masters in English from NYU, which fills me with awe. And awe isn't too far from the dream feeling, which is strong right now, attached to a new fear: AIDS.

Paul had sex with this kid Joey from San Marcos, who had sex with a thirty-year-old man in Phoenix. All the thirty-year-old gay men are dying. You'd have to be crazy to have sex right now. And Paul had anal sex with Joey, and Joey loves anal sex and I'm sure he had it with the thirty-year-old. I didn't sleep last night. I rolled from one side of my futon to the other, imagining Joey naked in bed with this guy who had one hidden purple lesion on the back of his calf. "A birthmark," he'd tell Joey, right before injecting him with the virus, which Joey would inject in Paul and Paul would inject in me. "Think about it," the movie said. "You aren't just having sex with your partner. You're having sex with every partner he or she has ever had. Think about it."

I am thinking about it. I had to get up six or seven times during the night to inspect my arms and legs for lesions. The two moles above my belly button are pretty dark brown, and they look like they might be turning purple. I've been coughing since yesterday. My throat itches. Pneumonia, I learned yesterday, is the leading killer of people who have AIDS.

I haven't told anybody I'm freaking out, but when Tania catches up to me on the way to Mr. Bryant's class, the first thing she says is, "What's wrong? Are you okay?" She's the most caring rock chick ever.

"Nothing," I say. Then: "I'm worried I have AIDS."

"Why?" she asks, hugging me.

"Yes," I say. "I've done all the things they said not to do in that movie."

"You have?"

"Yes." I tell her about Joey and the thirty-year old.

"So you mean Paul would have it too? And everybody he's slept with?"

"Yeah."

"Paul has slept with a lot of people."

"I know."

The bell rings. We're supposed to be in class. When we walk through the door, everyone is sitting down, and Mr. Bryant is still in the office behind his room. Somebody has written, in huge lavender letters, across the chalkboards on two walls:

LOOK OUT MR. BRYANT. JASON IS COMING.

I know it was Nick Brown. He's decided he hates me. After the JC Penney incident, we were "going out." Then he started "dating"

Nichole, but kept fooling around with me the whole time. Finally I told Nichole. Now he's telling everybody he's going to ruin my life. He knows about my crush on Mr. Bryant.

While I'm deciding whether to sit down or run out, Mr. Bryant walks out of his office, smiling broadly. "Hi guys," he says. "Have a seat." I squeeze into my desk. Mr. Bryant glances at the two chalkboards. The red is rising from his neck to his face as he grabs the eraser behind him and starts swinging it at the board. The lavender smears away, but the letters leave legible marks.

"Let's get to work," Mr. Bryant says as he finishes. "Timed writing today." He's not making eye contact with any of us.

"We're here because I'm disturbed by what I'm seeing on campus," Mr. Bryant says, "and I don't see anybody else doing anything about it."

The chairs are set up in a circle four layers deep, us "mods" on one side of Mr. Bryant, a massive hive of jocks and their girlfriends on the other. Mr. Bryant never showed any reaction to Nick's prank. He's been as nice to me as he always was, maybe even more.

"I've got these students everybody calls *mods*," he continues. We're nodding our heads *yes*. He understands.

The hand of the quarterback, Jason Bill, goes up. "If they're not mods, what are they?"

"They're people," Mr. Bryant answers. "Great people. Some of the kindest and smartest and most creative people you'll meet." The heads of jocks shake *no*. We shake *no* back at them.

"But they're not innocent either," Mr. Bryant says. "They hate jocks." Heads shake. Hands go up.

"Exactly," Dane Block says. "They're so busy trying to get attention, they hate everything normal."

I once got into a debate with Dane in economics class about immigrants. He thinks that an illegal immigrant in need of medical attention, say in a car accident, should be left to die so that we don't spend the money of American taxpayers.

"Wait, wait, wait," Mr. Bryant interrupts, holding his hand up like a stop sign. "Both sides will get their chance to talk. But I want to set one ground rule. You are not allowed to reduce anybody in this room to a category: stupid jock or mod freak. If you want to be treated like a human being, you have to give others that same respect. Respond to what people say, not their football jerseys or earrings."

Hands go up on both sides. "Kim," Mr. Bryant says.

"This year so far, I've had food thrown at me more times than I can count. Now, I'm a lesbian, I'll just say it. I know not everybody likes it, but that's my choice, and I'm proud of it. Some of my boy friends," she continues, "get punched on a regular basis. And spit on. I've been spit on too. By people in this room."

"Great. That was very articulate, Kim. Would anybody like to respond?"

"I just want to say," this dark-haired cross-country runner whose name I don't know begins, "that they're asking for it. They want attention."

"Hold on," Mr. Bryant says. "Do you really think they want to be spit on?"

"I think they want any kind of attention they can get. And I think they bring down the morale of the school. They don't go to games. They skip pep ralleys. They walk around sneering. One time I saw that kid," he says, pointing to me, "yelling across the quad, 'I am the Antichrist.'" Heads shake *yes* and *no* on their side, *no* on ours.

"He was singing," Gabby says. "It's a song. By the Sex Pistols. The lyrics are about political revolution."

"Revolution?" Dane Block says. "So they want to overthrow the government?"

"What we want," Gabby adds, "is the freedom to express ourselves."

"I'm sorry, but that's crap," Dane says. "The truth we all know is that these mods or whatever you call them are psychologically disturbed. They're acting out their mental problems."

"It's not crap," Scott says. "You need to see a little more of the world." Scott has lived in Chicago. "It's full of all different types of people. We're not disturbed. Non-conformists are the ones who change the world."

"The world is fine the way it is," Dane responds. "Who needs to change it?"

I raise my hand and start talking before Mr. Bryant can call on me. "It may be fine for you, but it's not for us. You're making huge generalizations about people you don't even know," I begin, not sure where the words are coming from. "Lots of people are psychologically disturbed," I say, thinking about Melissa's pathological lying, all the crystal Kim has been snorting, Roger on house arrest. "The clothes they wear are not how you diagnose them." Hands on the other side shoot up. Heads on our side nod *yes*. "But the worst thing about this situation," I continue, "is that it is condoned by the teachers and the principals. They watch while we get food thrown at us. Some of them blatantly mock us in class. Instead of protecting us from abuse, the teachers allow it to happen. Mr. Bryant is the only one doing anything about it."

Voices are talking on both sides. I know Eric Olgilvie has spoken. And Eowyn. I think she reinforced what I said about the administration. I heard the words "institutionalized abuse." By the time I regain equilibrium, Jason Bill is talking again.

"For me," he says. "I'm glad we had this meeting. I like what Gabby said about freedom of expression. It makes sense." Gabby is the one among us a jock could find sexy.

"I'm glad to hear you talk like that, Jason," Mr. Bryant says. "And I hope your friends will listen. I hope you'll be an example to them." Only a few heads, including Dane Block's, shake *no*. "Lunch is almost over, and this is only the beginning, but I hope every one of you in here will think twice about each other, as people, from here on out."

People are getting up from their desks, talking about what happened. Jason Bill walks toward us, toward Gabby. She walks toward him, like he's a magnet. He's almost a foot taller than her, in a football jersey cut off at the waist, the hair on his hard abs peeking through, in new-looking 501s. Gabby's wearing a Generation X T-shirt, cut off at the waist, her creamy abs peeking through, in new-looking 501s. Their voices are hushed, but their hands are moving a lot and their heads nod yes like crazy. Tania looks at them, looks at me. When they're done, Gabby walks over to us. "He asked me out," she says.

"What?" Tania says.

"Are you gonna go?" I ask.

"Yeah. Should be weird."

I know this could be a good thing for all of us, but I feel jealous, like Gabby is a traitor. This isn't a transformation. But it is a change. Things won't be quite the same after this. We already liked Mr. Bryant, but now he's become a hero.

In order to say, "If you were gay right now, you'd have to be crazy to have sex," Mr. Bryant needed to possess what some cognitive scientists call "theory of mind": the capacity to imagine another's mind or consciousness. My mom needed it to say, "This is not the way you were raised." Bernard Sumner of New Order needed it to sing *How does it feel to treat me like you do?* Theory of mind makes us social (as opposed to simply cognitive) beings. It enables us to empathize. It enables us to tell tall tales. It might have something to do with mirror systems in our brain. Research shows that when we witness others in action or feeling, synaptic patterns associated with those acts or feelings activate in our own brains. Nobody can feel another person's feelings, but we seem to be built to try.

It still honors me to think that Mr. Bryant, who was roughly my mom's age, used his theory of mind to imagine my consciousness. Even though it sent me into a bout of extreme anxiety, he took the time and care to imagine what consciousness was like for the sixteen-year-old me. He took the risk of trying to act on it. Like most risks, this one had unpredictable effects. It didn't stop me from having sex, but it did stick with me. The panic may have been enough to ensure that I was careful when I did have sex, which was, I'm guessing (using my theory of mind), what Mr. Bryant ultimately hoped to accomplish.

When Mr. Bryant gathered mods and jocks, he was hoping to get our theories of mind churning on each other, hoping we'd begin to imagine each other's qualia, consider each other's points of view. The results were unpredictable. Gabby and that guy Jason started dating, briefly. Mods and jocks still pretty much hated each other, but the strife and violence lost their thrill and waned. Again, this must have been what Mr. Bryant hoped to accomplish.

Theory of mind is imprecise. It gives us the ability to imagine another's thoughts, but not to get it right. You'd think we'd understand people with whom we share genetic heritages and daily living. You'd think hippies and newros, countercultural figures of two generations, could bridge their gaps. My mom didn't want her revolution smeared with lipstick or doused in hair dye, and I didn't want mine smeared in hippie filth or beat up by guys on heroin.

After the JC Penney incident, life tested our theory of mind—and our family mythology. While I was pretending to live by the rules of my restriction, putting my makeup on at school and scrubbing it off before my mom could see it, my punk cousin Bryan showed up schizophrenic, telling the tallest stories since Great-Grandpa Neves on the Golden Gate Bridge.

28

SCHIZOPHRENIC

I don't have to look to know that's the chug of Nanny's Mercedes pulling up to the curb, but I raise my blinds just a little to see what she's doing. Nobody told me she was coming over. She's on the sidewalk, bent into the passenger seat. She drags out her purse, one my mom made, soft leather with a beaded zebra on it. She must have washed her hair without setting it, because it's in ringlets.

I get to the door before she does. "Hi, Nanny."

"Hi, Jason."

"What are you doing here?"

"Where's your mom?"

"In her room."

"Is Ryan here?"

"He's in the backyard with Keith."

"Why don't you go get them?"

"Ryan," I call. "Keith," walking to my mom's door. She's sitting at her vanity table, applying blush from a clay pot. "Nanny's here."

"They found Bryan," Nanny says as we file into the living room.

"Thank God," my mom says. Bryan disappeared a few weeks ago, right after he cut his mohawk, started wearing a suit, and began talking about the Bible nonstop.

"In Arizona. Apparently he's been brainwashed or something," Nanny says.

"What do you mean *brainwashed*?" I ask.

"By a cult," she answers. "Apparently they kept him awake with drugs for a week and read the Bible to him. He's talking about Jesus and Noah and Satan and some plan. He says he's come back for us. All of us."

"To do what with us?" my mom asks.

"To take us back to Arizona."

"Where is he now?" Ryan asks.

"He was with his mother in Oxnard. But apparently he left Jeannie's, got on a bus to come down here, made some kind of scene, and got arrested. Now he's in a psych ward in Oceanside. Gary went to get him."

"What kind of scene?" my mom asks.

"He was preaching or something?" Nanny says.

"Preaching?" Ryan asks. "Bryan?"

"It's hard to imagine, isn't it?" Nanny replies.

"What are the doctors saying?" I ask.

"Well, Jeannie took him to this expert on deprogramming. He works with people who've gotten mixed up with these facacta cults. But he said Bryan was too weak. Deprogramming could push him over the edge."

"Isn't he already over the edge?" Ryan asks.

It's 105 degrees inside the tent. Bryan sits in the center of a circle, on desert sand. It's noon, but he doesn't know that. He's been awake four days, but he's lost track. The bodies around him are reading scripture, round-robin style, excerpts from both the Old and New Testaments, in no particular order: Revelation, Genesis, Numbers, Romans, Song of Solomon, Mark, Matthew, and Luke.

And the whole earth was of one language, and of one speech. [Genesis 11.1]

The words are like injections.

But those that encamp before the tabernacle toward the east, even before the tabernacle of the congregation eastward, shall be Moses, and Aaron and his sons, keeping charge of the sanctuary for the charge of the children of Israel; and the stranger that cometh nigh shall be put to death. [Numbers 3. 38]

They soothe, like satanic caramel.

Blessed are the pure in heart, for they shall see God. Blessed are the peacemakers: for they shall be called the children of God. Blessed are they which are persecuted for righteousness' sake: for theirs is the kingdom of heaven. Blessed are ye, when men shall revile you, and persecute you, and shall say all manner of evil against you falsely, for my sake. [Matthew 5.8-11]

He feels clear and well, like he's never felt.

Come, my beloved, let us go forth into the field; let us lodge in the villages. Let us get up early to the vineyards; let us see if the vine flourish, whether the tender grape appear, and the pomegranates bud forth: there will I give thee my loves. The mandrakes give a smell, and at our gates are all manner of pleasant fruits, new and old, which I have laid up for thee, O my beloved. [Song of Solomon 7.11-13]

Bryan is in the eye of his emergence, his purity. He knows what he has to do.

"Nourishment of the body comes at the expense of the spirit," his emergence partner told him. He swallows pills from his partner's palm. "To help with the hunger." At the end of a week, the time it took God to build the earth, Bryan will emerge whole, initiated.

His mohawk shorn, his punk clothes stuffed in a drawer in Ventura, his skin cleansed with sand, Bryan feels the purification. He spent the week previous to this banging on doors of the Ventura County School District, trying to cut the red tape that prevents a student from retaking the paragraph exit exam. He just needed them to let him write a paragraph. They failed him once, but he knew he would pass if he had another chance. Now he can hear whole passages of the Bible streaming through his head, advising, consoling, inspiring.

He thinks of Gary, Trever, and Jeannie. They will be stoked when they find out about purity and light. He thinks about Nanny. She'll be relieved. He thinks about Ralph. He can see now that Ralph was the missing piece. His return is a sign. Ralph returning from the dead three times is no accident. Ralph always said that *Neves* spelled backward was lucky *seven*. Three and seven are spiritual numbers. Ralph is the key. The rest will follow. He thinks about Cathy, Craig, Nichole, and Jason. They'll be impressed by his Biblical knowledge and his clear, well demeanor. They'll follow.

Bryan and I show up last. For summer in Escondido, this is a cool day: mid-eighties, pretty strong breeze moving the heat around. Kit Carson Park is freshly mowed, messy balls of cut grass here and there.

"Hola," I call, trying to sound natural. We're walking toward the group of people sitting Indian-style on the grass, under an oak, right near the Sombrero slide.

Amanda, Scott, Nichole, and I host picnics all the time, calling ourselves the Perpetual Picnic. The four of us are always together. After Scott arrived a few months ago, the demographics of our group shifted. But Nichole's on the coast and couldn't get a ride, so she's not here. I see a few other girls have joined us. "Hola," Bryan repeats, giggling. He's wearing Guatemalan pants in violets and blues, purple and red high tops, and a yellow tank top with a pinky orange sunset on it, his curly mullet hair and moustache bleached almost orange from the sun. The group is sizing him up.

"This is my cousin Bryan," I say. It might have been easier to stay home and fight with my mom about how much nicer I should be to Bryan, how it could be any of us, how most boys don't become schizophrenic until their late teens or early twenties and it could still be me, how Bryan used to dress weird like me and listen to "negative" music too.

"Let's eat," Amanda says. "My mom sent tuna salad and Orangina for everybody." Amanda's mom is Swedish, and in their house Orangina is a water substitute.

"There's plenty of everything for everybody," Scott adds, holding up a plate of cookies.

"I brought Brie and crackers," Amy says, "and they're melting."

I don't know if it's a side effect from his medication, but food is the one thing that can occupy Bryan's attention fully. I nibble on some grapes, try some Brie on a cracker, drink some Orangina. Bryan shovels chocolate cake with his fingers.

"New Order is playing at SDSU," Susan says, the first to speak. "My brother's getting tickets. Want to go, Jason?" She asks only me. People think she likes me. I heard she doesn't believe I'm gay. I met Susan a few weeks ago, at an Orange Glen dance.

"That would be cool," I say, remembering "Blue Monday" playing in my head when I was freaking out about AIDS.

"My cuz likes that shit," Bryan says.

"Shit?" Susan says.

"Music," Bryan says. "Shit. It's all shit."

"He has a point," Lisa says.

"Amen," Bryan says. "This chick's cool." Lisa laughs. She's never been called a chick.

"Jason," Susan says. "Let's go for a walk."

"Where?" I say, stalling.

"Up to the creek," she says. "It's shady."

"Maybe in a little while."

"Come on. What's stopping you?" she asks, looking at Bryan, who's busy with his cake.

"Go ahead, cuz," Bryan says.

We walk around the back of the Sombrero, a big cement slide in the shape of a Mexican hat. It's tipped at an angle and you slide down the brim. "Oh my god, what a case!" Susan says as we make our way to the creak.

"I told you he was schizophrenic," I say.

"I know, but he's just so weird."

"He can't help it," I say.

"Why'd you even bring him?"

"Why not?" I don't feel like telling her it wasn't my choice.

"God, those eyes. He makes everybody uncomfortable. He's ruining the picnic."

"He was punk before any of us." It's all I can think of. "It can happen to anyone."

"If it happens to me," she says. "I hope they lock me up."

"I'm going back," I say, walking away from her without looking.

As I leave the shadow of the Sombrero, I see the picnic spot is empty except for half-full bottles of Orangina, half a cake, and some shoes. There's a circle of people down below, near the adobe bathrooms, like the crowd that forms when there's a fight at school.

I can see Bryan's hair sticking up. I can hear his surfer accent, the volume turned way up as he addresses the crowd, part defense attorney, part preacher. Then he falls.

I run toward the crowd. Johnny sees me first. "Your cousin just wandered off," he says. "Next thing we knew, all these people were down here."

Bryan is tight and squirming under the restraint of two huge guys. I squeeze through the crowd. "He's with me," I say.

"I have a good mind to call the police," one of the guys says.

"Hey hey hey," Scott breaks in. "Everybody calm down." The two huge guys shake their heads, looking at Scott's pegged pants and the white fluff on his head.

"This lunatic is freaking my kids out," one of them says. Bryan's face is purple. The men loosen their grip, and Bryan squirms the tightness out of his body.

"Take him home," the other guy says. "Get him out of here." The crowd disperses.

"You want me to follow you home?" Scott asks me. We have matching cars, his white Beetle and my blue one.

"No, that's okay. I'm going to take him back to Nanny's in San Marcos."

"Call me later?" Scott says.

"Yeah," I say. "Maybe we can go to a movie."

"I love you, Jason," Scott says, while Bryan looks on in a daze, out of breath. Saying "I love you" is easy for Scott. It's one of the many things about him I marvel at. He was raised in a Christian house where they say it all the time.

"I love you too," I say. I've been practicing this. It feels forced, after an eight-year boycott on the word. Scott gives Bryan a hug, then gives me one.

"Come on, Bryan," I say. "Get in."

We were introduced to Bryan's schizophrenia in phases. At first we just thought his delusions were the result of the mind-control tactics of the cult. Then maybe that the drugs were a factor, like JP when he OD'd on PCP. But the delusions persisted. As we learned about schizophrenia, we integrated it into our lore. Bryan became the legacy of Great-Grandpa Neves.

As with bipolar disorders, psychiatrists agree in increasing numbers that schizophrenia isn't a single illness with a single cause, uniform set of symptoms, or predictable development. It's a spectrum of disorders marked by severe and prolonged hallucinations and delusions.

A hallucination is a false perception, and a delusion is a false belief. Hallucinations can involve any of the senses, but the most common hallucinations experienced by schizophrenics are auditory. They hear voices. Visual hallucinations are a distant second. Delusions are beliefs built on the foundation of hallucinations, but delusions also seize schizophrenics in the absence of hallucinatory evidence. To compound matters, a schizophrenic's hallucinations, mostly hearing voices, tend to support pre-existing delusions.

One in ten children of a schizophrenic eventually develops symptoms of schizophrenia, pointing to a genetic cause, a cellular web wrapped around our family. We're all crawling in the web, but Great-Grandpa Neves and Bryan are trapped and wriggling in the thick, sticky sections. One hypothesis suggests that genes instill a predisposition for schizophrenia. Because schizophrenia tends to emerge during late adolescence, particularly in men, there is debate about how and why a genetic predisposition would express itself at such a particular developmental period. An alternate hypothesis is grounded in the idea that though a given organism's DNA is constant in every one of the millions of cells of its body, the expression of particular genes varies, evolving as the organism develops. This hypothesis suggests that the genetic disorder is not apparent in early childhood but develops during puberty because it's a period of dramatic brain transformation, like the transition from infancy to early childhood. Periods of transformation, the theory suggests, create instability. Anybody, the theory suggests, could become schizophrenic.

Schizophrenics regularly challenge the perceptions and beliefs of the people around them. It's been common in various cultures and historical periods for people who hear voices to be treated as mystical visionaries. Schizophrenics *feel* like visionaries. They know they are hearing and seeing what the rest of us cannot. Whether or not this is a result of dopamine imbalances in the brain, the outcome is a picture of the world most of us can only imagine by analogy. A dream or a drug trip is as close as we get.

In fact, J. Allan Hobson has used the analogy between drugs, dreaming, and psychosis as the basis of his neural theory of consciousness. Hobson argues that all three of these altered states share a basis in common brain physiology. According to him, the reality we experience depends on three factors: perceptual input, the brain's current level of electrical activation, and the type of chemical modulation that processes the input. When we dream or hallucinate, our brains manufacture images of reality removed from the input they're processing.

"That's unreal," my uncle Gary loves to say. "Unreal" describes good stuff, bad stuff, anything mildly unusual or surprising. Hobson's theory feels right in the web of my family's devotion to the unreal. I'm not saying we want Bryan to be schizophrenic. I am saying that we become our family lore, but never quite in ways anybody could expect or predict. That's the point. We keep ourselves, and each other, on edge.

I dial Nanny's number. "Hello," she says, out of breath, after six rings.

"What's wrong?" I say.

"Well, the police just left."

"Why? What do you mean?"

"Your adorable cousin called them."

"Bryan? Why?"

"To tell them that his Nanny was stealing his money. He wanted them to arrest me." It's 1994, and Bryan's been living with Nanny on and off for six or seven years.

"And they came?"

"Actually, I had to convince them not to take *him* in."

"Why?"

"He was throwing things before they got here. And he pushed me into a corner and was screaming at the top of his lungs." Silence. "I don't think I can handle him anymore. I used to think he'd get better."

"I know."

29

ENDINGS

There I was in the *New York Times*, in one of those articles reporting a scientific study that explains what we never thought we'd understand about being human. I never quite trust these articles, but I recognize a version of me in this one.

In 2006, the *New York Times Magazine* ran this long story on psychological studies of resilience, "the springing back from serious adversity." The studies, conducted over two decades by Ann Masten and Norman Garmezy at the University of Minnesota, focus on "how a minority of maltreated children exceed expectations" when the majority of them seem more damaged by their experiences. They've identified a variation in a gene, 5-HTT, that may, under the right environmental circumstances, result in resilience. But the gene alone isn't enough; environmental circumstances have to be right too.

Where can I get tested? I asked myself when I read the article. *Do I have the 5-HTT variation?* As a kid, I had a tendency to bob and float, dodging the worst predators, often just before I was swallowed up. That's how it feels from here, inside a fleshy body that's always felt a little burdensome in its dependence on the laws of physics. But the burden lightens when I reflect on the efficiency of ganglia funneling inexorable streams of impulses, on a system that functions through the chaos and asymmetry of physiology to produce a guy like me writing words like these, a guy who can meld his own memories and fantasies with the oral history of a larger family organism and try to distill them into coherence. This coherence is fabricated, formed out of malleable perceptions, unreliable memories, wishful fantasies, and outrageous stories first told long before the day my eighteen-year-old mom refused the abortion. But that doesn't make it less real for any of us.

If there's a gene for resilience, Ralph—Lucky Seven—had it. If I have the 5-HTT variation, I got a watered-down version from him. But his resilience came at the expense of the horses he killed knocking other jockeys off him, of his six wives, of his privileged and bewildered children.

Maybe one day I'll find a doctor to map my DNA. For now, to tell the story of the kid I was, I have to give up on literal or complete truth and work with the chaos of his physiology, experience, and family lore. I have to tell a story that's like Maxwell's ether, a vague place where shared memories churn upon the inconsistencies between my version of my life and all the overlapping and competing versions that belong to others. My story, the details of growing up a hippie kid out of sync with his dropout world, a generation after his family had fallen from celebrity to poverty, is unusual but certainly not unique. Lots of kids are resilient. What preoccupies me is the peculiar experience of being conscious of my own self-preservation. I want to catch that in words—what it felt like to be me, bobbing and resilient.

We're on the green in the center of the Del Mar Racetrack, unofficially. Burying the ashes of a dead jockey here is illegal. Ralph will have no headstone, not even a shrub to mark his grave. We won't be able to visit or leave flowers. But he's where he belongs.

We each take a turn digging. My mom places the brass urn in the hole, about three feet deep. We each throw handfuls of earth over it. Gary pats it down. We stand in a circle around the grave. My mom cries. I'm on one side of her, my second cousin Patrick on the other. He puts an arm around her, holds her close to him.

The two of them took care of Ralph when he was really sick. The first time, when he had the heart attack a few years ago, my mom moved in with him. It was the beginning of the end of her marriage with Ryan. With her gone, he realized how much more peaceful his life was, and he started having an affair. I started getting hysterical phone calls from my mom in the middle of the night. When Ralph was diagnosed with lung cancer, the thing that finally proved he was mortal, Patrick moved into his mobile home to help.

"Right where he belongs," Gary says. We all nod.

Nichole and I ride in the backseat of Patrick's 1975 Cadillac. He's driving, my mom in the passenger seat. "You know," Patrick says, taking his right hand off the wheel and squeezing my mom's left. "During that last month, we got really close. Ralph told me I was like a son to him." Nichole and I look at each other. Patrick has AIDS and has been pretty sick himself. It meant a lot to him to be able to take care of Ralph. After all my panicking about HIV, it's weird to me that my cousin is sick with it. I look at him and think it could be me, grateful and guilty. But what he's saying can't be true. Ralph has never said anything even remotely as sensitive as this, to any of us, including Nanny and his three children.

Nanny is prone on an aluminum hospital bed in Mom's California room. I'm sitting on the couch. She's awake but quiet, except for her breath, which is raspy.

I keep wanting to make conversation. "How are you feeling?"

"Okay." She isn't moving at all, but she isn't still either. There is a palpable buzz in her skin. Her body is humming with neuralgic pain, a false message generated by the tumor. Its calcium-hard cells are impeding synapses, and so standard signals rendered impotent are firing at loose ends, their signals rioting. The buzz in her skin is a perception of something that isn't there. This false pain is constant and, according to the nurse's aide, probably unbearable. Three times daily we dose her with Elavil, which kills indiscriminately, speeding up the process of Nanny's evaporating self.

"Do you want me to adjust your bed?"

"I don't think so."

"Are you hungry?"

"Okay."

I've seen my mom feed her, and I know she does it a few times every day. Suddenly Mom seems incredibly brave. She has left some tamales, homemade by the old Mexican woman who works at the farm stand at the bottom of the mountain. "You put them in the microwave and cut them into four or five pieces, so she can pick them up. There's apple juice too. She can drink from a straw. She likes to. Use that plastic cup with the lid."

"Okay, Mom." I said I would handle it, and now I have to. My prohibition on *Mom* lasted longer than the one on *love*, but I finally gave it up my freshman year of college.

"We're having tamales. They're good. You love tamales," I add. I really want her to say, "I love tamales." I want her to get out of the hospital bed and make them herself. I want her to go outside, pick some tomatoes, and whip us up some salsa to eat with our tamales.

I go to the refrigerator and dig out the tamales and warm them in the microwave. "Not too hot," Mom warned. I feel the tamale with my finger. It needs to cool for a second. I cut it into tiny pieces. I taste a string of pork. I know it tastes spicy and that it's tender, but I have lost all connection to my senses. Where Nanny has feelings in the absence of sensory input, I'm developing a resistance to the input. This physiological apathy is a protective cover, of course, but it turns the air around me into vaporous glue that makes the simplest gesture a chore.

It's time, so I fill the sippy cup with apple juice and put a straw in it. I'm doing as instructed. Mom, after all, is a home health aide. She feeds sick people all the time, not just Nanny. "Do you want some juice first?"

Her nod seems to mean *okay*. I hold the cup to her mouth. She takes the straw between her lips and sucks. When she stops, I wait a minute to see if she's really done. I offer her some tamale. My mom told me that you let Nanny take the tamale in her hand but you help her hold onto it. I put the plate in front of her, and she gestures toward it. I guide her hand toward one of the pieces. She seems to want to show me that she can do this. I want her to show me. I'm letting her move her hand on her own, but it's slow and forced. I don't know if it's better to let her do it herself or just take over. I let her struggle. She seems to want to. I hold her wrist, but I don't move it. It takes forever, but finally she is nibbling on the tamale.

"How is it?"

She nods. She nibbles, and she actually eats the entire piece of tamale. I give her some more juice. Then another piece of tamale. I never get the hang of this. For each bite, I am caught in the impossible space between letting her eat on her own and helping her do it, between preserving her dignity and showing I care.

It started with headaches, stumbling, and lost memories. "I stumble sometimes," Nanny said to my mom on the phone.

"What do you mean?" my mom asked.

"I mean, I stumble!" she said. "That's what I mean." My mom called me, worried. Nanny wouldn't go to the doctor. She's always hated doctors, always put off going until it's too late.

Who put the tumor in her brain? Who made it suddenly turn from a grade II astrocytoma into a grade IV glioblastoma?

We finish the tamales. I go back to my couch. She sleeps and wakes and sleeps and wakes, until finally my mom comes home. "How'd it go? Did she eat?"

"Yes. A tamale and some juice."

"Good. How was it, Mom? Tamales, your favorite. They're the ones the little Mexican lady I told you about makes. I'm gonna have some right now."

My mom found a few records in Nanny's things when she and Gary and Craig were clearing out the mobile home. One of them was June Christy's *Something Cool.*

"You should take this record. Don't you and Dave like her?" my mom asked.

Dave and I have been together five years. He's a singer. Christy is a recent discovery, a voice we felt triumphant to resurrect. "You've got to listen to this," we'd tell friends. We'd drink Champagne to simulate the elegance time forgot. I can't stop imagining Nanny listening to June Christy in the fifties, a cocktail in her hand, enjoying the cynicism of Christy's bored-with-it-all phrasing. As with Nanny, genuine feeling simmers just beneath the surface of her nonchalance. I put the record on to see if Nanny will react. Christy is singing *I'd like to order something cool. It's so warm here in town, and the heat gets me down. Yes, I'd like something cool. My it's nice to simply sit and rest awhile.*

Nanny doesn't notice. The buzz of false pain is a wall between her and the sound. I think about how many synaptic networks unimpeded by cancerous hunks of calcinated tissue it requires to listen to this music, to enjoy elegance layered with ennui delivered with irony encircled with joy and despair. I decide to do a test. I hold up the cover. "Nanny, do you remember this record?"

"I remember that gal," she replies, the only full sentence she's spoken since I've been here.

Nanny's glioblastoma was a grade IV brain tumor, meaning it was fast-growing, invasive, and hard to treat. *Glio* is derived from *glial* cells, the brain cells that provide the nutrients and environment that allow neurons to function. A *blastoma* is an immature, embryonic, and undifferentiated cell. The *glioblastoma* grew in her brain when glial cells manufactured nonfunctional embryonic cells. They probably started in the cerebral hemispheres, but they spread throughout the brain with tentacle-like structures that made it impossible to excise completely through surgery.

Nanny's case was typical. The first symptoms of a brain tumor, especially a slow-growing one, are often overlooked. Nanny had them all: dizziness, nausea, headache, impaired perception and motor function. As the tumor grew, her memory got loopy and unpredictable. She never mentioned it, but her vision probably started to play tricks on her. She had seizures. She wasn't diagnosed until her symptoms became severe enough to warrant neurological examination. Surgery is the standard first treatment, to relieve pressure, explore the range of the problem, and slow the tumor's growth. Then radiation.

The treatment prolonged her life a little. However, a glioblastoma almost always recurs. According to the ABTA, research is currently underway to develop new treatments for severe tumors like these, including a variety of gene therapies that may be able to prevent the replication of tumor cells, promote molecules that interfere with tumor growth, sensitize tumors to drug treatments, or create viruses that replicate in tumor cells and "cause cell death." But it was too late for Nanny. Her brain, which made her, also killed her.

I feel like I'm still standing on the beach in front of the house on Nineteenth Street, the voices of hippie kids from thirty years ago bouncing off the insides of my skull. "Let's party at the Mausoleum. Midge is cool with it." Nanny must have spent more time on that stretch of beach than any other human being. If ether is real, I left some of mine there, with her.

My body is here on the driveway next to Mom's trailer in Lake Wohlford, talking to Charlie's father's family—Grandmother, Gramps, his sister Hallie, her husband Bill. "How did you ever come up with the topic?" Hallie asks, about my dissertation.

I haven't seen Hallie and Bill since my mom scared them off from converting me to Mormonism. We talk some more about my dissertation, the job search looming at the other end, how my life has turned out, how proud they are. I wonder what they expected, or feared, when they learned Charles had gotten that little Neves girl pregnant. I picture Nanny trying to find a way to relate to these people.

They can't stay long. People come and go at a wake. The word seems too old-fashioned. This is more like the afterparty for a funeral.

Somehow, I end up on the couch with Stanley. "You remember Santio and Tracy, right?"

"Yeah," I say, holding back the urge to say *of course, you idiot*, picturing Nanny watching this scene. The days when she thought Stanley was charming are long past. He became a slob, a drunk, and an asshole more than twenty years ago.

"They're both models," he says. "In LA." I've heard this before, but when I think about them, I see hippie kids with dirt on their cheeks.

"That wasn't exactly the happiest time in my life," I blurt, out of nowhere. He doesn't reply. That's as close as I'll ever get to telling Stanley off. Nanny's death gave me permission.

Jennifer, who overheard, takes Stanley's seat when he gets up. "Good for you, Toug," she says. "I'm proud of you." A lot of people are proud of me today.

"Thanks," I say.

"It's nice to see Nanny's things," Jennifer says. "She loved this stuff." This is five years before the fire that will destroy it all. "That chest—what is it, an apothecary chest?—it's just so Nanny. It's just Midge, you know?"

"Yeah," I say.

"And that birdcage," Jennifer says.

My mom told me on the drive up here that Gary and Craig want to put the rest of Nanny's stuff in a consignment shop, after we each take what we want. "Nichole should have the pearls," she said. I told her what I want: the painting of the girl from my dream, the gold mirror, the apothecary chest, the table with the glass top and the metal flower base. I want everything, but I don't say it. "We'll see," she said. "We have to work it out with Gary and Craig."

We won't work it out before I have to go back to New York tomorrow evening. Instead, I'll convince Nichole to drive to the mobile home park and get the stuff tonight, before we go to her house. I'll smuggle as many photos as I can, and we'll go. I won't get the mirror because it's too big, so I'll take a couple of small paintings. Gary will call me when I'm back in New York, asking me what I took, wanting it back for appraisal. I'll refuse. My mom will tell me I'm selfish and ask why I put her in this position. She'll ask me how we can all be so materialistic.

The important stuff won't go to consignment. Gary will forgive me. My mom will let it go after a few weeks. I will eventually ship the stuff from Nichole's house on my next visit, and Dave and I will find space for it in our apartment. Most of what remains will burn in the fire.

But part of me is back at the funeral, in front of the house where all this stuff used to live. The house was painted a greyer beige than it used to be, with light blue shutters instead of brown. The doors Nanny had made were still there, narrow and solid, with starfish and seahorses carved into them. Nanny's favorite creatures were seahorses and giraffes, animals you wouldn't believe were real if there wasn't so much evidence. The porch looked pretty much the same as it did when Nanny and Ralph sat on deck chairs to be photographed for the home section of *The San Diego Union*—clean, flat, glass doors letting beach sun into the house. The sand felt the same as when my mom and Charlie stood on it, in love.

There's something wrong with our blood, and it affects our brains. Nanny's tumor, the neurologists said, had been lurking for several years, hardly growing. In the last year, it became aggressive. Memories started to slip, then tangle. Nanny knew she knew me, but not how. "I know," she said. "You're Bryan. Hello, Bryan," she'd say. "It's so good to see you."

"It's Jason," I'd say.

"Oh, I know that. You're my grandson."

Motor neurons, which control muscle, received waning signals from the brain. Her movement slowed until she was confined to a hospital bed. Finally, the neuralgia seized her. Elavil masked the pain, along with most of the person who built this house.

Back on the beach, we gathered on the sand around a circle of flowers. We stood in three clusters, immediate family huddled, others staggered around us. I stood with Nichole and Jennifer, because my mom was inside the flower circle, dressed in white and accompanied by three strangers, friends from the massage school she was attending.

Five guys in wetsuits—Doug, Gary, Bryan, Trever, and Marty Fixx—dragged surfboards into the ocean. I was the only person here wearing a dry suit. *Nanny couldn't stand Marty Fixx. He hardly knew her. Who invited him?* I assumed, or hoped, that most people thought inappropriate thoughts at funerals. I bet Nanny would have. Nanny's kids never understood how important the things she couldn't stand were to her idea of herself. Part of me thought giving her something she couldn't stand at her funeral just made the whole thing more like her life.

"Perfect day," I heard a woman behind us say. "The blue sky looks just like her eyes." This woman was wrong. Nanny's eyes were more watery, more periwinkle than sky.

New age music wafted from a portable boom box. My mom and her friends began a choreographed tai chi ceremony, knees and palms rising slowly and descending, limbs bending and straightening. The guys scooted onto their boards, paddling over the breakers.

Nobody asked me if I wanted to go out. They knew I'd say no. But I felt jealous watching them. I wished I could be on a surfboard. I wished I could dig Nanny's ashes out of a box and sprinkle them over the plot of ocean that used to belong to her.

The six of them formed a circle. Gary had the ashes on the front of his board. We had to strain to see it, but Gary opened the box. It looked like Doug said something to him. When Gary started to scatter, the motion reminded me of throwing bread chunks to seagulls. Their heads disappeared for a moment behind the crest of a wave. The tai chi came to an end, and the four in the flower circle turned to face the ocean. My mom started to cry. Nichole wrapped an arm around me. Doug raised his two arms to the sky. Gary raised his too.

I thought about the fact that the ashes were going to mix with sand. Bits of tooth and bone are preserved when a body is cremated. These will toss with the current, get polished, wash up on shore. People will think they're pieces of shell.

The circle of boards unfolded. The six of them got into position, waiting for a wave. The tears started to unload. I had hardly cried since I was in middle school. But it was effortless, like a dam on overflow. I hugged Nichole. Jennifer hugged me. I hugged my mom, actually initiated it. "I love you," I said, half squeaking, thinking about the phobia that word carried for so long.

The waves, puny and slow, drew the guys back to shore. Doug stayed out a little while, alone. I knew it was wrong, but I spent those few minutes fantasizing that I had known Nanny better than anybody, that I was the one who understood her. Seeing Doug out there, I knew we'd all known her differently. He knew Midge in ways nobody else ever could.

This is the moment I'm savoring: tear-drenched, watching Doug straddle his board, finally turning to ride a wave in. The ghosts belonging to this place pass in and out of me. Charlie and my mom, bodies entwined, full of Jim Morrison's satanic caramel, beaming with chartreuse moonglow, watching silver dolphins shoot over the waves.

Bryan and Trever peeled down the upper half of their wetsuits. Trever hugged my mom, dampening her white blouse, put a shirt on, hugged me. Bryan marched up, towel around his neck, and hugged me, drenching the front of my suit. I tried to forget about the suit and just hug. I couldn't help thinking how Bryan got fat, from his drugs. I couldn't get my arms all the way around him.

I drove home with my mom, talking about how we'll miss Nanny, meaning different things by it. We laughed about the time Nanny called me in New York and said, "It seems your uncle Gary is in the hospital. You know he's been dating Paula, right? Well, it seems she got a little wild and broke his"—pause—"penis."

"What?" I was cracking up.

"Yes, Uni, you heard right," she said with signature sarcasm. "She *broke* his penis. Don't ask me what that means exactly."

Dave and I—we've been together eleven years now—are standing beside my mom and her husband Billy on the charred hill where their trailer used to be. The trees are bare, amputated, like they were freeze-dried mid-fire, limbs straining to uproot their trunks and float above the flames and heat. The plateau where the trailer sat is a series of chalky black piles, fragments of recognizable objects sticking out here and there.

"See the birdcage?" my mom says. "Over there? On its side?"

"Oh God," I say. "You're right." Dave walks over to look at it, poking at it to see if he can stand it upright. We met in 1993, right after I moved to New York. He met both Ralph and Nanny before they died. I can see in his eyes how awful this is. He's snapping his camera, for something to do and so we can revisit what we can't take in now.

It's been three weeks since the fire, almost four months since my mom and Billy's wedding. In high school, everybody knew him as the one black guy in a big group of white surfers. He's always been known as a nice guy, even when he was using. The wedding was in the "canyon" right beneath the trailer. My mom planted the hill with flowers. Gary and some of his buddies played. They were married by a huge Samoan woman. I gave my mom away, which meant I walked her down the hilly dirt aisle. She'd already had a couple of glasses of Champagne. Halfway to the altar, Gary started to play some song and she tore free from my arm and ran over and started yelling at him. They buried a whole pig, like they used to do in Del Dios. My mom fell on the dance floor at least twice. Looking down the blackened hill, it's hard not to imagine the wedding in a blaze.

Now the whole place is soot. Smoke still rises in some spots. But I had this fantasy that I'd find something precious, something everybody else had overlooked, maybe a knob from Nanny's apothecary chest, maybe a cache of photographs or a reel of Super 8 miraculously preserved, maybe Nanny's thirtyish smile beaming next to Betty Grable's. Maybe Ralph kissing a beauty queen square on the mouth.

All that's here is the birdcage, jutting at a sooty diagonal. When the evacuation was called, my mom panicked. She called for the cats. She grabbed her wedding album, a bottle of wine, and a pork loin she'd just roasted. I got her call from Sue Ellen's house, where she stayed almost a week before FEMA set them up in a temporary cabin at the base of the hill. "I keep telling your mother to calm down," Sue Ellen said. "Will you tell her?" I tried, but this time a little hysteria seemed warranted. Even Sarah Bernhardt's feelings must have been justified sometimes.

They wouldn't know until the following day that the trailer had actually burned. The path of the fire was chaos. Some trailers burned while their close neighbors were untouched. The film would have melted with the heat. And the photos would have curled before they caught flame. The apothecary chest was such dry wood it would have gone right away, the porcelain knobs probably melting later. Nanny's porecelain giraffe would have fallen when the loft bed gave out.

Nanny lived right here for three or four months while she was dying. A helicopter landed in the middle of this little canyon to fly her down to Palomar Hospital. Its propellers blew up a windstorm. The lights made the place look like *Close Encounters of the Third Kind*, my mom said. Nanny lasted two days at Palomar. Nichole, my mom, Gary, and Craig were with her the day she died. I was in New York.

"She loved that birdcage," Billy says. "Even I knew that." We stand around it, staring through the charry little bars. You can see the round swing in the center. Nanny kept a wooden parrot in there.

"It's intact," Dave says. "I wonder how you can get the soot off."

"Why didn't it melt?" I ask.

"The same reason the trailer next door didn't burn," Billy says. "Fire is random."

A lot of the evidence for our lore—our shared memory—burned in the fire. Reels of film documenting Nanny and Ralph in their early days, photos of my mom and uncles dressed up for big races and fancy parties, the furniture and art Nanny held onto until the end, refusing to sell them even when she needed rent or food. Objects are vulnerable to the forces of their environment. Eventually, they dissolve back into particles of matter. Fire sped that up, but it would have happened sooner or later. Our bodies will follow. Nanny's and Ralph's already have. The particles end up in other objects, other bodies, but do they carry traces of what they've been?

If they do, the traces are imperceptible. I'd like to hope you can tune your senses to the ether channel and find them. It's a hope I don't count on, though, and so I'm left with memory. I'm preoccupied with my own memory, but also with comparing my memories with others', both people who shared my experience and people who didn't.

It was a sociologist, not a psychologist, who made the idea of collective memory famous. Early in the twentieth century, Maurice Halbwachs argued that memories are social, not simply personal. A memory, he suggested, records interactions between people, where stories about X, Y, or Z event are shared, compared, and adjudicated. Everybody involved in the sharing comes away with reinvented memories. A family is like a Petri dish for collective memory. Halbwachs puts it this way: despite the "opposition of temperaments" and "variety of circumstances," members of a family have lived a constant "exchange of impressions." That creates a bond that's difficult to break: shared identity. Communities and nations do this too, but more loosely.

Halbwachs observes that consciousness is a prison. We all live in these prisons, cut off from the people around us who will never get inside our heads, never know what it feels like in here. We know each other through the visible evidence—gestures, words, inflections, actions, stories. We use theory of mind to imagine what these mean, what it feels like to be the people around us. But we never know for sure.

Most neuroscientists will tell you, these days, that consciousness is not a single thing. In fact, it's not a thing at all. It's a process, an experience, and it's composed of various parts and emerges from a variety of brain systems. One neuroscientist, Antonio Damasio, has proposed an elegant explanation of these parts. He calls them "core" and "extended" consciousness. Core consciousness is the moment—everything you might perceive in an instant. It's sensory, and it lacks story. Extended consciousness relies on memory and a sense of autobiography to connect one instant to other instances and make us feel whole, continuous, like people with autobiographies. Damasio makes the point that the objects around us make us who we are. We become conscious of ourselves when we are changed by the objects around us. These changes are literal, cellular. You can feel some of them in your private consciousness, but only some. Our awareness of ourselves responding to felt objects enables us to be aware of ourselves.

So we are always people without stories, imprisoned in core consciousness, interacting with the air we breathe, the sounds of trucks and birds, the feeling of the keyboard, the colors of summer sky and foliage—and most fundamentally, our sense of our own bodies, bounded in the instant. And we are always people with stories, people who live with others, exchanging impressions, building memories, becoming each other's "objects." And the objects, remember, make us who we are. That's where Damasio's ideas converge with the ones Halbwachs proposed almost a century earlier. We are each other's objects, and we build each other.

My family's collective memory tells a story of resilience just barely achieved. Great-Grandpa Neves didn't make it, but Ralph did. So did his children. We find ourselves in deep shit and we dig our way out. That's the spine of our story.

The stories are always unfinished because we need them to live, to be. For most of my childhood, my mom and I shared a fatherless life. Hers was married to a younger woman, living just two hours away, and mine was in and out of prisons, mostly in other states. But they were equally absent. They were objects missing from our lives, and missing objects are more easily mythologized than the ones we see and touch regularly. They require more imagination, they grow in vague and untouchable ways, and they seem impossible to evade. When they return, interacting with them becomes a bewildering negotiation. The mythical creation we've invented is more real in some ways than the flesh-and-blood person with a mind and a self.

Like us, our fathers are aging organisms and unfinished stories. We make them and they make us. But that doesn't make any of it easier.

I'm already looking for the pansies and sweet peas as I pull up to 1475 Summit Drive, imaging my mom, eighteen and pregnant, walking this same path nearly forty years ago. What I see instead is a series of formidable bamboo trellises. There may be some sweet peas here, but definitely no pansies, nothing at all close to blooming or climbing. I realize, as I get out of the car and walk the trellis-lined path to the front door, that I no longer have any idea how seasons work in California. *Could it be that sweet peas only grow here in winter?*

I'm aware that I'm walking the same path my mom took when she got up the courage to go see her mother-in-law-to-be that first time, when my fetus was already stretching her teenage belly. The house is the same red it's always been, the screen door the same passageway into the cool living room full of opera and Chinese porcelain. I see Grandmother sitting in the cushioned rocker before

I knock. As she's getting up, another figure rises. He opens the door before she gets there. For a second or two it's Gramps, only taller and a little meatier. The same close-cropped silver hair on a tan skull, similar long nose, deep-set eyes, gentle, stooping manner. But Gramps died in January. Grandmother wrote to tell me.

We hug, a sustained hug. We stare directly into each other's eyes for what feels like two or three more seconds. "You look just like your father," I find myself saying. *Was that the wrong thing to say?*

"Jason," he responds. I'm surprised and not surprised. I knew he lived here, and I mentioned in a letter to my grandmother a few months ago that I was no longer opposed to meeting him.

"Well, Jason. It's so nice to have you," Grandmother says. She looks good, though older and somehow smaller. "Let me look at you," she says. "I can't see you very well. My eyes are still recovering from the glaucoma and cataract surgery. Oh, there," she says. "I see you. You look wild." I guess she means the long curls on my head and the beard on my face.

The two of them lead me to the kitchen, where she and Gramps would sit reading the news, marveling at the corruption of politicians and fantasizing about someday attending a performance of the Metropolitan Opera in New York. It's 2007. There's no denying I'm a grown-up man, nor that Gramps is dead, nor that Grandmother is eighty-five, nor that by the time we meet, Charlie—*Charles*, she calls him—my biological father is silver-haired and drawn.

Some things have happened since 1997, when my mom finally kicked him out and got a restraining order. I was firm in my refusal to meet him or to respond to his letters. The decision was validated by the stories of violence my mother described, the police, and the hysterical phone calls in the middle of the night. Gramps had a heart attack, then heart surgery. Then gangrene from an untended bed sore. His leg was amputated up to the thigh. Last time I was here, he was in a wheelchair. We had lunch. He wanted me to see his stump. "Charles has been an enormous help," Grandmother said.

A few months before that visit, the phone rang in my office at Princeton. "Jason," a girl's voice said. "I'm your sister." I wrote down her number and told her I'd call her back from home that night. She was nineteen. She had three kids. She'd had the first when she was fifteen. Her mother and Charlie had been married, she said, while he was in prison. She knew him better than I did, though when I called Grandmother afterward, she said she wasn't convinced the girl was Charlie's daughter. She'd called them too. She wanted a relationship, family. She told me if she hadn't gotten me on the phone, she would have gotten on a plane. She told me she wanted to enroll in the police academy. Her last name is Tougaw. I feel weird about the fact that I can't seem to pull her first name out of my memory.

None of this comes up. "I've always wanted to change this ceiling," Grandmother says, glancing at the wood planks above us. "Phil and I exchanged many unkind words over this ceiling. It's always been so dark. Before he died, he told me I should do what I've always wanted with it. I want to put in a skylight. I'm thinking about whitewashing the planks."

Charlie grins at me. I can't tell if he's grinning because he's looking at his grown son or because he wants to distance himself from the old-fashioned, otherworldly sweetness of his mother. "Want to see the garden?" he says, practically in Grandpa's voice—deep, slightly hoarse, contemplative.

"I'd love to."

He grabs two colanders and we walk out the sliding door, down the concrete steps, into the courtyard between the main house and the guesthouse. We walk the path. Most of the fruit trees are gone. No plums, no persimmons. *I've written him in this spot*, I think as I follow him. I picture him pursuing my mom through fruit trees that are no longer here—or never were. *He doesn't know I've written him. Is it okay that I've written him*? I wonder. *What would he think if he read it? How accurate is my description? I wrote that scene based on stories told to me by my mom, Nanny, and Jennifer. There's no particular reason my imagining of the scene based on these stories would be any more or less accurate than his memory of events that took place thirty-eight years ago.*

I see the few remaining fruit trees as we turn the corner into the garden. What used to be an acre of neatly planted rows of thriving green vegetables is now mostly weeds and grass. The back of the field is dotted with apricots, peaches, and plums. There are a couple of beds of lettuces, kale, chard, peas, peppers, squash—a good-sized household garden, but nothing like what Gramps used to keep. "I don't know if this is stressful for you," he blurts. "I know it is for me. I never acted much like a father."

"It's strange," I offer, sounding calmer than I am and feeling guilty about it. "But I don't want to hold onto any bad feelings." This is as much as I can muster.

"Me either," he says. "I figured you didn't, or you wouldn't be here."

"I have very clear memories of this garden," I say. *Clear, but not accurate*, I worry.

"I found out my father wasn't who I thought he was," he says. The garden is the context for the comment. We both know it. There's something comforting and scary about not needing any other transition. "And then he died."

I pause, trying to figure out what to say, how to say it. "But you were here for a few years before he died, right? You took care of him when he was sick?"

"Yeah," he says.

"It seems like that's a lot better than not getting to know him at all."

"Yeah," he says.

"He went through a lot."

"He sure did."

"I guess those are the fruit trees I remember," I say, looking toward the back of the field. "But somehow I remembered them in a different spot." *He doesn't know I've written him in that spot, the one that doesn't seem to exist.*

"We're going to pick some of them," he says, handing me a colander.

He's squeezing peaches, plucking one off now and then. I follow his lead, but nothing I squeeze feels quite ripe. I want to pick something, just to feel normal, but I haven't found anything. "See my hideout," he says, pointing to a wide bamboo structure in the corner of the field, like an enclosed patio with a dirt floor and no windows. It looks peaceful, just a couple of chairs, some garden tools, lots of shade.

"Was that always there?" I ask—again, all I can muster.

"No, I built it," he says. "You can pick them even if they only seem almost ripe," he says.

It's like he read my mind. I start picking.

Other stuff happened that day. My cousin Leslie and her husband Bradley came. Leslie is an acupuncturist. Her husband is gregarious, small, nervous. We chat about how long it's been, about the disappearing bees ("hive collapse," Leslie tells us), about Leslie's family. Charlie makes us all tasty squash (from the garden) and cheddar sandwiches and serves them with apple juice. Leslie and Bradley have to leave. They're driving to Escondido to see friends.

There is no big talk, which is a relief. We don't exchange a lot of information. Grandmother tells me that Charles is a scavenger. He asks for the neighbors' dead bamboo, builds things out of it. He has been collecting groceries thrown out behind Vons, the local chain, and giving it to homeless people.

"Yeah," he says. "But I had to stop. It turns out they have an organization who does it for them. Because of who I am, they won't let me work for them."

Finally, I say I should go. I've been here four hours. Grandmother takes me out to the garage to show me Charles's bamboo projects. Dozens of bamboo wind chimes hang from hooks in the ceiling. They're simple, nicely engineered, made from polished bamboo hanging on invisible strings. *I guess this is recreational therapy,* I think. *This is my father doing something constructive.* "I'm sure he'd let you have one," she says. "Would you like one?"

"Yes," I say. I would. We're looking at them when Charlie comes out into the garage.

"You want one?" he asks. "Pick one you like."

"I'm torn between this one and this one," I say, pointing to one with a polished gourd hanging from the bottom and one with a round piece of flat wood.

"Well, I guess since you're my kid, you can take two."

ACKNOWLEDGMENTS

Thank you to Maud Casey and Vestal McIntyre, my earliest readers. Your enthusiasm, advice, and jokes made all the difference. As my friend Sheila likes to say, you both have "naughty eyes." Just what I needed in readers. To Robin Goldwasser, for reading at a stage when I'd written way too many pages and for gently helping me see the patterns in the excess. To Melissa Easton, for the depth and honesty of your interest—and for your curiosity. To Jill Grinberg, for reading fragments in a 'zine and remarking, "I don't usually say this, but I think you could write a memoir."

Thank you to Nancy K. Miller and Siri Hustvedt for your intellectual rapport, for caring and helping. To Victoria Pitts-Taylor for inviting me to spend two years co-organizing the Neurocultures seminar at the CUNY Graduate Center. You helped me transform and expand my thinking about those three pounds of flesh in our skulls. To Carrie Hintz, for listening, encouraging, and making me laugh. To Scott Cheshire, for camaraderie and knowing what's up. To Gloria Fisk, for being there for every step and reading, reading, reading. To Julia Greenberg, for listening, talking, and being a great friend.

To Sebastian Groes, for creating The Memory Network and for inviting me to read at University College London at a crucial moment. To Anna Stothard, for reading with me. I loved hearing you read my words, and I loved reading yours. I loved your objects, and I love that you coaxed me to make mine public. Lane Bryant, you were the first person to make me believe I was a writer, and your stories about New York convinced me it was where I should live. Kate McVey, you read my angsty teen song lyrics and said I could write and that I'd find my people. I'm glad you were right.

Thank you to Carrie Howland for working as much as an editor as an agent—and for being a human I can count on. Thank you to everybody at Dzanc Books for running a press dedicated to making good books (and for giving me a prize). To Guy Intoci for your no-bullshit tactics, your boundless humor and intelligence. To Michelle Dotter for your good sense and taste, your ear for language, and your ease. To Natalie Noland for the details, the sharpening, the polish. To Michael Seidlinger for spreading the word, packing books, and book-related cocktails. I love your nail polish.

Thank you to Ted Gideonse and Robert Williams for publishing an early excerpt in their collection *Boys to Men: Gay Men Write about Growing Up*. And to Deborah Williams and Cyrus Patell for publishing a later excerpt in *Electra Street: A Journal of the Arts and Humanities*.

Thank you to my family, both blood and extended, whose talent for telling our stories made this book inevitable—Cathy Allan (my mom), Midge Neves (we miss you), Ralph Neves (you were a piece of work, and we loved you for it), Jennifer Neal, Nichole Crane, Gary Neves, Craig Neves, Bryan Neves, Trever Neves, Doug Small, Buffy Benattou, Paul Slobodny, and Sue Ellen Appleby. To Nancy Tougaw for the kindness you've shown me all my life, for raising my father, and for your curiosity about the world. I love you all. Thanks also for agreeing to let me put my version of our shared story in a book.

Thank you to all the people who appear in these pages. I hope I've done you a little justice.

Thank you to David Driver, for being you, for singing the way I hope to write, for making a home and life with me, for being game, for being a superhero of multitalent. I love you.

ABOUT THE AUTHOR

Jason Tougaw is a professor of literature at City University of New York. He is the author of two nonfiction books, *Strange Cases: The Medical Case History and the British Novel* and *Touching Brains: Literary Experiments in 21st-Century Neuromania*. Excerpts from this book have appeared in *Boys to Men: Gay Men Write about Growing Up* and *Electra Street: A Journal of the Arts and Humanities*. He blogs about the relationship between art and science at Californica.net.